Christian Faith and
Social Justice:
Five Views

Christian Faith and Social Justice: Five Views

Edited by Vic McCracken

BLOOMSBURY
NEW YORK • LONDON • NEW DELHI • SYDNEY

Bloomsbury Academic

An imprint of Bloomsbury Publishing Inc

1385 Broadway	50 Bedford Square
New York	London
NY 10018	WC1B 3DP
USA	UK

www.bloomsbury.com

Bloomsbury is a registered trade mark of Bloomsbury Publishing Plc

First published 2014

© Vic McCracken and Contributors 2014

Scripture quotations are from the New Revised Standard Version Bible, copyright © 1989 the Division of Christian Education of the National Council of the Churches of Christ in the United States of America. Used by permission. All rights reserved.

Library of Congress Cataloging-in-Publication Data

A catalog record for this book is available from the Library of Congress.

ISBN:	HB:	978-1-6235-6119-2
	PB:	978-1-6235-6818-4
	ePDF:	978-1-6235-6796-5
	ePub:	978-1-6235-6241-0

Typeset by Fakenham Prepress Solutions, Fakenham, Norfolk NR21 8NN
Printed and bound in the United States of America

Contents

Conclusion

Contributors

Editor

Vic McCracken is Assistant Professor of Theology and Ethics at Abilene Christian University and co-convener of the pedagogy working group of the Society of Christian Ethics. In 2010 and 2012 he was recognized as the Honors College Professor of the Year at Abilene Christian University. *Christian Faith and Social Justice: Five Views* is his first book.

Contributors

Miguel A. De La Torre is Professor of Social Ethics at Iliff School of Theology. De La Torre is one of the foremost contemporary Christian ethicists whose recent book *Latina/o Social Ethics: Moving Beyond Eurocentric Moral Thinking* (Baylor University Press, 2010) offers a liberationist critique of and alternative to prominent approaches in Christian social ethics.

Daniel A. Dombrowski is Professor of Philosophy at Seattle University. Dombrowski has written extensively on issues ranging from animal rights to the philosophy of religion to the history of philosophy. In his books *Rawls and Religion* (SUNY Press, 2001) and *Rawlsian Explorations in Religion and Applied Philosophy* (Penn State University Press, 2011), Dombrowski articulates the case for Rawlsian liberalism against its religious detractors.

Jason Jewell is chair of the Department of Humanities at Faulkner University (Montgomery, AL), co-director of the Faulkner Patristics Project, and Associate Editor of the *Journal of Faith and the Academy*. Dr. Jewell also serves as an associate scholar at the Ludwig von Mises Institute in Auburn, Alabama, a prominent research and educational center of classical liberalism and libertarian political theory.

Elizabeth Phillips is Tutor in Theology and Ethics at Westcott House, a Church of England seminary, and lectures in the Faculty of Divinity at the University of Cambridge. Her publications include *Political Theology: A Guide for the Perplexed* (Continuum, 2012), and she is the co-editor with Craig Hovey of the forthcoming *Cambridge Companion to Political Theology* (Cambridge University Press).

Laura Stivers is Professor of Ethics and Director of the Graduate Humanities Program at Dominican University (San Rafael, CA). Her latest book, *Disrupting Homelessness: From Alternative Christian Approaches* (Minneapolis, MN: Fortress Press, 2011), explores the role of Christian communities in justice work among the American homeless. She is also co-editor of the latest edition of *Christian Ethics: A Case Method Approach* (Maryknoll, NY: Orbis Books, 2012), a major introductory text in the field of Christian ethics.

Acknowledgements

A collaborative volume of this sort depends on the expertise and commitment of many. I am most grateful to Dan Dombrowski, Miguel De La Torre, Jason Jewell, Elizabeth Phillips, and Laura Stivers for their willingness to contribute to this volume. This volume would not have been possible were it not for them. I am grateful to Bloomsbury Publishing for seeing the value of this project and agreeing to bring it to fruition. My former professors at Emory University—Elizabeth Bounds, Jon Gunnemann, and Timothy Jackson—first introduced me to the field of social ethics over a decade ago. I thank them for cultivating my interest in the topic of social justice and am grateful to them for the many ways they embody the ideal of socially-engaged scholarship. A special word of thanks goes to my students Rachel Helton Hart, Katie Cukrowski, and John Kern for their editing and research assistance. Their work was invaluable. I am grateful to Abilene Christian University's Graduate School of Theology and Honors College for the financial support that made their contributions possible.

Social Justice: An Introduction to a Vital Concept

Vic McCracken

Social Justice: Three cases

On September 17, 1998, sheriff's deputies from Harris County, TX entered the apartment of John Lawrence after reports of a domestic disturbance. Upon entering the apartment, deputies discovered Lawrence, an openly gay man, allegedly engaged in sexual activity with another man, Tyrone Garner. Lawrence protested, arguing that the officers had no right to intrude into his private residence. In spite of evidence that the sexual activity between Lawrence and the Garner was consensual, deputies arrested both men, citing them for engaging in deviant sexual behavior in violation of Texas's anti-sodomy statute, a class C misdemeanor.[1]

In 1999, Nikki White was diagnosed with lupus, a chronic but treatable autoimmune disease, while a college student at the University of Texas. Covered by her family health plan while in college, White lost this coverage after graduation. Unable to hold down a job with health benefits due to her condition, and with no private insurance company willing to cover the expenses of her treatment, White returned to Tennessee in 2001 to move in with her parents in order to seek coverage through the state's Medicaid program. She received coverage under Medicaid until 2005, when budget cuts to the program rendered her ineligible at precisely the moment when her health was deteriorating. Desperate to receive the care that she needed, White petitioned the Tennessee State Department of Human Services to make her eligible for Medicaid once again. Repeatedly denied coverage, White was eventually admitted to the emergency ward of Bristol Regional Medical Center after suffering kidney failure due to her illness. By then it was too late. In the spring of 2006 Nikki White died of health complications from lupus. She was thirty-two years old.[2]

---

[1] See Dale Carpenter, *Flagrant Conduct: The Story of Lawrence v. Texas—How a Bedroom Arrest Decriminalized Gay Americans* (New York: W.W. Norton & Co., 2012).

[2] See T. R. Reid's *The Healing of America: A Global Question for Better, Cheaper, and Fairer Health Care* (New York: The Penguin Press, 2009).

On September 18, 1989 three Muslim girls were expelled from their junior high school in Creil, France for refusing to remove their *hijab*s, or headscarves, in class. The girls claimed that God had told them to wear the headscarf and that "they would rather die than remove [them]," so they continued to keep themselves in close-knit groups apart from the other students and resisted the requests of teachers to drop their headscarves during class time. Through the 1990s a series of similar incidents plagued French schools. Intense public debate raged over the veiling of Muslim girls and the possibility of reconciling public displays of Muslim identity with the French commitment to a religiously neutral public sphere (*laïcité*). These debates culminated with the passage of the 2004 French ban on "conspicuous religious symbols," an amendment to the French code of education that banned the public display of religious attire in public primary and secondary schools.[3]

At first glance these three cases may seem unrelated. One is about sex. One is about healthcare. One is about religious practice. All three cases, however, share something in common. All are about *social justice*. In his seminal book *A Theory of Justice* philosopher John Rawls describes justice as "the first virtue of social institutions."[4] But what is justice, and what do we mean when we speak of *social justice*? This essay introduces readers to the broad contours of contemporary debates about this vital concept.

What is social justice?

Debates about the meaning of justice are not new. Nearly 2,500 years ago, Plato wrote *The Republic*, a Socratic dialogue revolving around the nature of the just society. Many of our most difficult political debates today—disagreements about same-sex marriage, healthcare, internet privacy, religious liberty, immigration policy, and the like—center on disagreements about the meaning of social justice.

The *Oxford English Dictionary* defines justice as "conformity (of an action or thing) to moral right, or to reason, truth or fact; rightfulness; fairness; correctness; propriety."[5] In the ancient world, writers listed justice as one of four cardinal virtues, along with prudence, temperance, and courage. Aristotle describes justice as a quality of character, a virtue that involves

---

[3] Bronwyn Winter, *Hijab and the Republic: Uncovering the French Headscarf Debate* (Syracuse, NY: Syracuse University Press, 2008).

[4] John Rawls, *A Theory of Justice* (Cambridge, MA: Harvard University Press, 1971), 3.

[5] The Oxford English Dictionary, 10th edition, s. v. "justice."

the right treatment of another person.[6] Justice is about giving people their due. In this respect, justice by definition is *social* because it is interpersonal. However, the phrase *social justice* today is somewhat controversial. Radio talk show pundit Glenn Beck, for example, warns, "Look for the words 'social justice' or 'economic justice' on your church web site. If you find it, run as fast as you can. Social justice and economic justice, they are code words. Now, am I advising people to leave their church? Yes!"[7] Such comments well demonstrate the contested nature of the topic.

Beck's histrionic reaction notwithstanding, the truth is that anyone who is concerned about the challenges of living in community must assume some vision of social justice. If justice is about giving each person his or her due, social justice is simply about how *communities* give people their due. More substantively, social justice is about the institutions—political and non-political, formal and informal—that coordinate our life together. Social justice is about the laws and practices that limit our actions or that steer us to embrace shared goods. Social justice is also about how communities ensure that all members are able to experience the benefits of our life together, and how communities rightly distribute the goods, burdens, and risks of that life. How should communities be organized to ensure that all people are treated fairly? What limits may communities place on their members? What do we have rightful claims to as individuals, and what burdens may society rightly impose on us? If community is about what we share in common— common goods, common rights, common responsibilities—then how do communities rightly recognize and affirm diversity? All of these questions are intrinsic to any vision of social justice.

While one need not be a Christian to be concerned about social justice, social justice should be of particular concern to Christians. The Hebrew words *mishpat* and *tsedeqah*, frequently translated as "righteousness" or "justice" in English bibles, occur 419 and 157 times respectively in the Hebrew Bible. The Hebrew Bible describes Yahweh as a "God of justice [*mishpat*]" (Isa. 30.18, NRSV) who "executes justice [*mishpat*] for the orphan and the widow, and who loves the strangers, providing them food and clothing" (Deut. 10.18). Yahweh calls Israel to be a community that embodies this same regard for the marginalized: "[L]earn to do good; seek justice [*mishpat*], rescue the

---

[6] See Aristotle, "The Nicomachean Ethics," *The Internet Classics Archive*, 2000, http://classics.mit.edu//Aristotle/nicomachaen.html (accessed November 13, 2013): "justice is often thought to be the greatest of virtues ... It is complete because he who possesses it can exercise his virtue not only in himself but towards his neighbour also ... For this same reason, justice, alone of the virtues, is thought to be 'another's good.'"

[7] Laurie Goodstein, "Outraged by Glenn Beck's Salvo, Christians Fire Back," *The New York Times*, March 11, 2010, http://www.nytimes.com/2010/03/12/us/12justice.html?_r=0 (accessed November 13, 2013).

orphan, plead for the widow" (Isa. 1.17). In the eighth century BCE, the Hebrew prophet Amos delivered a warning to the Israelites that God would soon bring judgment upon them because "they sell the righteous for silver, and the needy for a pair of sandals" (Amos 2.6). God cries out for Israel to be transformed, to "let justice [*mishpat*] roll down like waters, and righteousness [*tsedeqah*] like an ever-flowing stream" (Amos 5.24). God's own character, God's *justice*, is thus to be embodied within the covenant community— people for whom God's justice orients their relationships with one another and with the foreigner. But social justice is not only Israel's concern; God calls all nations to embody justice, as the prophet Daniel warns the Babylonian ruler Nebuchadnezzar: "atone for your sins with righteousness [*tsedeq*], and your iniquities with mercy to the oppressed" (Dan. 4.27).

In the New Testament, justice is no less a concern. The Koiné Greek word *dikaiosune* occurs 91 times and *krisis* 47 times and variously refer to God's own righteousness/justice (Mt. 6.33; 2 Cor. 9.9; Rom. 3.25, 26; 2 Pet. 1.1; 2 Tim. 4.8; 1 Jn 2.29), or the quality of a person who lives rightly (Rom. 6.13; Mt. 5.20; 2 Cor. 6.14; Heb. 1.9; 1 Jn 2.29). Paul's letter to the Romans is in large part an epistolary defense of God's justice (Rom. 1.17; 3.5, 21, 22, 9.28). Jesus pronounces a blessing on those who hunger and thirst for right-eousness/justice [*dikaiosune*] (Mt. 5.6) and criticizes those religious leaders who obsess over religious practices while neglecting the weightier matters of the law: "justice [*krisis*] and mercy and faithfulness." In parallel to the Hebrew Bible's depiction of God's commission to Israel, the author of the book of Acts describes the Christian community as one uniquely devoted to the wellbeing of the poor (Acts 2.43–7, 4.32–4).

While there is not space in this essay to detail the historical trajectory of social justice past to present, Christian leaders of the modern era echo this biblical call for justice. In the papal encyclical *Rerum Novarum* (1891), Pope Leo XIII offers a Christian vision of the just society, one in which regard for the wellbeing of the working class is a guiding norm:

> The members of the working classes are citizens by nature and by the same right as the rich; they are real parts, living the life which makes up, through the family, the body of the commonwealth; and it need hardly be said that they are in every city very largely in the majority. It would be irrational to neglect one portion of the citizens and favor another, and therefore the public administration must duly and solicitously provide for the welfare and the comfort of the working classes; otherwise, that law of justice will be violated which ordains that each man shall have his due.[8]

---

[8]   Leo XIII, "Rerum Novarum: Encyclical of Pope Leo XIII on Capital and Labor," *Libreria*

Christian theologian Gustavo Gutiérrez states the vital importance of social justice most succinctly:

> Where there is justice and righteousness, there is knowledge of Yahweh … To know Yahweh, which in Biblical language is equivalent to saying to love Yahweh, *is* to establish just relationships among men, it *is* to recognize the rights of the poor. The God of Biblical revelation is known through interhuman justice. When justice does not exist, God is not known; he is absent.[9]

Christians agree that being advocates for justice is critical to the Christian witness, but once we have agreed about the importance of justice, it quickly becomes apparent that Christians vary widely in their beliefs about what this commitment entails. What does social justice look like "on the ground," so to speak? Consider each case once again. John Lawrence and Tyrone Garner violated Texas's anti-sodomy law. The Texas penal code under which Lawrence and Garner were punished defines same-sex sexual activity as "deviant sexual intercourse."[10] Sodomy laws grew from the moral conviction that non-procreative sex (i.e., sexual acts that do not produce offspring) is immoral. Historically, the Christian belief that sodomy was "against nature" has served as justification for such laws.[11] But what should we think of laws like this? Lawrence and Garner were having consensual sex, after all. Is it just for communities to punish sexual behavior simply because some people believe sodomy to be immoral? If just communities may base laws on the moral beliefs of some, then what does social justice require when we *disagree* about the moral rightness of things like sodomy? Whose moral vision determines the laws that we will enforce? Perhaps social justice entails that we should simply "let a thousand flowers bloom"—just communities will simply let people live according to their own deeply held beliefs. But if this is so, then how far should this commitment to personal freedom extend? Does social justice require that we affirm the rights of private business owners to deny service to people on the basis of race?[12] What about other forms of racial or sexual discrimination?

Editrice Vaticana, http://www.vatican.va/holy_father/leo_xiii/encyclicals/documents/hf_l-xiii_enc_15051891_rerum-novarum_en.html (accessed November 13, 2013).

[9] Gustavo Gutiérrez, *A Theology of Liberation* (Maryknoll, NY: Orbis Books, 1973), 195.

[10] The relevant section of the state of Texas penal code is available at http://www.statutes.legis.state.tx.us/docs/pe/htm/pe.21.htm (accessed November 13, 2013).

[11] See William N. Eskridge, Jr., *Dishonorable Passions: Sodomy Laws in America, 1861–2003* (New York: Penguin Group, 2008).

[12] Llewellyn Rockwell, Jr., "Freedom of Association" (https://mises.org/daily/4465), argues that just societies must affirm the rights of business owners to segregate for any reason that they choose: "That a person has the right to make these choices on his or her own

Lawrence and Gardner protested against the injustice of their arrest. In 2003, the United States Supreme Court determined that the Texas anti-sodomy statute was unconstitutional. In his 6–3 majority ruling that struck down the statute, Justice Anthony Kennedy declared: "The petitioners [Lawrence and Garner] are entitled to respect for their private lives. The state cannot demean their existence or control their destiny by making their private sexual conduct a crime."[13] While many Christian organizations voiced support for the decision,[14] as recently as 2010 some Christian activists have continued to advocate the criminalization of consensual same-sex activity.[15] Legislators in Uganda have passed a law that increases the severity of criminal sanctions on homosexual offenders, including the subjection of those who engage in serial homosexual acts to life in prison.[16] Ongoing debate about sodomy laws, in short, revolves around disagreements about the nature of social justice.

Nikki White's story is tragic. Like tens of millions of uninsured Americans, White could not afford regular visits to her doctor or the expensive medicine that would have kept her disease in check. What does social justice entail for people like Nikki White? T.R. Reid observes that America has made a moral decision about healthcare that is at odds with the rest of the developed world:

> Despite all the rights and privileges and entitlements that Americans enjoy today, we have never decided to provide medical care for everybody who needs it. In the world's richest nation, we tolerate a health care system that leads to large numbers of avoidable deaths and bankruptcies among our fellow citizens.[17]

Many healthcare reform advocates argue for a system that is "fairer," one in which all citizens are guaranteed access to a basic level of care that is

---

cannot be denied by anyone who believes in liberty." (accessed November 13, 2013) Contrast this with Martin Luther King Jr.'s support for desegregation of private business in *Why We Can't Wait* (New York: Signet Classics, 2000), 111–12.

[13] See http://supreme.justia.com/cases/federal/us/539/558/case.html (accessed November 10, 2013).

[14] See the *Amici Curiae* brief, which supported overturning the Texas sodomy law: http://supreme.lp.findlaw.com/supreme_court/briefs/02-102/02-102.mer.ami.aob.pdf (accessed November 10, 2013).

[15] See Chris Matthews' 2010 interview of Peter Sprigg, senior research for the Family Research Council, where Sprigg defends the criminalization of consensual same-sex sexual activity, available at http://www.nbcnews.com/id/3036697/#35206587 (accessed November 10, 2013).

[16] Joanna Sadgrove, Robert M. Vanderbeck, Johan Andersson, Gill Valentine, and Kevin Ward, "Morality Plays and Money Matters: towards a situated understanding of the politics of homosexuality in Uganda," *The Journal of Modern African Studies* 50 (2012): 103–29.

[17] Reid, *The Healing of America*, 2.

publicly subsidized by taxpayers. From this perspective, social justice entails that healthcare be organized to ensure access to care, even for those who are unable to pay for it out of pocket.

But not everyone agrees that social justice requires such assurances. Some today argue that the systems of care that aspire to ensure access to care are themselves unjust. Medicare is a redistributive social program, after all, a mechanism that requires some people (i.e., taxpayers) to pay for the healthcare that other citizens receive. Says George Reisman, "the right to medical care does not mean a right to medical care as such, but to the medical care one can buy from willing providers."[18] From this perspective social justice requires that we let people make their own choices about healthcare and trust private charity to pick up the slack for people like Nikki White. Critics counter that such a system will leave the fate of the most vulnerable subject to the moral whims of strangers, potentially unable to receive the care that they need. Once again, disagreement about social justice abounds.

The *hijab* controversy in France is multilayered. At one level, debates about the *hijab* are fundamentally about identity. Some argue that the ban violates the religious liberty of Muslims and breeds intolerance. The *hijab* has become a symbol of identity and heritage for many, wearing the *hijab* a means of self-expression for Muslim women. Fareena Alam states: "Does this democratic society have any room for a British–Muslim woman like me who chooses to wear the hijab on my own terms? Isn't it the fundamental secular standard—that one cannot demand that any individual surrender an unobtrusive religious observance?"[19] Critics counter that the French public school system has as one of its principle aims the cultivation of the values of French citizenship, including a commitment to the practical separation of religion and the state. They claim that the display of Islamic headscarves undermines this commitment. How ought communities to reconcile the conflicts that attend the multivalent identities of their members? Does social justice entail that they should pursue practices aimed at instilling a sense of common purpose and identity, or ought communities to recognize and affirm cultural difference?

Furthermore, not everyone agrees that the *hijab* is best understood as a symbol of personal expression. Some feminist critics argue that for many young girls wearing the *hijab* is not an autonomous decision but one dictated by external coercion or peer pressure. From this vantage point the

---

[18] "The Real Right to Medical Care Vs. Socialized Medicine," http://mises.org/daily/3613#Sec_2 (accessed November 13, 2013).

[19] As quoted in "Viewpoints: Europe and the Headscarf" (BBC News Online, 10 February 2004): http://news.bbc.co.uk/2/hi/europe/3459963.stm (accessed November 13, 2013).

hijab is hardly a symbol of female self-assertion but rather an emblem of subjugation.[20] If this is so, does social justice entail anything with regards to the practice of life within this religious subculture? What would it mean to give women their due in the face of divergent understandings of gender and religious practice?

Social justice: Four challenges

As the three cases above attest, social justice is complex and controversial, touching on some of our deepest moral intuitions. The fervency of our disagreements testifies to how much we care about social justice. Even if we do not (yet) see eye to eye about what social justice requires, we agree that people should care about our life together. We might disagree about the shape of that life, but these disagreements beckon us to explore more deeply the sources of our discontent. Making sense of moral disagreements about social justice can be challenging. However, it is possible to make at least some sense of contemporary debates about social justice by noting four challenges that we face as we try to account for the nature of social justice in the Christian tradition.

Scarcity

Imagine a world of abundance in which there was an unlimited supply of resources that all of us desired. In such an imaginary world debates about the distribution of things like healthcare, food, and educational opportunity would be as necessary as debates over the distribution of air molecules. How much time have you spent debating whether or not we have enough air to breathe? Enlightenment philosopher David Hume observes that our world is one of *moderate scarcity*.[21] There are certain resources that all of us want or need, resources that are in limited supply. There are a finite number of doctors and hospitals, for example, and not enough transplantable organs for every person to be able to get everything he or she desires or needs. Thus, in the real world, communities must wrestle with the challenge of *distributive justice*. How does a just community organize itself so as to rightly distribute the scarce resources that all of us desire? As long as there is scarcity, the

---

[20] Winter, *Hijab and the Republic*, 26: "Whether secular or linked to pre-Islamic religious traditions, such traditional clothing practices are closely linked to patriarchal cultural and in particular to control of women's sexuality."

[21] David Hume, *An Enquiry Concerning the Principles of Morals*, ed. J. B. Schneewind (Indianapolis: Hackett Publishing Company, 1983), 20–26.

question of how communities rightly distribute these scarce resources is unavoidable.

Diversity

Communities face the challenge of diversity at a variety of levels. First, there is the challenge of *moral diversity*. Communities are made up of members who disagree about what is most important in life, what philosophers call "the good." What is a good life, after all? Many Christians believe that Jesus offers an ideal pattern for a life well lived and deem a life devoid of devotion to God as incompatible with living morally. Conversely, some public intellectuals today counter that religious devotion is both irrational and a source that inspires servility and unthinking acquiescence to evil.[22] This disagreement is but one example of the deep moral divisions that pervade contemporary life. So if we disagree about what kind of life we should aspire to live, what does a just society do? Does social justice require us to assume a singular vision of the good life, organizing society to cultivate a commitment to this vision? Or does social justice require that communities allow individuals space to pursue their own vision of the good without interference? If the former, then whose vision of the good life is allowed to dictate public policy? If the later, then what moral limits may society properly set on individuals?

Second, we also face the challenge of *racial, ethnic, and cultural diversity*. Communities today consist of people from wide-ranging racial, ethnic, and cultural backgrounds. What does social justice entail for how communities accommodate these differences? On the one hand, some visions of justice entail that racial, cultural, and ethnic differences be subsumed into a common identity. The historical metaphor of America as a great "melting pot" idealizes a communal vision in which cultural difference is not so much to be *valued* as it is to be *overcome*. On the other hand, critics counter that social justice entails not that we overcome these differences but that we instead affirm them, pursuing a multicultural *politics of recognition* in which community members learn to value racial, ethnic, and cultural diversity.[23] This conversation is all the more important due to the consequences of our own vexed histories in which racial, ethnic, and cultural difference have been principle sources of discrimination and inequality. What does social justice require if economic inequalities today are the consequences of the historical injustice of institutional racism?

---

[22] Christopher Hitchens, *God is Not Great: How Religion Poisons Everything* (New York: Twelve Books, 2007).

[23] Charles Taylor, *Multiculturalism: Examining the Politics of Recognition* (Princeton, NJ: Princeton University Press, 1994).

Third, we face the challenge of *gender diversity*. Increasingly, both secular and Christian ethicists have observed that historical conversations about social justice have tended toward highly abstract, theoretical analyses that de-emphasize the unique experiences of women. Some feminist ethicists today draw from these to advocate for revised conceptions of justice that account for these experiences. In her influential book *In a Different Voice* Carol Gilligan advocates for an "ethic of care" that replaces the abstraction of traditional accounts of justice with a theory that emphasizes empathy and the cultivation of caring relationships as the locus of moral concern.[24] Feminist scholars draw attention to the ways that traditional theories of justice have framed the concept in ways that reproduce gender inequality,[25] or have essentialized the male–female dichotomy in ways that are oppressive to people who do not fall neatly into these gender categories.[26] The social inequalities born out of long histories of gender discrimination raise important questions about the responsibilities of just societies as they deal with these outcomes.

Conflicting norms

Recently, Michael Sandel has argued that our contemporary disagreements about social justice stem from conflict among three important values that guide our intuitions about justice: welfare, liberty, and virtue.[27] Some theories of justice argue that a just society is one that maximizes the *welfare* of citizens. Communities in which a few people are able to live in luxury while the vast majority struggle to feed their families are unjust. Social justice entails that such societies be organized in order to enhance the *wellbeing* of society's members.

Other theories of justice emphasize *liberty* as the guiding norm. Just societies preserve space for individuals to pursue lives that they deem meaningful. Communities that regularly coerce people to conform to a single way of life, or that allow the majority to impose its will on the minority, or that steal what rightly belongs to a person or group of people are unjust; they violate liberty. Social justice from this perspective entails that societies zealously protect the property rights of individuals and that people have ample opportunity to live according to their own deeply held beliefs.

Finally, some theories of justice emphasize the importance of *virtue* as

---

[24] Carole Gilligan, *In a Different Voice* (Cambridge, MA: Harvard University Press, 1993).

[25] Susan Moller Okin, *Justice, Gender, and the Family* (New York: Basic Books, 1989).

[26] Judith Butler, *Gender Trouble: Feminism and the Subversion of Identity* (New York: Routledge, 1990).

[27] Michael Sandel, *Justice: What's the Right Thing to Do?* (New York: Farrar, Strauss, and Giroux, 2009).

the orienting value for a just society. Communities, after all, revolve around some sense of common purpose, some sort of common understanding about what is valuable, good, or right. A just society ought to orient community life in ways that cultivate these shared values, helping members to realize both the benefits and responsibilities of life in community. A just society ensures that all citizens have the resources necessary to become full participants in public life, and this society calls all members to be mutually accountable to one another.

While welfare, liberty, and virtue are all important, these values sometimes point to different conclusions about social justice. As Sandel argues, different theories of justice typically gravitate toward one of these values when they conflict. Those who emphasize the priority of welfare, for example, might see a progressive income tax that requires wealthier citizens to fund programs that benefit the poor to be just, while libertarians would fault this policy as an unjust infringement of the property rights of the wealthy. Or what about a society that permits commercial surrogacy contracts in which wealthier families pay poorer women to bear children for them? Assuming that poorer women are not forced into these contracts, libertarians might well permit such practices, in keeping with their commitment to individual liberty. If women rightly own their bodies, after all, then why not permit women to, in effect, "rent their wombs" to the highest bidder? Yet welfare concerns abound among those who fear that such practices effectively take advantage of poorer women in ways that are detrimental to their own wellbeing; virtue-oriented critics fault such market transactions as a perversion of the practice of childbearing. In short, disagreements about justice often emerge because we disagree about what values are most important in establishing the parameters of a just society.

Christian tradition

Scarcity, diversity, and conflicting norms are challenges that confront all theories of justice. For Christians, however, the Christian tradition itself poses another set of challenges to understanding social justice. Christian theologian Stanley Hauerwas warns that social justice is "a bad idea" for Christians.[28] Such a claim on its face might seem shocking, just another example of a privileged white male scholar aligning himself with the status quo. Hauerwas rejects this characterization and instead asks us to consider what Christians have lost by appropriating without question the language of social justice in Christian discourse. When Christians parrot secular

---

[28] Stanley Hauerwas, *After Christendom* (Nashville: Abingdon Press, 1991), 45–68.

appeals to social justice, argues Hauerwas, they too often forsake the virtues, values, and norms intrinsic to the Christian story of God's work in Christ. The Christian imagination has been co-opted by liberal presuppositions that obscure the distinctive claims that properly inform life in Christian community. Says Hauerwas,

> The current emphasis on justice among Christians springs not so much from an effort to locate the Christian contribution to wider society as it does from Christians' attempt to find a way to be societal actors without that action being colored by Christian presupposition.[29]

For example, while secular approaches to social justice might legitimate the use of violence for justice's sake, the Sermon on the Mount, a guiding articulation of ethics in many Christian traditions, teaches followers of Christ to love their enemies and turn the other cheek. Critics might well deem this rejection of violence unrealistic, but Christians who believe faithfulness to the way of Jesus to be essential to living justly cannot simply jettison what seems unintuitive to outsiders. The distinction between secular and Christian visions of justice matters. Rather than finding ways to reconcile Christian faith with secular reason, Christians should instead pursue a way of life that embodies the "politics of Jesus," so to speak, a politics that will seem alien to those outside of the church.[30]

Whatever one thinks of Hauerwas's critique of social justice, his comments point to an area of particular concern for Christians. With respect to social justice, the Christian tradition raises numerous questions. How does Jesus Christ's call that his disciples love God, their neighbors, and their enemies inform Christian visions of social justice? In Christian justice conversations, is the principle locus of concern the *Christian community*, as some argue, and if so what manner of life would constitute a just Christian community? What does the Christian faith entail for how Christians engage life outside of the church—in the political sphere, for example? And what are Christians to do about the theological disagreements that give rise to divergent Christian accounts of social justice? Not all Christians are persuaded, for example, that faithfulness to Jesus entails that Christians reject the use of violent force when necessary; the Christian just war tradition is alive and well.[31] Christian scholars must wrestle with questions about how the Christian

---

[29] Ibid., 58.

[30] See John Howard Yoder, *The Politics of Jesus*, 2nd edition (Grand Rapids, MI: William B. Eerdmans Co., 1972).

[31] For a recent defense of the Christian just war tradition, see chapter 3 of Timothy P. Jackson, *The Priority of Love: Christian Charity and Social Justice* (Princeton, NJ: Princeton University Press, 2003).

tradition intersects with broader societal conversations about the nature of social justice.

Social justice and Christian faith: Five views

Christian voices offer divergent, even conflicting perspectives about the nature of justice. This book intends to make sense of these differences. Five highly regarded Christian scholars will introduce readers to five rival perspectives on social justice and the Christian tradition: 1) libertarianism, 2) liberalism, 3) liberation theology, 4) feminism, and 5) virtue ethics. While the book aspires to offer a lucid introduction to each perspective, the purpose here is more than merely informative. The book is dialogical, structured so that the authors are able to model for the reader reasoned exchange among these perspectives. Each section of this book begins with a foundational essay in which a contributor introduces and defends a distinctive vision of social justice. Following this foundational essay, the other contributors respond, noting areas of agreement and disagreement and raising questions of one another. The book concludes with a final section in which each author presents a closing response to the other contributors.

A book of this sort cannot hope to be comprehensive. Observant readers will note some prominent secular and theological perspectives not represented here. There is no section devoted to utilitarianism, for example. The varieties of liberationist perspectives and the diversity within Christian liberalism are not well accounted for in this volume, nor is the Christian natural law tradition given the substantive attention that it merits. The vastness of social justice discourse poses a challenge to a project of this sort, which must of necessity narrow the scope of conversation. While some may find reason to fault the editorial decision to exclude certain perspectives while including others, a strong case can be made that the five perspectives included in this volume are important enough to contemporary social justice discourse that they merit the attention they receive here. If this volume does not provide a final resolution to what it means to be committed to justice, at the very least it will offer readers a window into how some contemporary Christian scholars answer this question.

This book is structured as follows. In Chapter 1, Jason Jewell makes a case for a libertarian theory of justice. The growing prominence of libertarian thought, with its critique of big government and forced taxation, in contemporary US politics makes Jewell's essay a fitting one with which to begin. Libertarian justice, says Jewell, is about *means*, not *ends*. Libertarians object to the initiation of violent force (*aggression*), even if for a worthy cause. States by nature are *aggressive*. Forced taxation robs individuals of property. Morals legislation (e.g. laws against drug use and pornography) violate individual liberty. Thus, a just society would ideally minimize the role of the state in human life. Jewell defends an alternative vision of society in which voluntary association and contractual exchanges largely or entirely replace the state. Appealing to the Christian natural law tradition as well as biblical prohibitions against aggression, Jewell argues that his libertarian theory of justice best articulates the Christian tradition's own vision of the state, elevating charity while reducing levels of actual or threatened violence in society.

Not everyone is persuaded by the libertarian voice, of course. In Chapter 2, Daniel Dombrowski introduces readers to the influential work of philosopher John Rawls, whose seminal book *A Theory of Justice* has largely set the agenda for academic debates about justice since its 1971 publication. Beginning with the empirical observation that reasonable people disagree about basic questions of the good, Dombrowski presents Rawls's logical argument in defense of a politically liberal society. Like libertarians, Rawlsian liberals value individual liberty. But unlike libertarians, liberals believe that just societies will arrange themselves to ensure that natural and economic inequalities will not hinder opportunities for those on the margins. Dombrowski explores the practical ramifications of Rawls's theory of justice, arguing that this philosophical theory of justice is fully compatible with the Christian tradition. Christians motivated by Christ's call to love their neighbors will find much to appreciate in a liberal society arranged to provide the greatest benefit to the least-well-off members. A just society will ensure that a robust social safety net exists that ensures the wellbeing of those that libertarianism might otherwise leave behind.

In Chapter 3, Miguel De La Torre introduces readers to a liberationist perspective on social justice, a radical departure from both libertarianism and liberalism. Representative of prominent mainstream theories of social justice, these perspectives, argues De La Torre, are rooted in class, gender, racial, and ethnic assumptions that render them suspect, and in the end both libertarianism and liberalism do little more than justify the status quo. De La Torre defends a revolutionary theory of justice that entails Christian solidarity with the poor and oppressed, those on the "underside" of history. Just as God sides with the poor against the rich and powerful, so are Christians to align themselves with the poor against the unjust powers that prevail in the world. Today, such solidarity requires a radical posture, an ethic *para joder* in which Christians "screw with" the system, disrupting prevailing modes of thinking and living to open up new, more just possibilities. In doing so, Christians take Christ's own life—his own solidarity with the suffering—as a model for their own lives.

In Chapter 4, Laura Stivers introduces readers to a Christian feminist theory of justice. Similar to the liberationist perspective introduced by De La Torre in Chapter 3, Christian feminists are fundamentally concerned with the particular forms of injustice that people on the margins, especially women, experience. Calling into question abstract, ahistorical approaches to justice such as those defended by libertarians and liberals, Stivers argues that social justice entails a commitment to unmasking forms of systemic and cultural oppression that are dehumanizing to the most vulnerable. Distributive justice is critical, yes, but the pursuit of economic equality is inextricable from critical analysis of prevailing beliefs about gender, race, and class. Too often these assumptions have provided justification for inter-secting forms of oppression experienced by the most vulnerable. The call for justice requires not simply an understanding of what injustice is, but more importantly a personal commitment to *justice-making*, a willingness to engage in practices that undermine the complex web of power, privilege, and patriarchy that undermines self-worth and inhibit right relations. To make justice is to do nothing less than heed the divine call for us to become disciples of Jesus.

Over the last several decades, virtue has reemerged as a prominent concern in Christian social ethics. In Chapter 5, Elizabeth Phillips intro-duces readers to how the concept of moral virtue can orient a contemporary Christian vision of justice. She argues for a vision of justice which is guided by the Christian virtues of faith, hope, and love, and which points towards a vision of the common good. Phillips observes that justice is not simply about knowing what is right, but also about becoming more just people, and that modern approaches to justice, by focusing narrowly on questions of duty and the right, have neglected the role that communities play in cultivating moral dispositions and practices indispensable to human flourishing.

This book is purposefully *conversational* and *argumentative*. Its contrib-utors intend to make the case for their distinctive visions of social justice, and they intend to persuade readers that the other perspectives represented in the volume are problematic in one way or another. Readers have the opportunity to witness Christian scholars in dialogue, often disagreeing with one another, sometimes stridently so. In a sound-bite age dominated by partisan cable news networks, each spinning their respective vision of the world, serious intellectual exchange can be hard to come by. This book aspires to offer readers a window into the constructive possibilities of such exchange.

1

Libertarianism and Social Justice: A Christian Approach

Jason Jewell

Todd and Sarah are both Christians who advocate justice. They both believe that the just society is one in which all children receive a decent education, people of all races, genders, and social backgrounds have equal opportunities, and huge disparities in wealth do not exist. Their social vision is *egalitarian*.

To advance his vision of the just society, Todd donates a portion of his income to a ministry that provides scholarships at a local Christian school for children from low-income families. He volunteers at a homeless shelter run by another ministry. He knows that his actions help many people, but he is also painfully aware that the social problems he sees around him are much bigger than he is. He decides to increase his income by acquiring more job training and starting a part-time business on the side. He devotes most of the resulting income to ministry efforts. Todd also works to raise awareness among the affluent people in his community of the problem of homelessness and the need for Christian education. He secures pledges from them to fund scholarships for children, and job training and counseling for the homeless. In schools, the inner city, and the suburbs, Todd lets his acquaintances know that his Christian faith is what prompts him to sacrifice in this way. His example provides a powerful inspiration to those around him. Over time, he hopes to build a network of like-minded contacts among local churches and businesses who will work with him to create opportunities and jobs for those on the lower rungs of the socio-economic ladder.

Sarah also donates her time and money to worthy causes locally. However, she becomes discouraged when thinking about the scale of the social problems in her community, and she doubts that the institutions she supports will ever make a significant impact. She knows there is wealth in her community. She is frustrated when she sees affluent people choosing to enjoy luxuries when she knows those resources could be doing significant good for the poor. She believes she would be a better steward of those resources than the people who now control them. However, Sarah also knows that stealing is wrong, and she would not consider simply robbing the wealthy in order to help the poor. So Sarah decides to devote her energy to political activism. She knows that the state is the largest and most powerful institution in society, and she thinks that it is the only entity that can realistically fix the problems she sees. She hopes to persuade the state to take away the "excess" wealth of the affluent people in the community and use it to provide opportunities to those who are less well off. She works to increase the power of the state, trusting that good people who end up in office will exercise that power responsibly. She knows that government programs are relatively inefficient, with overhead costs far exceeding those of the ministries she supports, so more money will have to be taken in taxes to receive the same results her ministries achieve. She also knows that relying on the state for poor relief, education, and other aspects of social welfare will prevent her and other Christians from using these avenues as opportunities for evangelism, but she considers this an acceptable price to pay for the alleviation of some of the big social problems she sees around her.

Which of these strategies, Todd's or Sarah's, is more Christian?

Nancy and Dave are both Christians who advocate justice. They both believe that God created men and women with different strengths and weaknesses, suiting them for different social roles. They also believe that each individual's status as a unique creation with a unique potential will inevitably result in a "natural elite" that controls a disproportionate amount of social wealth, and that there's nothing inherently wrong with that. They believe that the just society is not one in which everyone gets the same material breaks, but rather is one in which a high level of public morality is maintained so that people, especially children, are protected from harmful influences and temptations that could lead them astray. We might call their vision *complementarian* or *traditionalist*.

In addition to her charitable giving, Nancy volunteers at a local ministry that provides resources like a mothers'-day-out program for stay-at-home moms. She also contributes to a non-profit organization that provides marital counseling for couples who are considering divorce and another that provides rehab for recovering addicts. When she receives her next raise at work, she plans to donate to an adoption agency that successfully placed a child with a friend of hers last year. Nancy knows that in the big picture her individual efforts will not solve the problems she is fighting, but she knows she is helping many people and strengthening her community.

Dave also engages in charitable giving and approves of the kind of work Nancy's organizations do, but he is dissatisfied with what he considers the small headway these private efforts are making against the enormous problems of broken homes and hedonism in his community and in society at large. He believes there must be a faster way to address these issues. So Dave turns to political activism. He lobbies against the proposals for drug decriminalization that have been making their way on to the ballot in his state. He writes letters to his federal and state representatives urging them to impose tighter controls on the internet and the airwaves to prevent obscene material from circulating. He also argues for the government to do more routine surveillance of the population in the hopes of catching drug traffickers.

Which of these approaches, Nancy's or Dave's, is more Christian?

In each of the scenarios described above, one Christian pursues a vision of the just society through purely voluntary or "private" avenues. The other pursues the same vision through political means. Thus although Todd agrees with Sarah on how society ultimately ought to look, his efforts to nudge society in that direction actually bear a closer resemblance to Nancy's than to Sarah's. Conversely, Sarah's focus on leveraging the institution of the state to accomplish her social vision looks more like Dave's approach than Todd's.

The *libertarian* system of thought is concerned more with the strategies employed to achieve desired social outcomes than it is with those outcomes themselves. In other words, it is primarily about *means*, not *ends*. In the above examples, libertarian theory does not make a judgment as to which vision for society, the egalitarian or the traditionalist, is better. However, it does argue that Todd and Nancy are taking the ethically correct (socially just) approach in advancing their respective social visions, whereas Sarah's and Dave's tactics are ethically incorrect (socially unjust).

Libertarianism is a set of claims about the use of *violence* in society: when it is ethically permissible to resort to violence, and when it is not. This makes libertarianism a *political philosophy* and not a comprehensive theory of ethics. This point cannot be overemphasized, but to explain it fully I must devote considerable space to a discussion and analysis of the central institution of modern society: the state. Only with a solid understanding of this institution will the ethical conclusions of libertarianism make sense.

What is the State?

Nearly everywhere we look in the world today, we find the state. We have grown up with it, and we take many or most of its operations for granted. It delivers our mail, puts out fires, operates schools in our communities, and sends monthly checks to our senior citizens. It also takes portions of every paycheck we earn and regulates many aspects of our lives. But what is it, exactly? What distinguishes the state from the other institutions we encounter in our daily lives, such as Home Depot, the Boy Scouts, or the Rotary Club? After all, non-state institutions can and often do perform the same services the state performs. UPS delivers packages at least as quickly as the US Postal Service. Claims agents for private insurance companies often track down stolen goods more quickly than the police. Private schools generally educate children as well as or better than state-supported schools. The Red Cross outshines the Federal Emergency Management Agency in providing disaster relief. Of course, churches and numerous other charities help alleviate poverty in our communities, just as state welfare programs do. I could go on listing examples, but these make the point.

So once again, what makes the state different from all of these private institutions and organizations? The answer is that whereas the private organizations listed above support themselves through sales to customers, investment, and donations, the state claims the right to support itself through *force*. The twentieth-century sociologist Max Weber expressed this most famously in his lecture "Politics as a Vocation" (1919) by stating: "A state is a human community that (successfully) claims the monopoly of the legitimate use of physical force within a given territory."[1] Weber's characterization of the state has become standard in the field of political science.

Weber's phrase "legitimate use of physical force" refers to the authority to *initiate* force against others. Everyone agrees that muggers, rapists, and murderers use force illegitimately in part because "they started it," whereas someone who tries to fend off an assailant with pepper spray or fingernails is not in the wrong because the victim did not initiate the violence. The state, on the other hand, claims that when it initiates force no moral outrage occurs. In other words, *the state claims that it does not have to follow the same rules as every other individual and institution in civilized society.*

We do not always see this clearly because we usually employ different terms to describe similar actions by state and non-state actors. If I take your money against your will, we call it "theft," but if the state takes your money against your will, we call it "taxation." If I force you from your home and into my service, we call it "kidnapping" and "enslavement," but if the state does the same thing to you, we call it "conscription" or "the draft." If I force you to pay me money to open a business on your own property, we call it a

---

[1]   Max Weber, "Politics as Vocation," in *From Max Weber: Essays in Sociology*, ed. and trans. H.H. Gerth and C. Wright Mills (New York: Oxford University Press, 1946), http://www.sscnet.ucla.edu/polisci/ethos/Weber-vocation.pdf (accessed February 1, 2014).

"shakedown," but if the state does it, we call it "the permitting process." If I intentionally kill people who have never harmed me in any way, we call it "murder," but when the state does it, we often call it "an act of war."

Saint Augustine of Hippo provided perhaps the best illustration of the double standard applied to state action in his *City of God*:

> Indeed, that was an apt and true reply which was given to Alexander the Great by a pirate who had been seized. For when that king had asked the man what he meant by keeping hostile possession of the sea, he answered with bold pride, "What [i.e., the same thing] you mean by seizing the whole earth; but because I do it with a petty ship, I am called a robber, while you who does it with a great fleet are styled emperor."[2]

Some might respond to this discussion of the state's coercive nature by saying "It may be true that the State initiates force, but so do corporations and other powerful interests and individuals in society. Walmart forces mom-and-pop stores out of business everywhere it opens a new store. There's only one cable company that services my neighborhood, so I'm forced to use it. The bank forced me into refinancing my mortgage on very unfavorable terms when I couldn't make my payments for a couple of months." This counter-argument makes sense only if we accept a very broad definition of "force" extending beyond the realm of physical violence. None of these examples involves the initiation of violence against anyone. Walmart does not send enforcers out to break the kneecaps of its competitors. Instead, it persuades shoppers to come to its stores by offering them better deals. The local cable company doesn't threaten anyone with violence for refusing to sign up for its most recent special. Anyone not satisfied with the service it offers is free not to use it (and not to pay for it). The bank has not committed any aggression against the delinquent homeowner who has broken his promise to pay back his loan on schedule. In fact, the homeowner agreed *in advance* to the refinancing of the loan or the repossession of the home when he signed the loan documents in the first place and received a considerable sum of money from the bank. He might not like his present situation, but it's hard to see how the bank's actions could be called "force" when the homeowner gave his consent up front. We are left with our original contention that *only the state* asserts a legitimate monopoly on the initiation of force.

Here again the skeptic might respond by saying, "What about crony capitalism? Big banks received hundreds of billions of dollars in bailouts following the 2008 financial crisis. That local cable company got a sweetheart deal from the city council locking out its competitors. Walmart got the land

---

[2] Saint Augustine of Hippo, *City of God*, Book IV, Chapter 4.

for its new store from an eminent domain seizure." What must be remembered in each of these situations is that the state is involved, and that is where the coercion occurs. Whether it is the transferring of taxpayer funds to corporations, the granting of a compulsory monopoly, or the forcible seizure of private property, the state is what enables Big Business and other powerful interests to exploit ordinary people.

A moment's reflection tells us that the state is making a bold claim in saying it has the right to initiate force against others. It's important to realize how this initiation of force is tied to nearly everything the state does. The overwhelming majority of state activities are funded by taxation. This includes military operations, social programs like Medicare and food stamps, running of schools, scientific research, subsidies to farms and corporations, maintenance of parks and roads, and a host of other functions. In some of these cases, such as the maintenance of parks and the operation of state universities, operating funds come partly from donors' gifts and users' fees, e.g. tuition payments. However, these funding sources do not cover all the operating costs, and the state taxes its citizens to make up the difference. In other words, all of these state functions rely on coercion.

I must dwell on this point (the coercive nature of the state) a bit longer because so many people resist recognizing it and its implications. They look at a state function such as the operating of a public school and think, "There's nothing violent about educating children. How could anyone consider this a coercive activity?" The answer is that *ends cannot be divorced from the means that are employed to achieve them.* In this case, the state pursues the education of children not only through compulsory attendance laws, but also through coercing citizens to pay property, sales, and income taxes, which are used to pay the public schools' faculty, staff, and administrators. Most people have a decent aversion to accepting stolen goods as gifts or as payment for debts, so it makes them uncomfortable to reflect that "free" services they receive from the state, e.g. the education of their children, have been obtained in a similar fashion. However, we must squarely face the reality that anything the state provides us, it does so *via* force or the threat of force, even when the service itself is not inherently coercive.

The libertarian view of the State

The foregoing analysis of the state should clarify my statement that libertarianism is a political philosophy because it makes a set of claims about when violence is morally permissible in society. In its simplest form, libertarianism condemns the initiation of force. This stance is often referred to as the Non-Aggression Principle or Non-Aggression Axiom, and it is the "classic" libertarian starting point for evaluating the legitimacy of social interactions, including those in which the state is involved.[3] Philosopher Gerard Casey defines it this way: "No one may initiate or threaten to initiate the use of coercive physical violence [aggression] against the person or property of another."[4] Put more simply, the Non-Aggression Principle is the consistent application of what we all learned in kindergarten: don't hit others and don't take what doesn't belong to you. These simple rules seem obvious and just to nearly all people, but they also have a philosophical foundation.

Libertarians often justify the Non-Aggression Principle through an appeal to intuition and natural law, a 2,000-year-old philosophical tradition that holds we can discover basic truths about the natural order and ethics through the proper use of reason. We all intuitively sense that we "own" ourselves, in that we possess volition and naturally control our own actions. We also naturally acquire a sense of ownership of things in the physical world for which we have worked or traded with others. If someone takes these things away from us against our will, we feel violated in some way. Gerard Casey writes that there is a natural argument for the Non-Aggression Principle based on reciprocity: "Why should the NAP [Non-Aggression Principle] be respected? Because transgressing this principle results in the violation of the basic liberty of other people, their liberty to dispose of themselves and their lawfully acquired property as they see fit."[5] Thus the Non-Aggression Principle is a negative expression of the Golden Rule: do not do to others what you would not wish to have done to you.

I must stress again that libertarianism is not a comprehensive theory of ethics. Libertarians do not claim that all non-aggressive actions are moral or just, only that aggressive actions are unjust. In other words, the Non-Aggression Principle provides a *minimum threshold* of justice. To evaluate the morality or justness of a non-aggressive action, a libertarian must bring a complementary system of ethics—a system of ethics compatible with the Non-Aggression Principle—to bear.

Libertarians are a diverse lot who have radically different ideas about what constitutes a good or just society. Some favor traditional mores, while

---

[3] The writings of Murray Rothbard (1926–1995) provide much of the theoretical framework for libertarianism. See especially *For a New Liberty* (1974) and *The Ethics of Liberty* (1982), both available at the Ludwig con Mises Institute website: http://mises. org.

[4] Gerard Casey, *Libertarian Anarchy: Against the State* (New York: Continuum Books, 2012), 38.

[5] Ibid., 43–4. The quoted passages come from Crispin Sartwell, *Against the State: An Introduction to Anarchist Political Theory* (New York: SUNY Press, 2008), 21, 103.

others wholeheartedly endorse alternative moral norms. Some wish to see wealth evenly distributed throughout the society, whereas others are less troubled about the existence of pockets of relative wealth and poverty. Some hate corporations, and others love them. Some are atheists who would like to see religion disappear from the public square, but others are Christians who hope to restore the cultural dominance once enjoyed by the Church.

What unites libertarians is their insistence that aggression is not the way to achieve a good society. Ends do not justify means. Most people do not find these assertions controversial. However, what separates libertarians from mainstream thinking about aggression is that libertarians deny the state's central claim that it is justified in initiating force against others. *They insist that the State follow the same rules expected of everyone else in civilized society.*

Given the lengths to which I have gone to demonstrate the essential connection between the state and coercion, you may wonder if libertarians must necessarily be anarchists, i.e., people who favor the complete abolition of the state. In fact, many libertarians have embraced a philosophical anarchist position. Because the term "anarchist" still conjures up for many people mental images of the violent European, anti-state protestors and assassins of the nineteenth century, libertarian anarchists frequently call themselves "market anarchists" or "anarchocapitalists" to emphasize that they do not oppose peaceful commerce.

Other libertarians, sometimes called "minarchists" (*not* "monarchists"), believe that the state does have a few legitimate functions related to protecting citizens from the aggression of others. For example, they may favor state operation of a strictly defensive military, police force, and court system. Of course, if the state were limited to these functions, its size, revenues, and budget would be a fraction of current levels in any Western country, making the differences between the anarchists and minarchists seem negligible in the current political context.

Many people will consider a society without the state as its central institution a ludicrous notion. Hasn't the state always been with us? It may surprise you to learn that the answer is no, or at least not in its modern form. Although elites of various kinds have coercively oppressed people throughout nearly all of human history, the state as we know it, with its bureaucratic structure, general taxing authority, and claims of sovereignty, developed only in the sixteenth and seventeenth centuries in Europe and spread around the world thereafter. Many state services we take for granted today were provided adequately by private entities until the twentieth century, when the state crowded them out.[6] Yet most people today cannot

---

[6]   Cf. Marvin Olasky, *The Tragedy of American Compassion* (Wheaton, IL: Crossway, 2008).

envision any sort of social organization in the absence of this relatively new institution. The truth is that the state in general, and individual states in particular, did not fall from heaven. They are historically contingent, and we do have examples of societies that organized themselves without anything that could reasonably be called a state.[7]

The implementation of non-aggression throughout the various levels of government would bring many changes, and libertarians have intramural disagreements concerning strategies to make the transition, but nearly all agree that the following steps would be positive.

1) Military and foreign policy

Libertarians condemn aggression against and provocation of other countries, advocating a "Golden Rule" in foreign policy. Nearly all libertarians condemned the wars against Iraq beginning in 1990 and 2003, the war in the Balkans throughout much of the 1990s, and similar attempts to impose American will around the world. They oppose military conscription.

2) Economic policy

Libertarians support replacing the current coercive regulatory system with a stronger enforcement of property rights combined with a voluntary system of accreditation such as exists in many industries already. This includes the elimination of subsidies to businesses ("corporate welfare") and all barriers to open competition in the marketplace. They also call for the repeal of legal tender laws to remove the state's monopoly power over our money and for the eventual abolition of central banks such as the Federal Reserve.

3) Education

Libertarians oppose the coercive nature of the public education system. They favor the repeal of compulsory attendance laws and the various restrictions on private and home schools. They call for voluntary funding of public schools, colleges, and universities through measures such as existing state lotteries. Eventually they would hope to achieve a "separation of School and state," returning education fully to voluntary associations and families, with the possible exception of military academies.

---

[7]   Thomas Woods and Gerard Casey, "Ireland: Stateless for 2,000 Years?" at http://www.libertyclassroom.com/casey, accessed June 27, 2013. See also David Friedman, "Private Creation and Enforcement of Law: An Historical Case," *Journal of Legal Studies* (March 1979): 399–415, http://www.daviddfriedman/Academic/Iceland/Iceland.html (accessed June 27, 2013).

4) Other social programs

Social programs such as Social Security, Medicare, and Medicaid are unsustainable in their current form, with unfunded liabilities exceeding the GDP of the entire world. Libertarians argue that the coercive nature of these programs makes them immoral apart from their unsound financial status. They call for a phasing out of these programs and their replacement with the private action—for example, the restoration of the multigenerational household, where the elderly live with their children—that used to provide these social functions.

5) Civil liberties

Libertarians oppose aggression as a means of enforcing moral or other community standards of behavior. Thus they favor replacing current laws against drug use, pornography, prostitution and the like with a system of voluntary covenants, deed restrictions, etc., that can provide incentives to moral behavior in a non-aggressive way.

These are just a few of the policy proposals libertarians have put forward, but they should give a general idea of their political direction.

Christianity and libertarianism

To what degree is Christianity compatible with a libertarian political philosophy?

On its face, the compatibility of the two seems obvious. Nowhere in the New Testament do we find an endorsement of the use of violence for the furthering of Christian goals. To the contrary, aggressive acts such as murder and robbery are condemned. The libertarian Christian repudiates such actions and insists that the state refrain from them as well.

This is a particularly important point in modern democratic societies, where the citizenry has some influence, however indirect, over public policy through the electoral process. Christian teaching deems theft (the forcible taking of someone else's property) immoral: "Thou shalt not steal." Christians should not steal even to support good causes, such as relief of the poor. Nevertheless, many Christians see no problem with voting for, say, state welfare programs, which are, fundamentally, institutionalized aggression with the goal of poor relief. It's as though some modern Christians interpret the command as reading "Thou shalt not steal, except by majority vote." The libertarian sees this stance as inconsistent, arguing that there is no difference between stealing and deputizing the state to steal ("tax") for the purposes you favor. Christians should not "do evil that good may result" (Rom. 3.8) with or without the state as a proxy.

Christians often respond to this line of argument by asking, "But what about Romans 13? It tells Christians to pay their taxes!" This passage from Saint Paul is indeed important for understanding the Christian's relationship to the "powers that be"; the message is basically "Don't give the emperor an excuse to persecute the Church." However, Romans 13 is not a blanket endorsement of state activities. In fact, if we look at all the biblical passages that directly bear on political powers, such as Genesis 11, 1 Samuel 8, Psalm 2, and various chapters of Revelation, we would have to conclude that the biblical writers were not huge fans. When we recall that our system of numbering chapters and verses is a later addition to the biblical text, it's significant that Paul's comments on Christian submission to the powers that be in Romans 13 immediately follow his command to "overcome evil with good" at the conclusion of Romans 12.[8]

Another point of overlap between libertarianism and Christian teaching is in the use of natural law. I have already mentioned the basis of libertarian thought in this tradition, which stretches back to the ancient Stoics and Cicero and continues to develop in the modern era through thinkers such as John Locke and Lysander Spooner. Christian recognition of natural law dates from Saint Paul, who wrote in Romans 2: "For when the Gentiles, which have not the law, do by nature the things contained in the law, these, having not the law, are a law unto themselves." Christian philosophy through the centuries has drawn heavily on natural law, with figures such as Saint Thomas Aquinas and Richard Hooker producing powerful syntheses of reason and revelation. Libertarian thinkers and Christian philosophers thus appeal to similar concepts, such as the rational nature of human beings, even if they sometimes favor different strands within the natural law tradition.

One aspect of libertarianism that sometimes does not "click" with Christians is the emphasis on property rights. "Everything belongs to God," a Christian might say, "and so we don't really have rights to property the way libertarians say we do." This objection misconstrues the libertarian position, which does not conflict with the doctrine of God's sovereignty, but merely tries to sort out which human beings have the proper authority to control and dispose of "stuff." Just as the command "thou shalt not commit adultery" presupposes the institution of marriage, the command "thou shalt not steal"

---

[8]   For a more detailed discussion of Romans 13 in context, see Norman Horn, "Romans 13: New Testament Theology of the State," http://libertarianchristians.com/2008/11/28/new-testament-theology-2 (accessed July 1, 2013). See also Andy G. Olree, *The Choice Principle: The Biblical Case for Legal Toleration* (Lanham, MD: University Press of America, 2006), 105–27.

presupposes individuals' rights of property. God delegates to each of us a tiny piece of His creation. To some He delegates more than to others, just as the master in the parable of the talents (Mt. 25.14-30). Each of us ultimately will give an account of how we have used God's resources, but in the meantime, we are commanded not to steal from each other.

Christian libertarians insist that this prohibition applies to the state as well. Acknowledging God's ultimate ownership of all property and resources is not grounds for concluding that the state can take from individuals what it pleases for the purposes it favors. The inconsistency in that position should be obvious: if God's ownership means that individuals do not have property rights, it also means that the state has no right to property either, unless one equates God with the state. The nineteenth-century philosopher G. W. F. Hegel (arguably) actually attempted to do this, but Christians who adhere to any version of orthodoxy do not. To the contrary, the most cursory reading of the story of Naboth's vineyard in 1 Kings 21 should lead us to conclude that it is illegitimate for rulers to confiscate others' property. Would King Ahab get a pass from Israel's prophets or from modern Christians if he had seized Naboth's vineyard via eminent domain, or if he had changed the zoning ordinances to prohibit agricultural use of Naboth's land? I certainly hope not.

Common objections to libertarianism

Anyone who has discussed libertarian ideas for any significant period of time has encountered certain objections from listeners. Some of these arise from simple misunderstandings of the libertarian position. I list a few of them here in the hope that we can dispense with them quickly.

1) "Libertarians are hyper-individualists who have an atomistic view of society and ignore the way individuals influence each other." No libertarian denies that individuals constantly influence each other as they pursue their various goals or that the cumulative impact of individuals' actions on society, environment, etc., can be significant.

2) "Libertarians are libertines and hedonists who condone all sorts of reprehensible behavior." Some libertarians probably do fit this description, but libertinism and libertarianism are very different things. Libertarian theory is not a comprehensive theory of ethics and makes no claim about the moral validity of "alternative lifestyles."

3) "Libertarians are utopians who believe that all people are good." The assumption behind this objection is that only the state can restrain whatever

evil tendencies people may have, so that if libertarians object to the state, they must be dismissive of people's potential for wickedness. However, this assumption is incorrect. Far from denying our propensity to do evil, libertarians will usually ask why an inherently violent institution *controlled by people subject to the same evil tendencies as everyone else* is supposed to be the solution to this problem.

4) "Libertarians believe that individuals are completely rational, always know their own interests best and act accordingly." This misconception often arises among those who think that libertarian thought is derived from the classical economists like Adam Smith, who frequently assumed rational economic action on the part of individuals. But libertarian thought does not assume wisdom on the part of individuals any more than it assumes goodness. It only denies the propriety of aggression when attempting to steer individuals toward better decisions.

5) "Libertarians are heartless people who don't care about _____ [insert particular concern]." The unstated assumption here is that one who cares about X will automatically want the state to see to X. Thus if libertarians dislike the Environmental Protection Agency, they must not care about the environment. If they have a problem with Medicare, they do not care about affordable healthcare for seniors, etc. As Frédéric Bastiat wrote more than 150 years ago, this misconception stems from a confusion of the distinction between the state and society.[9] Libertarians call for society to provide important services and protections on a voluntary (non-state) rather than a coercive (state) basis.

6) "Libertarians are on the side of Big Business." The plain fact is that Big Business has no desire to see politics move in a libertarian direction. It has invested huge sums of money in creating a fascistic system of "corporate welfare" and legal barriers to its competitors, whether foreign or domestic, through a manipulation of the state. Libertarianism threatens this arrangement with its insistence on the ending of monopolies, subsidies to businesses, and the regulatory apparatus that makes it prohibitively expensive for potential competitors to enter industries. Anyone who peruses the writings of libertarian thinkers at any length will find plenty of criticism of the ubiquitous collusion between corporations and the state.

To the political conservative concerned with public morality and with law and order, the libertarian points to historical examples of societies that

---

[9] See Frédéric Bastiat, *The Law*, available at http://bastiat.org/en/the_law.html (accessed November 30, 2013).

have maintained order with a minimal state or even with no state.[10] Many conservatives in recent years have come to realize that the conservative focus on political solutions to the "culture wars" of recent decades may have been a serious strategic error. Legal bans on immoral behavior have often become the cure that is worse than the disease, as they create black markets run by violent gangs. In the meantime, conservatives have failed to instill their values in the rising generation and are increasingly facing defeat at the ballot box in the twenty-first century. The libertarian stands with the conservative in opposing state policies and programs that encourage immoral and disorderly behavior, such as welfare regulations that discourage single mothers from marrying the fathers of their children.[11] In other areas, the libertarian invites the conservative to refocus efforts on culture rather than politics, rebuilding and strengthening the truly productive institutions of society: families, churches, and voluntary associations.

To the political left-liberal or progressive concerned with poverty and the distribution of wealth and influence in society, the libertarian points to the enormous theoretical and empirical evidence that markets, i.e., free associations and exchanges of goods and services, produce more wealth even for the least well off in society than state planning of the economy. As early as the 1920s, classical liberal economists Ludwig von Mises and F. A. Hayek demonstrated that central planners in places like the Soviet Union faced an insuperable obstacle—the impossibility of rational economic calculation when allocating resources in the absence of a price system—in their efforts to create economic growth and provide a robust standard of living for their citizens.[12] It took many years for economists on the left to concede this point, but most of them finally did after the Soviet Union collapsed and everyone realized just how decrepit its economy had become.[13] Nevertheless, the problem of economic calculation continues to plague bureaucracies charged with tasks such as humanitarian aid because their source of funding is divorced from their ability to receive and interpret important signals

---

[10] Cf. Casey, *Libertarian Anarchy*, 83–116.

[11] See Patrick F. Fagan, "Encouraging Marriage and Discouraging Divorce," *The Heritage Foundation*. March 26, 2001, http://www.heritage.org/research/reports/2001/03/encouraging-marriage-and-discouraging-divorce (accessed January 21, 2014).

[12] See, for instance, Ludwig von Mises, "Economic Calculation in the Socialist Commonwealth," trans. S. Adler (Vienna: The Ludwig von Mises Institute, 1990), http://mises.org/econcalc.asp (accessed January 21, 2014).

[13] For instance, the well-known socialist Robert Heilbroner wrote in the 1990s, "Many believed the Mises-Hayek argument had been demolished. In fact, we now know that their argument was all too prescient." Robert Heilbroner, "Socialism," in *The Concise Encyclopedia of Economics*, http://www.econlib.org/library/Enc/Socialism.html (accessed July 3, 2013).

concerning needs and preferences from the populations they are supposed to serve.[14]

Faced with the failure of central planning, most left-liberals and progressives have made their peace with some level of private ownership of property and markets, but they often still put their faith in the state as the agency that can and will redistribute (along the lines they prescribe) the wealth produced by a market economy. This faith is misplaced. The view that state officials are motivated primarily by the public good was discredited decades ago by the work of economists from the Public Choice school, which includes Nobel Prize winners James Buchanan, George Stigler, and Gary Becker. Public Choice theorists have shown that bureaucrats and other government officials are guided by self-interest, seeking larger budgets, more access to media and powerful people, etc., and that this tendency very often leads them to strike sweetheart deals and otherwise make decisions not in the best interests of the public. Attempts to put democratic pressure on the bureaucracy fail because the concentrated benefits (to special interests and the bureaucracy itself) and diffused costs (to millions of taxpayers) of this "rent-seeking" make it nearly impossible to motivate rational voters to take the pains to learn about the system and demand change. Thus, even conceding the desirability of the left-liberal/progressive goals of wealth redistribution, there is little reason to think that they can be accomplished *via* the state in a way that will satisfy the sincere egalitarian. The libertarian stands with the progressive in attempting to roll back state encroachments on civil liberties and otherwise invites the progressive to seek a more equal distribution of wealth and opportunity through voluntary means.

The world has created a monster in the modern state, an institution which has killed hundreds of millions of people in the last century with its wars, purges, and efforts to remake society according to the preferences of its controllers. There is something disturbing about the notion that civilized people would create an institution based on aggression, entrust it with enormous resources and power over practically every area of their lives, and then spend their time struggling for control of it. Yet that is where we are today. We have put nearly all of our eggs in one basket, thinking that we "just need good people" to operate this institution to everyone's benefit. Then we are surprised when people who enjoy exercising power over others are attracted to the institution, seize control of it, and use it for their own purposes.

The libertarian invites people to consider a different path, one where

---

[14] Cf. Chris Coyne, *Doing Bad by Doing Good: Why Humanitarian Action Fails* (Stanford, CA: Stanford Economics and Finance, 2013).

fighting over political spoils is not necessary because almost no political spoils are to be had. It is a path where violence does not underlie our social relations. It is a path where Christians show the light of Christ not through laws rammed down the throats of others, but through virtuous lives and works of love.

Libertarian justice: A liberal response
Daniel A. Dombrowski

Jason Jewell is to be thanked for trying to justify the libertarian view on a Christian basis. On his account, society can be morally improved through purely voluntary means. Whereas various private organizations (e.g., The Red Cross) support themselves through voluntary exchanges or donations, the state arises and continues to exist through an implicit appeal to violence. Hence the former are to be preferred to the latter, according to Jewell. He even goes so far as to say that when a thug takes your money it is called theft, but when the government does so it is called taxation.

Jewell is at his best when he reminds us of the fact that it is the state that enables Big Business to exploit people. But rather than issuing a call to reform the state, he counterintuitively calls for its dismantling or at least for its diminishment. As he sees things, the ends of the state cannot be divorced from the means used to enforce them. The state claims a monopoly on the use of force. It is surprising that, given Jewell's opposition to this claim to monopolization of the use of force on the part of the state, he does not indicate his own view of violence. Although I am not sure about this, I doubt if he is a Christian pacifist. Does he think that violence will be less of a problem if there were no police forces or if each voluntary mutual protection society had its own militia? Robert Nozick's famous defense of libertarianism in *Anarchy, State, and Utopia* makes it clear that there are good reasons why the state claims a monopoly on the use of force in that without such a claimed monopoly there would be, if not a Hobbesian war of all against all, at least a free-for-all among various individuals and groups who would be armed and dangerous.

It must be admitted that Jewell distinguishes between two sorts of libertarian thinkers: one group moves toward anarchism and the abolition of the state, whereas another group moves toward a minimal state that would involve a strictly defensive military and a police force. The latter would involve only minimal "taxation" (it seems that in order to be consistent, Jewell should say "theft"). But it is not clear which of these two sorts of libertarianism Jewell professes. In any event, it is to Jewell's credit that he argues that there is no eternal Platonic form of the state in that the state as we know it today is a contingent historical artifact. But this in itself does not necessarily support the case for its radical diminishment or dissolution.

To be frank, I resonate positively with libertarianism's foreign policy as articulated by Jewell: aggression should be condemned and *if* military power is justified it would have to be defensive in character. And libertarians are to be commended for opposing the wars in Iraq in the 1990s and from 2003 until the present. But little rapprochement between Jewell's libertarianism and Rawlsian political liberalism is possible in economic policy. Jewell would dismantle the state's ability to regulate commerce; however, he would also be willing to use state power to solidify property rights and to enforce anti-monopoly law. He would eliminate the state's monopoly on the issuing of money (analogous to the state's monopoly on the use of force) and he is opposed to any central banking system like the Federal Reserve. Perhaps Jewell has an explanation regarding how his views regarding economic policy are compatible with Christian ethics, but this connection is not explicated in any detail.

Look under any rock and libertarians find the abuse of force by the state. For example, the public education system is seen to be coercive in character because it is funded by forced property taxation and enforces compulsory attendance laws. Jewell is correct in claiming that there is a New Testament basis for being suspicious regarding the use of violence. However, it seems to me that it is quite a stretch to see public education and government welfare programs as institutionalized aggression. For example, public education can plausibly be seen as having a crucial role to play in enhancing liberty by ensuring that children develop the skills and virtues that are necessary to become participants in civil and political society and in the economy. It is also hard for me to see how libertarians can claim to have a defensible environmental policy if, in principle, they are in favor of dismantling the national park system and selling off the land to the highest bidder. Perhaps the land would be bought by private environmental interests like The Nature Conservancy. Or perhaps it would be bought by developers who would want Mt. Rainier National Park to be turned into a ski resort and casino complex. I think that almost all reasonable people would see this latter alternative as a disaster.

Jewell's intellectual honesty is in evidence when he tries to reach rapprochement with both liberals and progressives, on the one hand, and with political conservatives, on the other. But his idea that a more egalitarian and just system of distribution of wealth could be brought about by strictly voluntary means is a real cipher. And it seems hyperbolic to claim that the state is a real monster.

I would like to be as clear as possible regarding what I take to be the greatest strength and the greatest weakness of Jewell's view. From a politically liberal perspective, the greatest strength of his view is that he has clearly recognized the fact of pluralism in contemporary society and that it would be unjust for any one individual, group (religious or otherwise), or even the state to impose its own comprehensive doctrine on others who are unwilling to receive it. That is, I have full confidence that Jewell's political philosophy is both democratic and genuinely driven by a desire to be fair to everyone, regardless of the comprehensive doctrine that is affirmed, so long as it is reasonable.

However, the greatest weakness of his view from a politically liberal perspective is that, despite his desire to be fair to everyone, libertarianism is not fair. The fact that it is not fair is in evidence when it is realized that no rational person would ever choose it in a decision-making procedure that is itself fair. In the next chapter I defend a theory of justice that invites us to consider what rational people would choose behind a "veil of ignorance." Whereas we may very well know crucial facts about ourselves in reality, when we are behind a veil of ignorance we have to think about which principles of justice we would agree to if we did not know these facts. We have to imagine the possibility that once we leave the original position, we might have to live in the society we create with different characteristics from those we have at present.

Imagine someone who was natively very bright and who came from a wealthy or upper-middle-class background and from a very prominent family. It would not be surprising for this person to advocate for libertarian low levels of taxation and little government involvement in the affairs of a capitalist market. Behind the veil of ignorance, however, this person would have to think about the possibility that, once the veil was lifted, he or she would not be natively bright and/or would come from a lower-middle-class or poor background in a rough neighborhood. The upshot here is that although in reality many people obviously defend some version of liber-tarianism or *laissez-faire* capitalism, no rational person who was deliberating about a just society behind a veil of ignorance would choose libertarianism or *laissez-faire* capitalism! This is a remarkable result that should lead us to wonder about the defensibility of this economic system.

Granted, people differ in their comfort levels regarding risk. It is certainly rational to buy a $1 lottery ticket each week in the hope that one might hit it big. But it would not be rational to develop the habit of betting one's entire paycheck every week. There are limits beyond which it is irrational to accept risk. Betting one's entire paycheck on the lottery is strongly analogous, I claim, to choosing a libertarian economic system behind a veil of ignorance. The risk is too great, for example, that we will end up with a system in which even healthcare is a commodity on the market such that even in the wealthiest country in the world tens of millions of people would have no real access to modern medicine. Perhaps this is why in the social democratic states of northern Europe, which more closely approximate the Rawlsian view of justice than the United States, people live longer than do people in the United States, yet with far less wealth. We can do better than libertarianism.

Libertarian justice: A liberationist response

Miguel A. De La Torre

The libertarian approach to justice, as articulated by Jason Jewell, is probably the best illustration of a Eurocentric upper-class ideology in action. This is obviously an ethical motif for Todd, Sarah, Nancy, and Dave and not for José, María, Mirta, and Enrique. When Jewell writes "Libertarians are a diverse lot," he provides philosophical examples, not racial or ethnic. One simply needs to peruse the crowds that followed libertarian politicians like Ron Paul, Paul Ryan, or Rand Paul to notice the lack of "color." Jewell presents us with a conservative, white methodology for defining justice in the name of freedom; however, the freedom he calls for is for the few at the expense of the many. Freedom (liberation) can never be achieved by those lacking resources like education or healthcare or who are prevented from achieving them due to racism, classism, and/or sexism. Those who define freedom as limiting the power of the state never depended on the state to pass laws preventing child labor, slavery, or the infringement of civil rights. While liberationists like me make a preferential option for the oppressed, Jewell's libertarianism makes a preferential option for their oppressors.

I do agree with Jewell's assertion that "libertarianism is not a comprehensive theory of ethics." It is an economic ideology from the early part of the twentieth century that influences the political; it creates a neat dualism between the centralized economic organizing of the early Soviet Union (which no longer exists) and Social Darwinian capitalism before the rise of multinational corporations. Perhaps libertarianism had something to say in that bygone age; but in today's globalized, neoliberal economic structures the problem is not so much the state, but rather the state-less multinational corporations that co-opt states under the libertarian platitudes of "unhindered free-markets," "deregulation," and "limited government."

Because the politics advocated by libertarians has negative effects on the lives of those on the margins of society, an ethical response is required. Although much in Jewell's essay deserves a more detailed and nuanced rebuttal, for the purposes of this response I will concentrate on the thinkers undergirding the libertarian approach Jewell advocates, specifically the political theorist John Locke and the economist F. A. Hayek (to both of which he refers).

Locke's emphasis on property and the property rights associated with land is problematic, especially when we consider Locke's social context and location. He viewed property as an institution of nature, not a social convention based on human laws.[1] Locke argued for the right of each person, based on self-preservation and personal interest, to keep whatever property he or she possessed despite the means of its acquisition or his or her ability to use all of its resources. The state, constructed to preserve the rights of the individual to life, liberty, and property, is duty-bound to insure these inalienable rights.[2]

Missing from most analyses of the Eurocentric concept of private property is how the property was first acquired. Most of our modern western understanding of private property is based on Locke, who was an international slave trader[3] (hence some humans are also property) and who worked as a business manager for a colonial land-holding corporation. Eventually he moved beyond being a mere colonial bureaucrat to owning a minority share in the Carolina Province along with a seat in the colonial legislature of the Carolina territory. As Tink Tinker reminds us, Locke's ethical philosophy justified the theft of Indian land via a facade of legal and moral propriety. God, according to Locke, wanted the English to take the "vacant" lands of North America. Even though indigenous people lived on the land, their failure to develop (capitalize) the land forfeited any legal rights to it.[4] According to Locke, who had a vested interest in the colonial venture:

> God and his reason commanded him to subdue the earth ... He that in obedience to this command of God, subdued, tilled and sowed any part of it, thereby annexed to it something that was his property, which another had no title to, nor could without injury take from him.[5]

As Jewell reminds us, "The *libertarian* system of thought is concerned more with the strategies employed to achieve desired social outcomes than it is with those outcomes themselves. In other words, it is primarily about *means*, not *ends*." Hence the end Locke pursued (the theft of Indian land) is not the concern; it is the means, the philosophical defense of property, that matters. When private property and free markets secure the liberty of the wealthy class, with the help of the government, it is generally done at the expense

---

[1] John Locke, *The Second Treatise of Government*, ed. Thomas P. Peardon (Indianapolis: Bobbs-Merrill Educational Publishing, 1952), 17.

[2] Ibid., 5–6.

[3] Locke was part owner in a slave-run plantation, Bahamian Adventurers, and a slave acquisition and selling firm, Royal Africa Company.

[4] George Tinker, "John Locke: On Property," in *Beyond the Pale: Reading Ethics from the Margins*, eds. Stacey Floyd-Thomas and Miguel A. De La Torre (Louisville, KY: Westminster John Knox Press, 2011), 56.

[5] Locke, *The Second Treatise*, 31.

of the marginalized who become increasingly alienated. The interests of the common person (specifically those who are poor and of color) become subordinated to the interests of this ruling class. Because the privileged will be in an economic position to acquire immense portions of wealth through so-called "free-markets," they can impose laws upon those who need jobs, loans, or services for basic subsistence. In exchange, the disenfranchised must recognize the supreme authority of the wealth-builders (thieves?).

Hence it becomes somewhat naïve to argue that no one forced the poor to shop at Walmart or obtain a subprime mortgage. "None of these examples," as Jewell argues, "involves the initiation of violence against anyone." Yet, violence does not solely come from the barrel of a gun. Violence is also caused by the economic, social, and political structures which become the unintended consequences of Jewell's libertarianism. The multinational corporations Jewell's libertarianism privileges act violently when they maintain social structures (in partnership with co-opted states) that inflict prolonged harm or injury upon a segment of the population which is disenfranchised due to race or economic standing. The normative everyday experience of violence found throughout the global south, affecting the world's most vulnerable members, is closely linked to the reality of socio-economic injustice, ecological destruction, militarization of society, uneven distribution of wealth, poor access to education and health, poverty, unemployment, racism, ethnic discrimination, gender inequality, and global economic policies that benefit a small portion of the world's population at the expense of the many. True, the act of flying a plane into a skyscraper is an act of immediate and bloody violence. The death of a child due to lack of food or sanitary conditions over a period of years may not be immediate nor bloody, but it is no less violent.

When society is constructed on the fundamental principle of private ownership, the state must protect property by enacting laws against trespass and theft. Economist Franz Hinkelammert states that the unconditional recognition of the right to private property deprioritizes all other rights, leading to global dispossession. Protecting private property is maintained at the expense of rights "to satisfy basic needs in food, shelter, medical attention, education, and social security."[6] In effect, property rights trump human rights. For the hungry to jump a fence and take a fallen apple rotting on the ground is a convictable offense, even if the motivation of the trespasser was to feed her or his hungry child.

As Locke provides the political undergirding for libertarianism, Friedrich

---

[6] Franz J, Hinkelammett, *The Ideological Weapon of Death: A Theological Critique*, trans. Phillip Berryman (Maryknoll, NY: Orbis Books, 1986), 120.

von Hayek provides the economic justification. The resurgence of Hayek has resonated with many Tea Party activists due mainly to his warnings that society is sliding toward despotism (i.e., Obama's presidency), and his defense of a minimal state (i.e., anti-Obamacare sentiments). Ironically, even though Hayek rejects socialism as tyranny, nevertheless, he still endorses some commitments to the common welfare at the expense of unfettered free markets. Jewell should consider the state welfare and healthcare which Hayek endorses. Hayek writes:

> Nor is there any reason why the state should not assist the individuals in providing for those common hazards of life against which, because of their uncertainty, few individuals can make adequate provision. Where, as in the case of sickness and accident, neither the desire to avoid such calamities nor the efforts to overcome their consequences are as a rule weakened by the provision of assistance—where, in short, we deal with genuinely insurable risks—the case for the state's helping to organize a comprehensive system of social insurance is very strong.[7]

Elsewhere in the book *The Road to Selfdom* Hayek supports state aid for victims of natural disasters,[8] and government policies to regulate working hours, provide sanitary arrangements, and control poisonous substances.[9]

For Hayek, any form of government action or political liberalism becomes an inevitable slide into totalitarianism. The fallacy of such slippery slope arguments is the assumption that individuals or governments cannot stop and change directions. Worse is that in defense of libertarian principles, liberation is sacrificed on the altar of economic expedience. For example, in a 1979 interview, Hayek had no problem supporting Chile's military dictator Pinochet, who combined totalitarianism with free-market economics. The goal of radical (economic) freedom advocated by libertarians comes only at the expense of (political) freedom for people who look like me. Hayek states it best: "I have seen in some South American countries the most extraordinary progress. In that much condemned country Chile, the restoration of only economic freedom and not political freedom has led to an economic recovery which is fantastic." He goes on to show his true colors (and those of modern libertarians) when he concludes: "You can have economic freedom without political freedom, but you can't have political freedom without economic freedom."[10]

---

[7]   Friedrich von Hayek, *The Road to Selfdom*, ed. Bruce Caldwell (Chicago: University of Chicago Press, 2007 [1944]), 148.
[8]   Ibid.
[9]   Ibid., 86.
[10] John M. Geddes, "New Vogue for Critic of Keynes," *The New York Times*, May 7, 1979.

Libertarian justice: A feminist response
Laura Stivers

Asking whose perspective—whether that of Todd, Sarah, Nancy, or Dave—is more Christian seems a fruitless endeavor to Christian feminists. Analyzing who is more virtuously Christian is not high on their agenda, but even more problematic for them is the implied starting point for thinking about justice. Todd, Sarah, Nancy, and Dave all have the money and time to devote to charitable causes, and presumably they live comfortable lives. The majority of people in the world are not as well situated, and certainly most women do not fare this well. Even in the US context, both Sarah and Nancy are likely to be married, considering over a third of single female-headed households are poor.[1] What does it say to women and other marginalized people when a conception of justice begins from a perspective of power and privilege? When the perspective is not concerned about "end states" but only about "means"? When private property rights have more value than basic human needs? When no attention is paid to the multiple oppressions people face—sexism, racism, classism, heterosexism, to name a few? And when inequality is seen as natural and even divinely ordained (e.g., "To some He [sic] delegates more than to others")?

While there are many critiques Christian feminists have of a libertarian theory of justice, I will focus on three. First of all, ignoring oppression, power, and privilege in the way our society is structured means that a "free market" will simply support the status quo of inequality to the detriment of most women and other marginalized people. The libertarian perspective is far from "neutral," as it claims, but advocates a particular "lifestyle" of privilege for a few. Second, focusing on taxation as a *means* of theft and violence and denying the importance of actual *outcome* is counter to the Christian values of human dignity, solidarity, and the common good. A Christian feminist emphasis on right relationship as well as human dignity and capability to flourish entails support of policies that produce just outcomes. Thus, feminists would not view progressive taxation as theft, but instead as a powerful means of distributing wealth more equitably. Third, focusing on the state as the primary institution that is coercive, aggressive, and violent ignores the immense power capitalism and corporations have

---

[1] "Poverty in the United States: A Snapshot," *National Center for Law and Economic Justice*, http://www.nclej.org/poverty-in-the-us.php (accessed November 13, 2013).

to destroy both people and the Earth. Christian feminists have no need to idealize the state, but they do critique *any* institution that does not support gender justice and the flourishing of all life. Furthermore, idealizing the family and church as "productive institutions of society" completely ignores the patriarchy and oppression in these institutions.

While advocates of a libertarian perspective on justice are aware of inequality, they do not account for the pervasive structural oppression in our society and the world, and the consequent unequal playing field. They assume that all people are free with equal agency to make decisions. According to libertarians, Walmart doesn't "force" us to shop at its stores, but if I am a single mom on welfare and Walmart is the primary store left in my community (after the mom-and-pop stores closed) that sells the basic necessities I need, do I really have the option to shop elsewhere? The Waltons (owners of Walmart), who presumably would be the target of any substantial progressive taxation to redistribute wealth, did not get their wealth simply through their own hard work. They made huge profits by paying their workers low wages with limited benefits, by selling goods produced in countries with few laws to protect the environment, and by relying on an economy of scale to "bargain" (not force, according to libertarians) for lower-priced goods to sell in their stores.

Libertarians only focus on how taxation steals the wealth of hardworking people (especially the rich because they pay the most), with no mention of the "theft" of whole livelihoods and environmental resources to create that wealth. Sexism, racism, and classism within our society serve to bolster capitalist profit. Simply look at who works in Walmart's stores for unlivable wages and produces the products that Walmart sells for a low price: primarily poor women and people of color. The libertarian emphasis on a minimal state could mean the elimination of minimum wage, overtime, or child labor laws. Furthermore, the libertarian theory of justice offers no real way to protect the bargaining rights of workers, nor does its emphasis on a free market offer effective regulation to protect the environment from the exploitation of corporations.

With their emphasis on right relationship and human flourishing, Christian feminists support policies that substantially lessen inequality. Feminists believe that a just society will ensure universal access to those resources that everyone needs to survive (e.g. food, shelter, and clothing) and will be organized in ways that enable people to participate democratically. For them, justice is about outcome, not simply means. Christian feminists can agree with libertarians that the state can be "what enables Big Business and other powerful interests to exploit ordinary people;" however, they do not agree that the solution is to get rid of the state. Instead they would opt for public policies that limit corporate influence on the state so that democracy has a chance. Taxation is but one tool that the state uses to distribute goods and power more equitably (what Christian feminists see as a more just outcome). Taxation as a means is not in and of itself unjust, but is an efficient way to collect money for public goods that everyone should have access to, such as education, police protection, roads, green space, and more.

Christian feminists believe regressive taxation that distributes wealth up the income scale and increases inequality is unjust. By contrast, progressive taxation based on solidarity with the poor and marginalized and in support of the common good is just. While feminists are not opposed to private property, they give priority to meeting basic needs, promoting human dignity, and furthering the common good. Christian feminists also argue that the libertarian emphasis on private provision of goods, such as education, healthcare, and social security, limits access to these goods (e.g. high number of people without basic healthcare and young people unable to afford college in the US). Furthermore, relying on voluntary contributions for public goods such as police protection, as some libertarians advocate, gives the rich immense power as "benevolent benefactors." Christian feminists argue that the Hebrew prophets and Jesus critiqued societal structures that benefited only a minority, and repeatedly equated justice with promotion of human dignity, the common good, and solidarity. Jesus himself did not care about property and called his disciples to a different form of "abundant life."

Christian feminists ask why libertarians are so focused on critiquing the coercive, aggressive, and violent state yet disregard the inherent violence of capitalism and the dominating, and fast-growing power of multinational corporations. Furthermore, they wonder why libertarians think families and private non-profits, especially churches, are the "truly productive institutions of society." Advocates of a libertarian form of justice seem oblivious to the patriarchal nature of family, church, and many voluntary institutions. No feminist assumes the family is just. One need only look at the statistics for domestic abuse and for poverty of single female-headed households. Furthermore, many churches continue to exclude women, people who are openly homosexual, and others from leadership positions, and sometimes even membership. While all institutions are created and managed by humans and thus never fully just, enforcement of civil rights has always required state intervention. Christian feminists include the state in any analysis of injustice, but note that fifty-one of the largest economies in our world are not countries but corporations.[2] Furthermore, they argue that

---

[2] "Corporate Power Facts and Stats," UNESCO Teaching and Learning for a Sustainable Future, http://www.unesco.org/education/tlsf/mods/theme_c/popups/mod18t04s01.html (accessed November 13, 2013).

the inherent logic of capitalism for increasing profit comes at the expense of the poor (the majority of the world's population) and the earth. Last of all, Christian feminists argue for justice-making in relation not only to particular institutions, but also to larger economic and political systems as well as societal patterns and practices.

Libertarians believe that a minimalist state would free voluntary associations to serve the needs of the least more capably via *charity*. Christian feminists argue that private organizations, without state regulation, can choose whom they think is deserving (or undeserving) of help, allowing discrimination and other forms of institutional oppression to flourish. More importantly, however, Christian feminists would never equate charity with justice. Even if charity resulted in a just distribution of goods (which is doubtful), it can never promote justice of recognition because people cannot participate as equals in a society based on patronizing charity and philanthropy. Such a system assaults human dignity and does not challenge unearned privilege and human-created oppression. God might have given each of us different gifts and abilities (what libertarians identify as inequality), but that does not mean that God supports human-created inequality, domination, and oppression. Justice requires challenging a system where a minority has power and privilege at the expense of the majority. Christian feminists do not aim to squash human initiative through policies for more equitable distribution of goods and power (as libertarians argue), but instead they seek to empower human initiative by giving all people the capability of using their distinct talents in life.

Libertarian justice: A virtue ethicist's response
Elizabeth Phillips

Throughout my reading of Jason Jewell's essay on libertarianism, a single question was ringing in my mind, a question from classical philosophy which has been taken up by liberation theologians: *cui bono*? (to whose benefit?). The heart of libertarianism is the maintenance of freedom (as Jewell articulates it, the freedom from aggression, coercion, and violence). My question for libertarians is: freedom for whom? Who genuinely benefits from the vision of freedom espoused by libertarianism?

Libertarianism itself cannot answer this question because, as Jewell notes, it is a political philosophy which is concerned with means, not ends. As I note in my essay and in my response to Daniel Dombrowski, approaches to ethics and justice which rule out the relevance of teleology are, at their heart, irreconcilable to the virtue approach, regardless of any areas of commonality we might find on specific issues.

The answer to the question *cui bono*?—freedom for whom?—is clear to me: libertarian freedom is for those who are already most free. Notice the common thread running through the steps Jewell offers for the "implementation of non-aggression throughout the various levels of government": voluntarism. The military should be voluntary, not conscripted. Markets and industries should be guided by voluntary systems instead of government regulation. Funding for schools should be voluntary. Voluntary "private action" should replace the social safety net. Voluntary covenants should replace vice laws. The consistent stress on voluntary activity which is central to libertarianism is a stark example of the assumption that all moral agents are equally free, untroubled, healthy, able, rational, and independent. In other words, only those people and entities who are already so privileged as to enjoy unusually high levels of freedom can benefit from the freedoms promoted by libertarianism, as they depend on everyone's ability to choose and act voluntarily. Those who are born into poverty, who experience severe disability, and who are oppressed by the mechanisms of racism, are involuntarily located in circumstances which severely constrain their freedom. Many of the systems which libertarianism calls aggressive are actually meant to account for these inequalities of freedom in circumstance.

As a Christian pacifist (a conviction which is not necessarily part of virtue ethics, but which is common to many, though not all, figures in the recent revival of virtue), I obviously found some resonance with certain passages and suggestions in Jewell's piece questioning the employment of violence and force. If indeed libertarianism were only and truly "a set of claims about the use of *violence* in society: when it is ethically permissible to resort to violence, and when it is not," as Jewell claims, we would have much more common ground to discuss. I share with him a concern about the way most citizens casually accept promiscuous employments of violence by the state which they would clearly recognize as immoral if perpetrated by any other entity or any individual. However, my pacifism and Jewell's "non-aggression" are not kindred perspectives; they are rather two trajectories which begin and end in entirely different places from one another but happen to cross paths at a certain specific point along the way. The most important differences between us have to do with why violence is wrong and what the state is meant to accomplish.

The fact that Jewell and I have different horizons governing our refusals of violence becomes clear in his indiscriminately interchangeable uses of "aggression," "coercion," "violence," and "force." Whether or not one is a Christian pacifist, and if one is a pacifist, what type one chooses to be, are integrally related to the distinctions between aggression, coercion, violence, and force; their use as synonyms is unacceptable. Anyone who, like myself, categorically rejects the use of violence must be very clear about what violence is. There have been absolute forms of non-resistant pacifism which would seek to reject all forms of force, aggression and coercion along with violence. I think this is both mistaken and impossible. It is mistaken for Christians because the form of nonviolence which we see practiced by Jesus in the gospels is not non-resistant or passive. I believe "non-resistance" arises from a mistranslation of Matthew 5.39, which is more accurately something like "do not violently retaliate against an evildoer," instead of "do not resist evil." The way of Jesus and the prophets before him is a way of active resistance against injustice, and this resistance may sometimes be "aggressive" or "forceful," depending upon how one defines those terms. I would call his act of protest in the Temple (Mark 11.15-19 and parallels) an aggressive and forceful act intended to unmask the financial exploitation which had overtaken the Temple courts. Resisting injustice requires the assertion of justice; this is not ruled out by the kind of Christian pacifism I and many others practice. All forms of retaliation and violent aggression or coercion *are* ruled out.

For Christian pacifists who also share the virtue approach, nonviolence is about cultivating and living the Christian virtues and practices of patience, enemy love, and justice. Contrary to the arguments of many Christians who insist that violence can and should be used as a last resort, pacifism is not choosing to love the enemy instead of actively seeking justice. It is seeking justice as Jesus has shown us is God's way in the world, through active, non-violent giving of ourselves, instead of how the world and our sinful human nature will always want to exercise justice, through punitive and retaliatory action against others. Non-pacifists always pose the question: aren't you seeking to establish peace without justice? Can there be true peace if we are not willing to use violence when necessary to enforce and establish justice? My reply is that true justice cannot come from violence; there cannot be true justice if we are willing to succumb to the cycles of violence and domination of which every violent act is a part.

Given that this is my understanding of violence, and why it is not an acceptable means for Christians, it may be clear why I can share a momentary agreement with Jewell in opposition to certain wars, or the coercive practice of conscription to the armed forces. However, the agreement is only momentary. When Jewell goes on to classify welfare and public education as equally coercive forms of force exerted by the state which are equivalent to violence, well, the mind boggles. To my way of thinking, certain measures of redistribution and the public funding of universal education are precisely the sorts of positive, non-violent enactments of justice we want the state to employ.

What is at stake in this difference with Jewell is not only the definition of "violence" and the other words he uses interchangeably with it, but also a different understanding of the purpose of government in human life. Libertarianism takes a particularly bleak and suspicious view of government, and libertarians seek either to abolish or severely limit the state. Jewell suggests that the natural law tradition is a common source for philosophical and theological libertarians. However, most Christian employments of natural law are much more deeply and directly indebted to the teachings of Saint Thomas Aquinas, who believed that the forming of governments was part of the goodness of creation—that it is part of how God created us to live. Aquinas recognized, of course, that there are good and bad forms of government, as well as good and bad individual rulers. But he also believed that government has a positive purpose and role, which is to make it possible for humans to pursue the flourishing life. In other words, governments must positively promote the common good. The common good is absolutely central to a virtue approach to justice.

I have a very critical view of the modern nation-state and believe it cannot on its own provide what is needed for human flourishing; government cannot in itself create and sustain the common good. I believe this sort of critical distance is a necessary stance in relation to any government so that Christians can function both as prophetic voices who are not bound by governments and thus are free to speak truth to power, and as pioneering agents of new possibilities which are not constrained by what can be accomplished within government. However, I also believe that government is needed for human flourishing; the common good cannot be protected and cultivated in large-scale social bodies without some form of government.

Publicly funded education and healthcare, two of the systems to which libertarians are most vociferously opposed, are precisely the sorts of places where the prophetic/pioneering and positive/common good views of government have met in Christian history. Prophetically seeing the social necessity of education and access to medical care, Christians pioneered the development of schools and hospitals. To my way of thinking, it is a matter of joy that these pioneering efforts were adopted and funded by modern states (though to differing degrees in different nations). Our role now is to continue to engage critically with these systems, ensuring that they are drawn ever closer towards justice, while also moving on to pioneer new ways of making our societies more just. Where Jewell sees the failure of the state through coercion and aggression, I see a victory of Christian justice which is worthy of celebration, though it is an extremely limited victory, and has created systems which are in dire need of critical engagement in order to call them more towards their intended purposes. Libertarians promote privatization of these systems, but I see their decline into capitalist systems governed primarily by the market as a tragic refusal of their *telos* in human flourishing.

2

Political Liberalism, Social Justice, and Christian Faith

Daniel A. Dombrowski

Introduction

The purpose of the present chapter is to explore the implications of the politically liberal philosophy of John Rawls (1921–2002) for Christianity and to indicate in a short space what a Rawlsian society would look like in practice. Rawls is the most influential political philosopher of the past century and a half, although the implications of his thought for the relationship between politics and religion are often either ignored or misunderstood. In due course I will make clear what I mean by "political liberalism," but here at the outset I would like to make it clear that I mean something that is somewhat different from what "liberalism" means in everyday American discourse, where "liberalism" is contrasted to "conservativism" or where blue states are contrasted to red states.

Rawls himself grew up Episcopalian and at one point in his life thought about becoming an Episcopal minister. He wrote an undergraduate thesis while at Princeton that indicated his traditionalist Christian beliefs at that time. However, personal experiences as a soldier during World War II relating to theodicy (the problem regarding how to reconcile the existence of evil with the existence of God) caused him to abandon traditional Christian doctrine. He nonetheless apparently remained a fideist (someone who has faith in God without rational justification for such belief) for the rest of his life.

In his best-known book, *A Theory of Justice* (1971), he offered his famous thought experiment regarding the "original position," to be discussed below, and he defended a view of human persons that relied heavily on the thought of the eighteenth-century German philosopher Immanuel Kant. Later, in *Political Liberalism* (1993), he developed a distinction between an individual's own comprehensive doctrine (whether religious or non-religious) and the principles to which one would have to commit in order to facilitate the realization of a just democratic society, in general.

Before liberalism

Liberal political philosophy originated in the early modern period (sixteenth–eighteenth century) in Europe. Pre-liberal political philosophy or political theology concentrated on two major tasks: a) to figure out the characteristics of *the* good (the definite article is crucial here) and *the* truth about what to believe or *the* correct way to behave; and b) to figure out how to get those who understood *the* good and *the* truth and *the* correct way to behave into power and to make sure that they were succeeded by rulers who were equally knowledgeable. This characterization of pre-liberal political thought applies equally to thinkers who are otherwise quite different: Plato, Aristotle, Saint Augustine, Saint Thomas Aquinas, Martin Luther, John Calvin, etc. They may have differed in their accounts of the good, but they agreed that one of the main tasks of political thought was to come to grips with it intellectually. And they may have differed regarding how many individuals were equipped to understand the good, how difficult it would be to get them into power, and how best to solve the problem of having good rulers succeeded by other good rulers, but they agreed that the overall goal was to get those who understood the good into power and to keep them there.

One very interesting feature of pre-liberal political thought was that in these views toleration was not seen as a virtue. Indeed, it was a vice. The reason why pre-liberal political theorists wanted those who understood the good to be in power was to guard against those who did not understand it. To cite just three examples, think of Plato's expulsion of the poets from the ideal city; Saint Thomas Aquinas's willingness to have unrepentant heretics put to death; and Calvin's willingness to kill Servetus. An admirable ruler, in pre-liberal political thought, guarded the populace against heresy or against anything else that would lead them away from the good. In fact, not to do so would be to fail to do one's duty as a just ruler, as rulers' very success was measured in terms of the degree to which they could lead the populace toward an approximation of the good.[1]

---

[1]   See Plato's *Republic*, 605b. Also see Saint Thomas Aquinas, *Summa Theologiae* 2a2ae, q. 11, a. 3. Finally, see Daniel Dombrowski, *Rawls and Religion: The Case for Political Liberalism* (Albany: State University of New York Press, 2001), chapter 1.

Liberal political theory

In the early modern period in Europe something of a crisis occurred in political theory as a result of the wars of religion. What are we to do when two competing religions or conceptions of *the* good (in Rawlsian terms, competing comprehensive doctrines which could be either religious or non-religious) each claims to have *the* truth (once again, the definite article is crucial here)? What are we to do when each claims absolute political authority, such that as a result society is ripped apart in religious warfare? *Either* one could wait until one of the competing religions or comprehensive doctrines eventually got the upper hand and dominated the other *or* one could develop a political theory that would allow adherents to competing religions or comprehensive doctrines (whether religious or non-religious) to co-exist in peace. Rawlsian political liberalism is the disciplined effort to think through carefully and to justify the latter approach.

In contrast to pre-liberal political thinkers, political liberals see toleration not as a vice but as a virtue. Indeed, it is seen by political liberals as the key virtue that is necessary for people to not only survive but to flourish in a state with a plurality of religions or comprehensive doctrines. By ending both theoretically and practically the wars of religion that plagued Europe in the early modern period, it can be said without exaggeration that political liberalism can be seen as one of the great achievements of human civilization!

In order to bring about justice in a condition of a plurality of competing religions or comprehensive doctrines, however, questions regarding *the* good have to be largely taken off the table *in politics*, although it makes sense to debate them elsewhere, say in universities. That is, politics is not the place to debate *ultimate* questions regarding the purpose of human life, the meaning of death, the existence of God, or the theodicy problem. Rather, political questions are *penultimate* (important, but not ultimate) and concern the conditions under which defenders of different religions or comprehensive doctrines can nonetheless get along with each other in a peaceful and fair manner. In short, Rawls and other political liberals concentrate in politics on justice or fairness in contrast to *the* good or *the* truth of any comprehensive doctrine, whether religious or non-religious, or *the* right way to behave.

The argument in this section goes as follows. a) Pre-liberal conceptions of just societies assumed that there was a single way of life that people should pursue (i.e., a single version of *the* good) and that just societies were those that ensured that people would devote themselves to this single way of life. b) The wars of religion in the early modern period forced thinkers to pursue a vision of a just society that allowed for a wide range of ways of life (i.e., multiple conceptions of *the* good) to coexist in peace and justice. And c) a liberal theory tries to make sense of what is *required* in order to bring about justice in societies inhabited by people who are deeply divided about what is most important in life.

Love

Something more needs to be said. It is not enough to argue that religious believers *could* be good citizens in a just (or approximately just) society. It is also important to point out the *positive* connections between Rawlsian justice and the social goals of those who defend religious beliefs.

At this point I would like to introduce that part of Rawls for which he is most famous. In *A Theory of Justice* he asks us to imagine a decision-making procedure in which we are to design a social contract that would outline the abstract principles that would govern a just society. He calls this situation the *original position*. In order to prevent us from tailoring principles of justice to fit our own cases (i.e., in order to prevent us from stacking the deck in our own favor), he asks us to deliberate in the original position behind a *veil of ignorance*. What this means is that, whereas we know crucial facts about ourselves in reality, when we are behind the veil of ignorance we have to think about which principles of justice we would agree to if we had radically different crucial facts about ourselves. We have to imagine the possibility that once the decision-making procedure is over in the original position, we might have to live in the society we create with different characteristics from those we have at present. For example, a person who is a Methodist has to consider the possibility that once the veil of ignorance is lifted, she will turn out to be a progressive Catholic, or a traditionalist Catholic, an orthodox Jew, a reform Jew, a Greek Orthodox believer, a Hindu, an atheist or an agnostic, etc. The key idea is that injustice in religious matters is less likely if the principles of justice are chosen in a fair decision-making procedure wherein our biases are held in check.

The process becomes more complicated when it is realized that, in addition to religious beliefs (or lack thereof), participants in the original position are to remain ignorant of many other features that might characterize them in the just society they are devising: race, ethnicity, economic class, sex, sexual orientation, health status, level of intelligence, age, present or future generation (which has enormous implications for environmental justice), etc.

Once again, imagine someone who was natively very bright and who came from a wealthy or upper-middle-class background and from a very prominent family. It would not be surprising for this person to advocate for low levels of taxation and little government involvement in the affairs of a capitalist market. Behind the veil of ignorance, however, this person would have to think about the possibility that once the veil was lifted, he or she would not be natively bright and/or would come from a lower-middle-class or poor background in a rough neighborhood. The upshot here is that although in reality many people obviously defend some version of *laissez-faire* capitalism (or what Rawlsians would call a system of unrestricted utility), no rational person who was deliberating about a just society behind a veil of ignorance would choose *laissez-faire* capitalism! This is a remarkable result that should lead us to wonder about the defensibility of this economic system.

Or again, imagine someone who in reality came from a lower-middle-class or poor background and from a historically marginalized ethnic group who assumed that a just society would have to be a Marxist one where all vestiges of free enterprise would have to be eliminated. Behind the veil of ignorance, however, this person would have to think about the possibility that once the veil was lifted, he or she would not only be natively bright, but also by disposition a hard worker with entrepreneurial ability (although clearly the poor can also be hard workers). That is, behind the veil of ignorance this person would have to think about the opportunity costs and incentives that might be appropriate for someone who engaged in all of the hard work involved in becoming a physician. Behind the veil of ignorance one would seriously consider the conditions under which it might be just to get a larger slice of the pie than others such that *some* version of a market economy (if not *laissez-faire* capitalism) might be just.

In the decision-making procedure found in the original position behind a veil of ignorance, reasonable/rational beings would, Rawls contends, universally and willingly contract into two major principles of justice. (A reasonable being is one who is willing to get along with others if the terms of agreement are fair, whereas a rational being is one who can follow arguments, weigh evidence, etc. In effect, it takes a reasonable being to be willing to deliberate about justice in an original position behind a veil of ignorance, whereas it takes a rational being to deliberate there and follow the arguments.) The first concept that would be agreed to in the original position behind a veil of ignorance can be called the *equal liberty principle*. The basic idea here is that in a just society primary goods would be distributed equally. These would include formal primary goods like freedom of speech and religion, the social basis for self-respect, equality under the law, etc. But it would also include the material bases required in order for these basic freedoms to have their meaning; these material bases would include access to food, shelter, healthcare, etc., so that one could exercise meaningfully one's freedom of religion, say. Freedom of speech might not seem to mean very much if one is dying of a starvation related disease.

The second principle of justice concerns the distribution of all of the other goods made possible by living together in a society; this second principle, in turn, has two parts. Goods beyond the primary ones can be distributed unequally (i.e., some citizens can get a larger slice of the pie than others), but only if such unequal distribution is open to all (e.g., women and blacks would not be prohibited from educational opportunities and careers). This can be called the *opportunity principle*. Further, such goods can be distributed unequally, but only if such unequal distribution benefits everyone, especially the least advantaged, say through a system of taxation. This can be called the *difference principle*. Behind a veil of ignorance it would make sense even to the least advantaged members of society to reward those with talents if such reward benefits everybody, especially the least advantaged members of society.

The defenders of Rawls think that he preserves the best in defenses of both free enterprise and socialism. That is, the equal liberty principle, when supplemented by the opportunity and difference principles, would if implemented lead to the most egalitarian *and* democratic and free society on the face of the earth. Once again, if it is asked *why* we should adopt these two principles of justice (actually three in that the second principle has two parts), the Rawlsian response would be as follows: because they are the principles that would be adopted by us as reasonable/rational beings *if* we were to deliberate about justice in a fair decision-making procedure wherein various distorting factors (both our own biases as well as the curse of money) were not present.

Because a problem of justice does not even arise unless there is a significant difference of opinion on some serious issue, it does not make much sense to assume that the disputing parties are perfect loving agents. Rawlsian justice as fairness models the separate interests of individuals and associations that conflict in terms of the assumption of mutual disinterest in the original position. This is quite different from stating the (dogmatic) claim that human beings are, by their very nature, egoistic. The parties in the original position are assumed to be mutually disinterested for the sake of the method used in this decision-making procedure.

The issue here should be of intense interest to religious believers who privilege agapic love (from the Greek word for "love" in the Christian scriptures: *agape*) when dealing with social issues. If agapic love involves the desire to advance the other person's good, a difficulty arises when the claims of various persons to be loved conflict. One can legitimately wonder about what "love of humankind" could possibly mean. As Rawls sees things, benevolence is at sea as long as its many loves are in opposition.

Love or benevolence is here seen as a second-order notion in that it seeks to advance the good(s) of beloved individuals with the good(s) in question already given. That is, at the concrete, primary level, people love different things; hence if we love all humankind this love would have to be at a more abstract, secondary level. If the distinctness of persons is respected, even loving agents need conceptual help. This help is ably provided by Rawls's two principles of justice, as mentioned above. Love is guided by what reasonable/ rational individuals themselves would agree to in a fair initial situation. We can now see why nothing would have been gained by attributing benevolence to the parties in the original position. To be sure, the sense of justice and love are compatible. Indeed, they can easily work in tandem even if love is wider than the sense of justice in that love prompts supererogation (going above and beyond the call of duty) that is not necessarily encouraged by justice.

In sum, agapic love is a natural attitude that both undergirds the effort to approximate a just society, on the one hand, and extends the effort beyond what is required in its exhortation to go above and beyond justice, on the other. In other words, it *frames* justice. One who utterly lacked a sense of justice would probably be a person who felt that he or she was never loved and hence who felt the need to selfishly resist all appeals to reasonableness. For all our sakes it is to be hoped that such people remain few in number.

The very early Rawls's remarks on love (in his undergraduate thesis at Princeton) help to illuminate what he says in *A Theory of Justice* about the relationship between love (or benevolence) and justice. Many religious believers are turned off by Rawls's theory of justice because it strikes them that, even though Rawls's social contract is not based on a cunning inspired by Thomas Hobbes, it is nonetheless cold and overly "rational," in the pejorative sense of the term such that it prohibits love and other partial affections. One can imagine mutual criticisms being thrown back and forth: in Rawls there is much talk about justice but nothing about love, whereas in the Christian scriptures, say, there is a great deal of talk of love but little about justice.

Actually, both accusations are false. The accusation against religious ethicists that they are overly agapistic is due to the fact that the many instances of the ancient Greek *dike* and its cognates in the Christian scriptures have typically been translated as "righteousness" or "uprightness," etc., whereas this same term and its cognates when they appear in Plato's dialogues are always translated as "just" or "justice." That is, the impression that religious ethics is not focused on justice is to a considerable extent the result of the difficulties of translation rather than of anything integral to Christianity, in particular, or to religious belief, in general. Admittedly this impression is accurate to the extent that some thinkers, like the very early Rawls, try to distance themselves as much as possible from Greek thought, including Greek thought regarding justice. There has to be some reason, after all, why scriptural translators often render *dike* and its cognates as "righteousness" rather than as "justice."

The above-mentioned accusation against Rawls is also inaccurate. In the design of an appropriately defined decision-making procedure, Rawls cannot stipulate that the participants in the original position are perfectly loving agents in that he would then be criticized for stacking the deck in his favor. Nor can he stipulate that these participants are selfish to the core in that such beings would be incapable of justice. Rather, he adopts the moderate position that they are capable of *reciprocity* by way of judicious deliberation. The important thing to notice here is that the mutually disinterested imaginary agents found in the original position *when constrained by* the veil of ignorance produce a conception of justice that is very close to what would result if a just society were planned by purely loving agents! For example, the difference principle is strongly analogous to the preferential option for the poor urged by the contemporary Catholic Church and by the World Council of Churches. This is one of the best-kept secrets in Rawlsian philosophy, despite the explicit statement on this point in the text.[2]

In the very early Rawls it is clear that the ability to respond to love is what enables one to enter into any sort of community with others, including, we are to assume, what will later become the mega-community of liberal citizens in an approximately just society. Thus it is not strictly accidental that love and justice coincide in their results in *A Theory of Justice*. The impulse toward love and justice runs deep in Rawls, from his very early period to his latest works, even if the religious manifestation of love starts to look more and more above and beyond justice from the time of *Political Liberalism* on. But the fact that he never repudiated the difference principle, say, indicates that, in a peculiar way, his very early religious ethics endured until the end.

It might be asked why we should take the hypothetical decision-making procedure of the original position, with its veil of ignorance, seriously. The proper response to this question is to say that as a result of this procedure we are better able to get a clear view of the standard of justice against which we can judge actually existing societies like our own. A just society would

---

[2] See John Rawls, *A Theory of Justice*, revised edition (Cambridge: Harvard University Press, 1999 [1971]), 128–9.

have the following features, as determined by a social contract that would be agreed upon by reasonable/rational agents in the original position:

- Reasonable people would be free to worship (or not worship) as they pleased without fear of retribution or ridicule.
- In addition to the freedom of religion mentioned in the previous point, other basic freedoms (freedom of speech, freedom to participate in the democratic political process, etc.) would be distributed equally.
- In order to have the above freedoms really mean something, there would also have to be a minimum material standard of living for all citizens.
- The standard of living mentioned in the previous point would include universal access to healthcare.
- In order to make possible the equality of each citizen in the political process, there would be public funding of elections so as to eliminate the curse of money in politics, whereby some wealthy citizens have greater influence than others over the democratic process; that is, campaign contributions would be seen as bribes.
- Likewise, in order to insure that each citizen would be secure in the social basis of self-respect, the government would be seen as the employer of last resort such that all who were willing to work would find meaningful employment.
- There would be no barriers to educational or employment opportunities that are based on arbitrary criteria related to race, ethnicity, sex, sexual orientation, etc.
- Further, talented people would be rewarded for the opportunity costs they incur in order to work in their professions and they would be provided an incentive to work hard in their professions.
- The unequal distribution of wealth mentioned in the previous point would nonetheless be to the benefit of everyone in society, especially the least advantaged.
- Levels of taxation would be high enough so as to make sure that primary goods would be available for everyone, yet low enough to cover the opportunity costs and incentive costs required in order to encourage talented people to work in their professions.
- Quality public education would be available to all children so as to facilitate equality of opportunity.
- The peaceful and prosperous workings of a domestic society that is approximately just would encourage the society in question to interact with other societies in a just manner according to the law of peoples that would be agreed to in some version of an international original position.

The above features of an approximately just society point us toward a realistic utopia, both domestically and internationally.

Deeper reasons

Thomas Pogge, who is heavily influenced by Rawls, speaks as follows in what I take to be a remarkable passage. He imagines what a liberal religious believer might say to herself just before she engaged in political discourse:

> I know which political outcome would be pleasing to God. But I cannot demonstrate this knowledge to my fellow citizens in a way that is accessible to them. Forcing the correct decision on them without being able to show them why it is correct—this would not be a service to God but would, on the contrary, negate their God-given freedom ... In public political discourse, I should therefore appeal to the values and facts all citizens can acknowledge together and should support whatever political decisions seem most reasonable on this basis.[3]

This fictional piece of reasoning captures well the claim that religious believers respect the duty of civility *not in spite of* their religious beliefs but *because of* them. That is, the separation of the right or the just from *the* good poses no threats other than the usual ones to the unity of the self in that, once one comes to grips with the fact of reasonable pluralism, it is relatively easy to distinguish one's own comprehensive religious view from the principles that would be appropriate for the determination of a just society.

Pogge emphasizes the point that in the Rawlsian view one is not only *permitted* to provide deeper foundations for the freestanding character of Rawlsian justice as fairness as a political doctrine, one is *encouraged* to do so. That is, the broadening of overlapping consensus among people who affirm different religions or comprehensive doctrines is not at all at odds with deepening one's justification of respect for persons. Perhaps it will be objected that if someone thinks that he or she is in possession of religious truth that this person will have less reason to observe the duty of civility than others. The proper response to this objection, again rightly noted by Pogge, is that reasonable religious believers affirm that the duty of civility just *is* part of religious truth. In effect, religious intolerance has come to be seen by most religious believers themselves in democratic societies as a diminished (at best) or distorted (at worst) form of religious belief itself. Once again, we

---

[3]   Thomas Pogge, *John Rawls: His Life and Theory of Justice* (New York: Oxford University Press, 2007), 141.

have all (perhaps unwittingly) been morally improved by political liberals like Rawls.

Sin

Rawls's undergraduate thesis at Princeton dealt primarily with the concepts of sin and faith. The former was defined as the repudiation and destruction of community, whereas the latter was defined as the affirmation and enhancing of community. The sort of relations that were *communal* were those between persons (including God as personal), relations that were *natural* were those between a person and an object, and relations that were *causal* were those between objects. Egoism was seen as a type of sin wherein communal relations were turned into natural relations (e.g., when people were treated as objects). Egotism (with a "t") was a more basic type of sin that consisted in self-love. In fact, egoism was claimed to be an external manifestation of egotism such that the latter was really the master sin. Whereas egoism fails to embrace personal relations and settles for natural relations, egotism embraces personal relations only to destroy them from within. At this early stage in his career Rawls anticipated a third sort of sin to appear in the future: despair. This was because the prime result of sin was aloneness, which was seen as the most terrible condition for a human being. Even Rawls's early view of sin was primarily social rather than metaphysical. Despair is a type of hopelessness, suggesting that living without hope is a type of sin. One is reminded here of Rawls's later attempt to sustain reasonable hope for liberal democracies.

Although the root of sin was passion (specifically, in the passionate tendency toward self-love), and although the ancient Greeks gave a great deal of attention to passion, they did not arrive at an adequate conception of sin. The early Rawls view of sin was heavily influenced by the neo-orthodox theologians popular in the mid-decades of the twentieth century, who in turn were influenced by Saint Augustine. This included the influence of original sin. It is ironic, given his later stance, that the very early Rawls saw the view of society as based on mutual advantage (i.e., social contract theory) as sinful. At this point in his career he also saw both bad institutions and anxiety as signs of sinfulness. That is, he rejected the view that sin was due to a cause external to us. Rather, we deprave ourselves, which is the heart of the doctrine of original sin when interpreted not literally as the inheritance of Adam's sin but as a metaphor for humanity's tendency to foul its own nest, as it were.

Later in his career Rawls identified Kant's moral psychology as Augustinian in that our moral failures were seen by Kant as due to the exercise of our free power of choice. By contrast, Jean-Jacques Rousseau criticized Saint Augustine's doctrine of original sin in that he saw our moral failures as due to external causes. In this regard the mature Rawls was more like Rousseau than Kant. He even came to see Saint Augustine (along with Fyodor Dostoyevsky) as one of the two "darkest minds" of Western thought. Indeed, in his very late essay "On My Religion" (1997) he came to see the doctrine of original sin as "repugnant." This strong language is surprising given that one of the reasons for deliberation behind a veil of ignorance is the pervasiveness of bias in theorizing about justice, a pervasiveness that makes sense on the Augustinian belief in original sin. Rawls's repudiation of the doctrine of original sin is required to understand his view to the effect that if a reasonably just society, or a global society of peoples, is not possible, then the explanation would probably be due to the inability of the members to subordinate their power to reasonable aims. If human beings are incurably self-centered (which Rawls denies), then Rawls wonders "whether it is worthwhile for human beings to live on the earth."[4]

Conclusion

From the perspective of political liberalism, religious belief can actually facilitate the goals of a just society in two ways that might not otherwise be easily possible. The first of these was treated in the section above on love: the mutually disinterested imaginary agents found in the original position when constrained by the veil of ignorance produce a conception of justice that is very close to what would result if a just society were planned by purely loving agents! This is a remarkable view. It should not escape our notice at this point that some philosophers like Charles Hartshorne have claimed that the whole point to theistic metaphysics is to better understand the claim that God *is* love. Indeed, this claim was his deepest conviction. For these reasons religious believers in general should be strongly motivated to take Rawls seriously and to willingly contribute to the sort of society that he defends. That is, theists should embody the reasonableness (as before, the willingness to abide by fair terms of agreement) that is required for high-level discourse concerning a just society.

A consideration of the second way can be introduced in terms of the following oddity: that someone who is influenced by some version of

---

[4] John Rawls, *Law of Peoples* (Cambridge: Harvard University Press, 1999), 128.

materialistic reductionism, and who views a human being as nothing other than protoplasmic stuff that is the accidental byproduct of blind evolutionary history, might nonetheless belong to Amnesty International. It is precisely this oddity that leads us to ask: *why* should we view human beings as politically free and equal and worthy of moral respect? As far as I can tell, there are three stages in Rawls's career relative to this question.

1) The very early (again, undergraduate) Rawls gives abundant evidence of support for the thesis that human beings are made in the image of God, hence there is something heroic or semi-divine about a human life that makes it special. On this basis, it makes perfect sense to pay one's dues to Amnesty International. As an image of God, a human being is thereby capable of entering into community with the same in that a personal God is in the divine nature itself communal; hence to be made in the image of such a being is to share in some fashion this communal nature. Further, it is because human beings are made in the image of God that the very early Rawls thinks that they can be held accountable for their actions.

2) There is also the Kantian view of the human person in *A Theory of Justice*. Given what the very early Rawls says in defense of the *imago Dei* (image of God) hypothesis, we can see why it makes sense to suspect that behind Rawls's Kantian view of free and equal persons lies a natural rights view or something else that has a family resemblance to the Judeo-Christian view of the human person that derives from Genesis. And it also makes sense for Marxists to suspect that behind the Kantian view of the human person as an end-in-itself (adopted by Rawls in *A Theory of Justice*) lies theistic metaphysics. It is understandable why some think that the human rights movement has been heavily insured; it has been living off the capital of the religious ages for quite some time now, but not necessarily by paying the premium required in terms of an explicit defense of theism.

3) It is also understandable, given the fact of pervasive pluralism, why Rawls in *Political Liberalism* moves away from the comprehensive Kantian view of the human person in *political* philosophy. One gets the impression that Rawls's own comprehensive doctrine remained Kantian (and hence implicitly theistic or at least fideistic) until the end, including a Kantian conception of the human person.

As I see things, this third stage need not be as problematic as some scholars think it is. From a *political* point of view, theists like myself are free *both* to indicate why we think that it makes sense to defend the thesis that rational human beings and sentient beings of whatever species deserve moral respect *and* to ask religious skeptics who are materialistic reductionists to provide the reasons that provide the justificatory warrant for their Amnesty International membership. But this latter freedom should be exercised at the associational level, rather than at the political one, in that deep metaphysical reasons for one's political beliefs are themselves not political.

The Rawlsian method of reflective equilibrium (or dialectic) itself eliminates the requirement that there be absolutely secure starting points in political philosophy, say those that would be provided by the *certainty* that human beings are made in the image of God. That is, even with the insecure starting points provided by our intuitions, the back-and-forth process of reflective equilibrium (or dialectic) from intuition to objective rationality (as in the Rawlsian original position), back to intuition, etc., leads to a conception of justice as fairness that is as secure as a reasonable being would, in good conscience, want it to be, given the fact of reasonable pluralism.

Political liberalism: A libertarian response

Jason Jewell

> To the extent that Christianity is taken seriously, I came to think it could have deleterious effects on one's character.
>
> John Rawls[1]

In 2006, Will Wilkinson of the libertarian-leaning Cato Institute coined the term "Rawlsekianism" to refer to a tendency among some intellectuals to bring together what they consider the best ideas of John Rawls and F. A. Hayek. Rawlsekian thinkers affirm the Rawlsian idea that society should promote liberty and the welfare of its least-well-off members. They also affirm Hayek's contention that only a market economy can sufficiently coordinate society's activities (through the price system) to sustain modern life.[2]

Although Hayek identified himself as a (classical) liberal, not a libertarian, many libertarians consider him one of their own because of his many works on economic and social theory that emphasize the harmful effects of the state on society.[3] Rawlsekians believe that if conventional Rawlsians absorb Hayek's insights on social co-operation and the benefits of markets, their policy proposals will move in a libertarian direction. Are Rawlsian liberalism and libertarianism truly compatible? Furthermore, is Rawlsian liberalism compatible with a Christian understanding of the world?

Let's first compare Rawls's theory of justice to the libertarian Non-Aggression Principle described in my foundational essay. As described by Daniel Dombrowski, Rawls's theory hinges on two fundamental grounds: the *equality principle*, which deals with "basic goods," and the joint operation of the *equal opportunity* and *difference* principles, which deal with "nonbasic goods." The equality principle is a vision of a particular end; whatever process society goes through, everyone should end up with an equal portion of basic goods. The equal opportunity and difference principles are a vision of both

---

[1]   John Rawls, "On My Religion," in *A Brief Inquiry into the Meaning of Sin and Faith*, ed. Thomas Nagel (Cambridge, MA: Harvard University Press, 2009), 265.

[2]   Will Wilkinson, "Is Rawlsekianism the Future?" (Washington: Cato Institute, April 12, 2006), http://www.cato.org/blog/rawlsekianism-future (accessed September 13, 2013).

[3]   See, for example, *The Road to Serfdom* (Chicago: University of Chicago Press, 2007), *The Constitution of Liberty* (Chicago: University of Chicago Press, 2011), and *The Pure Theory of Capital* (Chicago: University of Chicago Press, 2007).

an end and means to achieve it. Specifically, the end is the betterment of all groups in society (especially the least well off), and the means is allowing individuals to accumulate unequal portions of nonbasic goods as long as everyone has an equal chance to acquire the larger portions.

If my representation of Rawlsian justice is accurate, we may not find any *inherent* conflict between it and libertarian justice. In my foundational essay, I described libertarianism as a theory that prescribes only means (non-aggression), not ends, in the quest for justice. Egalitarian libertarians agree with Rawls's equality principle, and libertarians with a sense of general benevolence (often the same as the egalitarian libertarians) agree with Rawls's goal of increasing the welfare of society's disadvantaged groups. Furthermore, all libertarians, as far as I know, are willing to see an unequal distribution of nonbasic goods in society.

So *in principle* it seems that Rawlsian liberals and libertarians can join forces to make progress toward the ends they may have in common. This is why the Rawlsekians entertain hopes for a sort of liberal–libertarian political alliance in the foreseeable future; theoretically, there is nothing to prevent it from happening.

However, *in practice* the two groups often find themselves at odds with each other on a variety of issues. One obvious reason for this situation is that some libertarians reject Rawlsian ends, but since this has nothing essentially to do with their being libertarians, we can put that source of disagreement aside for the purposes of this discussion. The more significant reason for the disagreement lies elsewhere.

One potential problem is that Rawls's category of "basic goods" includes both civil liberties and material goods. In the area of civil liberties, if we understand the equality principle to mean there should be no state prohibitions on the exercise of free speech, a free press, etc., then libertarians are in full agreement with Rawls. On the other hand, if the equality principle means that anyone can say anything on anyone else's property, libertarians will object. To take one example, a militant atheist does not have the freedom to walk into a church on Sunday morning and shout down the minister who is attempting to deliver a sermon. Agents of the church would be perfectly within their rights to eject the heckler.[4] Perhaps Dombrowski can clarify his understanding of the equality principle in this regard.

The other part of the equality principle involves distribution of material goods. In a market economy, this distribution is the result of the choices of individuals (acting either alone or as agents of families, businesses, and voluntary associations) directing their resources (e.g., labor or money) in

---

[4] I assume here an American context where the church in question is not state-owned.

the absence of aggression. In a society characterized by Christian morality, we can easily envision an equal distribution of basic goods without any state involvement whatsoever. Indeed, the history of the Christian church's role in society is largely the redistributing of wealth (through tithes and offerings) in the form of food, shelter, healthcare, and education to those who were not born with access to them or who had lost access to them through some misfortune. Other non-profit organizations with non-Christian affiliations perform similar work and can do much to assist the less-well-off members of society.

However, this sort of redistribution of wealth is not what Rawls and most liberals have in mind. Rawlsians tend to assume that the welfare state is both necessary and desirable to fulfill the equality principle as well as the difference principle. If they see a market outcome of an unequal distribution of basic material goods or of non-basic goods not benefiting the least-well-off members of society, they call for wealth confiscation (taxation) of society's more-well-off members and state-directed redistribution of that wealth (minus a large percentage for overhead costs) to its less-well-off members.[5] Libertarians object to this means of redistribution as a violation of the Non-Aggression Principle.

In the interests of space, let me turn now to a consideration of the potential compatibility of Rawlsian liberalism and Christianity. As the quote at the beginning of this essay indicates, the mature Rawls was no friend to Christianity. Dombrowski acknowledges as much in his essay. Of course, this fact alone should not prevent Christians from adopting Rawlsian political philosophy. All truth is God's truth, no matter who utters it. On the other hand, identifying some residual influence of Christian teaching on Rawls is not enough to lead us to embrace his position, either. Most if not all of the perspectives in this volume are products of unbelieving minds that had a "Christian hangover" to some extent.

As I stated in my foundational essay, one of the points in favor of libertarianism is its foundations in the natural law tradition upheld by the Church throughout its history. Rawls, by contrast, rejected natural law explicitly.[6] Dombrowski has also noted that the mature Rawls's thinking was much closer to that of Jean-Jacques Rousseau, who believed that our

---

[5] If my generalization of the position of Rawlsian liberals is incorrect, I welcome correction from Dombrowski. As for Rawls himself, we find throughout his writings statements such as this: "The second part of the distribution branch is a *scheme of taxation* [emphasis mine] to raise the revenues that justice requires. Social resources must be released to the government so that it can provide for the public goods and *make the transfer payments* [emphasis mine] necessary to satisfy the difference principle." John Rawls, *A Theory of Justice* (Cambridge, MA: Harvard University Press, 1971), 278.

[6] Rawls, "On My Religion," 268.

problems originate in our environment, not in ourselves. The Rousseauist and Rawlsian prescription for social problems is thus environmental: use the state to fix institutions. The Christian who holds to historic orthodoxy knows that Rousseau and Rawls have misdiagnosed the problem and should thus be skeptical of their proposed solutions.

Rawls's construct of the original position, which results in his prescriptions, is vulnerable to charges of circular reasoning. Christian philosopher Nicholas Wolterstorff, who is by no means a libertarian, has noted this internal problem in Rawls's system. As Dombrowski has stated, Rawls insists that one's arguments for legislation be made in terms likely to be acceptable to "reasonable" citizens who have different conceptions of the good. Political philosophers call this "public reason." What does it mean to be "reasonable," though? In essence, it means you have to accept public reason; if you don't, your comprehensive doctrine is "unreasonable" and does not even have to be admitted into discussion. It's not much of a stretch to argue that Rawls is employing rhetorical sleight-of-hand to avoid having to deal with views not compatible with his own brand of liberalism.[7]

I believe the Rawlsian view suffers from other internal problems, but space prevents me from exploring them further. To conclude, to the extent that Rawlsian liberalism relies on the state to achieve its vision of justice, libertarians oppose it. If the Rawlsekians have their way, and the Rawlsians adopt voluntary means to advance their vision, libertarians will have no further political conflict with them.

---

[7]   Nicholas Wolterstorff, *Understanding Liberal Democracy* (New York: Oxford University Press, 2012), 81–4.

Political liberalism: A liberationist response
Miguel A. De La Torre

Experience has taught those of us who are scholars of color in the academy that unless we assimilate to liberal academic paradigms (and even then) we will be viewed with suspicion. Unless scholars on the underside of the academy learn to explain reality through a Euroamerican male lens (i.e., Rawls) and assimilate to the dominant culture or forsake their social location through a "veil of ignorance," their work will be seen as lacking. The liberationist attempt to function as an organic intellectual rooted in the experience of the marginalized is diametrically opposed to the compromises inherent in Rawls's attempt to create an objective abstract procedure for defining justice.

To do ethical analysis as a liberationist means, by definition, to raise consciousness concerning complicity with oppressive structures so that said structures can be explored and challenged. While many within political liberalism were and continue to be vocal on issues important to the disenfranchised—issues concerning racial and ethnic reconciliation, economic justice, and the dangers of an imperial foreign policy—they remain complicit with empire-building.

No doubt there are areas of commonality between liberationists and political liberals, specifically in areas concerning the eradication of poverty and a more inclusive approach to the accessibility of social services. Still, as attractive as liberalism may appear to be, its ultimate goal is to "reform" the empire, not create new just structures that fairly redistribute power and wealth. Even when Euroamerican liberals join in solidarity with people of color concerning issues crucial to dispossessed communities, some still refuse to place justice over social order.

Let us not forget that it was the liberal progressive clergy's criticism of the timing of Martin Luther King, Jr.'s organized march that led King to write his famous *Letter from Birmingham Jail*. No doubt the eight religious leaders to whom King formally addressed his letter were among the few white residents of Birmingham who publicly opposed Governor Wallace's defiance of federal desegregation orders. Still, King recognized that the greatest stumbling block to liberation was not the hooded Ku Klux Klan member, but the co-option of any liberative movement by well-meaning Euroamerican liberals who de-radicalize the movement's goals to make it more palatable to Euroamerican sensibilities.[1] King understood that well-meaning liberals were quick to profess solidarity with noble concepts like equality, justice, and dignity; but, when it came to actually implementing social change, they tended to discourage action that could threaten their privileged positions within the social structures and/or upset the societal equilibrium that provides them and their families with security.

Liberalism's understanding of justice, especially via Rawlsian thought, can be more damning to the social location of the marginalized than that of neoconservatives on the political, economic, and/or religious right. Rawls's theory of justice as fairness "carries to a higher level of abstraction the traditional concept of the social contract."[2] He hopes to carry this abstraction to even higher levels than thinkers like "Locke, Rousseau, and Kant."[3] The abstract objectivity for which Rawls strives is simply the subjectivity of Euroamericans who possess the power to make their subjectivity objective, regardless of whether they are hiding behind a veil of ignorance. This produces a harmonious narrative based on value-neutral abstract analysis concerning the definition of justice, which is normalized and legitimized for all. Because most liberationists are troubled by this Euroamerican tilt toward the abstract, away from the actual trials and tribulations of the disinherited or any theoretical reflection rooted in praxis, the Rawlsian social ideal of justice advocated by Daniel Dombrowski is usually viewed with suspicion.

For a group to decide "what is to count among them as just and unjust,"[4] Rawls provides us with his well-known concept, the veil of ignorance. As Dombrowski reminds us, we are "to imagine a decision-making procedure in which we are to design a social contract that would outline the abstract principles that would govern a just society." This group of persons deliberates in the original position, meaning, they arrive at consensus ignorant of crucial facts that they know about themselves (i.e., their gender, race, class, ethnicity, orientation, etc.). They would have to consider the possibility that once the principles of justice are decided, they might have to live in the society they created from a different social location. Such an exercise might have proved useful if not for the fact that we are more a product of our social location than we are willing to admit. We simply cannot divorce ourselves from the social location to which we were born, which nurtured us, and which constructed our concepts of right and wrong. Simply stated, individuals cannot ignore their capital (be it social, economic, or cultural)

---

[1] Martin Luther King, Jr. *Why We Can't Wait* (Boston, MA: Beacon Press, 1963), xii, 60, 98.

[2] John Rawls, *A Theory of Justice* (Boston: Harvard Press, 1999 [1971]), 3.

[3] Ibid., 10.

[4] Ibid., 11

and step outside of their habitus. For this reason, we must jettison Rawls's veil of ignorance because ultimately it is impossible to achieve.

Rawls's method for constructing principles of justice based on existing practices only reinforces the prevailing Euroamerican worldview that fails to consider how power permeates all aspects of society. For example, if the Euroamerican systems of democracy and capitalism allow anyone to succeed because they are generally given a fair chance, then these systems are what most rational persons would pick while behind the veil of ignorance. Hence Rawls justifies the status quo, no doubt calling for some reform, but definitely not implementing revolutionary praxis. Regardless of the veil of ignorance, those with power will still fail to see their Others as reasonable and rational persons, a requirement for Rawls to participate in defining the principles of justice.[5]

For example, let us consider that a group of Southerners used the veil of ignorance in 1850 for the purpose of creating a social contract that defines, once and for all, what justice means. Because their worldview is based on the inferiority (if not bestiality) of blacks, even if they were to assume a position of ignorance about their own race, the foundation of their worldview is based on beliefs about the differing value of people to such an extent that they will still construct a concept of justice that justifies slavery. Rawls may rely on the "convictions of common sense"[6] to arrive at the principles of justice, but we must ask: whose common sense? The common sense of rational beings who are slaveholders? The common sense of the slaves who are considered irrational? What would happen if blacks joined their slaveholders behind the veil of ignorance? Blacks (as well as women) may very well participate in Rawls's exercise today, but in the early nineteenth century, they would not join white men in this exercise because they were not considered rational beings. Even if they had, their minds might be so colonized that a few might see and define themselves through the eyes of their oppressor, or do so in order to survive.

Rawls's concept fails because it ignores the prevalence of power structures and how power creates knowledge as well as identity. Whether behind the veil of ignorance or not, a slave—like any other farm animal—is not a human being. Hence, slaveholders could argue that even if they were to come out of the veil of ignorance as blacks, it does not change the fact of black inferiority and their need for paternalistic treatment. The end result would be a "kinda, gentla" slavocracy.

In fact, we see a justification for social and economic inequity in Rawls's priority rule (especially his second point), where he writes: "a less than equal

---

[5]   Ibid., 17.
[6]   Ibid., 24.

liberty must be acceptable to those citizens with lesser liberty."[7] Because inequalities can be just if they benefit the least, those who are less than human (the least) benefit under the caregiving of the patriarch, thus justifying why blacks must accept "a less-than-equal liberty."

On a different note, Dombrowski's understanding of *dike* is interesting. When he writes "that the many instances of *dike* and its cognates in the Christian scriptures have typically been translated as 'righteousness' or 'uprightness,'" he is obviously speaking about the English Christian scriptures. So when he goes on to explain the fact "that religious ethics is not focused on justice is to a considerable extent the result of the difficulties of translation rather than of anything integral to Christianity," he is fusing and confusing religious ethics with Euroamerican religious ethics. Those of us who read the Bible in Spanish practice a very different Christian justice than do Euroamericans because we have the ability to read the Bible with our own eyes.

When I read the Bible in Spanish, *dike* is translated to the Spanish word *justicia*, which corresponds to the English "justice." This changes the way these scriptures are read and what concept of justice is communicated. The dictionary defines "righteous" as "morally right or justifiable, acting in an upright, moral way."[8] This term implies action which can be performed privately. However, "justice" can only be exercised in a flesh-and-blood community. A solitary individual can be righteous through prayer and God-based thought. Justice, however, requires others to whom justice can be administered. By using the words *justo* and *justicia*, the Spanish translation reinforces communalism as opposed to the hyper-individualism connoted by "righteousness," and which is reinforced by Rawls's methodology.

While Dombrowski may wonder why scriptural translators often render *dike* and its cognates as "righteousness" rather than as "justice"; those who are not part of the dominant culture understand the power relationships that led to this translation decision. Could it be that the translators, working for the king (James I), wanted to move away from concepts of social justice lest their benefactor be held accountable to the biblical text? Then the king could remain righteous without having to dispense justice. Based on such power analysis, ethics as practiced in the English-speaking world becomes alien to those who read the text in Spanish.[9]

---

[7] Ibid., 220.

[8] "Righteous," *Dictionary.com*, http://dictionary.reference.com/browse/righteous?s=t (accessed January 21, 2014).

[9] Space prevents a thorough exegetical word study or a historical review of how the biblical text was translated; nevertheless, for those seeking a more detailed analysis of these points, please see Miguel A. De La Torre, *Reading the Bible from the Margins* (Maryknoll, NY: Orbis Press, 2002), 146–8.

Dombrowski concludes by asking why we should take the hypothetical decision-making procedure of the original position, with its veil of ignorance, seriously. He responds by stating, "as a result of this procedure we are better able to get a clear view of the standard of justice against which we can judge actually existing societies like our own." I would argue that rather than achieving his hope of an objective principle of justice, this procedure, because it ignores how power creates knowledge and identity, will only reform our current social structures, which continue to be oppressive to those on the underside of what Dombrowski signifies as "existing societies like our own."

Political liberalism: A feminist response
Laura Stivers

While the liberal ideals of freedom, equality, and justice are clearly important for addressing the oppression of women and others, many Christian feminists are concerned that the abstract individualist conception of the human person that liberalism is based on undercuts the liberatory potential of Rawls's theory of justice for women. Clearly, applying Rawls's difference principle would radically challenge the substantial domestic and global inequality and demand policies that reign in corporate-led free market capitalism that is impoverishing multitudes of people. Christian feminists would certainly support such change, but believe that such reform would not go far enough in addressing injustice. Of the feminist critiques of Rawls's theory of justice I will outline two that are closely related. One critique developed by Susan Moller Okin is that Rawls restricts justice to the public realm without applying justice to a primary site of women's oppression, the family. The other critique relates to the theory's inability to address the full realm of structural injustice that women and other oppressed groups experience, primarily because its focus is confined to distributive justice with no attention to the ways culturally constructed knowledge buttresses the status quo.

Rawls's theory of justice, and liberalism in general, assumes a generic human viewpoint, and under the veil of ignorance sex is one of the "morally irrelevant characteristics." While feminists realize the veil of ignorance is hypothetical, the resulting "gender-neutral" principles and laws end up being discriminatory for women. Susan Moller Okin writes: "There is strikingly little indication, throughout most of *A Theory of Justice*, that the modern liberal society to which the principles of justice are to be applied is deeply and pervasively gender-structured."[1] For example, offering family leave to both men and women sounds like an empowering policy, but without policies that protect women when they take leave and financial supports for women to do so (as women are more poor than men), the law simply offers formal legal equality, not actual equality. Feminist philosopher Martha Nussbaum addresses this point in substantial depth with her capabilities

---

[1]   Susan Moller Okin, *Justice, Gender, and the Family* (New York City: Basic Books, 1989), 89.

approach. Rather than assuming all people have similar needs, she asks: "What are people actually able to do and to be?" People with disabilities, for instance, will have particular needs that others might not have to be capable of functioning, and will most likely require more support. Formal equality or equal distribution of resources will not result in capability equality, especially in a society with systemic structural oppression.

Okin argues that all of our major social institutions assume that women will take care of the young and old, and will perform all of the "reproductive labor" (unpaid work of the home). Okin critiques Rawls's theory for not challenging this assumption but furthering it with his distinction between the political and the private and his belief that family institutions are just. Feminists have argued for years that the gendered division of labor in the home is not just and furthermore that this division affects how women fare in the workplace and public realm. Okin's solution is not to repudiate but to embrace Rawls's original position as a powerful tool for challenging the gendered assumptions and practices within families. She argues that Rawls's principle of fair equality of opportunity requires justice within the family. Okin envisions radical transformation of our culture's gender-dominated social relations and advocates for a "genderless family" in which all responsibilities of parenting, elder care, and other household labor are equally shared. Only then, she believes, will women truly have equality of opportunity.

While all feminists support justice within the family, many are not as optimistic that Rawls's theory can challenge oppressive gender role expectations in the way Okin argues. His emphasis on distributive justice does not address many forms of oppression that women and others face. While the actions of people in power sustain subordination, the structural processes and dominant discourses and ways of knowing that privilege some at the expense of others are larger roots of oppression. Iris Marion Young argues that focusing only on what individual people possess precludes the social processes and institutional relations that affect their life chances. Young writes: "A distributive understanding misses the way in which the powerful enact and reproduce their power."[2] Individuals are part of social groups based on race, class, and gender, and these social identities affect their ability to develop and exercise their capacities, not only because of the ways in which others perceive and relate to them, but also due to internal conditioning. Girls, for example, are taught from an early age to be caregivers, not leaders. These gender expectations affect the way they are treated in the educational system, workplace, and broader society. Women are paid less for

---

[2] Iris Marion Young, *Justice and the Politics of Difference* (Princeton, NJ: Princeton University Press, 1990), 32.

the work they do, they deal routinely with sexual harassment, and they are not represented adequately in positions of power. Oppressive gender conditioning also influences women's own "choices" of what to do and be.

Rawls's theory lacks a fully developed understanding of oppression, exploitation, and power to address the ways groups of people are affected by structural processes, which is in part a result of the "social contract" tradition and its view of free and consenting individuals who are not constrained or supported by cultural ideologies and conditioning. Simply granting women or other marginalized groups free exercise of their basic rights and a larger distribution of primary goods will not challenge sexist, racist, and classist cultural worldviews that negatively affect individuals' agency and capability to function. We need an understanding of personhood that emphasizes interdependency, dignity, and moral worth instead of the Rawlsian view of humans as contracting agents who are free, equal, and independent. An understanding of ourselves as relational beings with a purpose or *telos* to be in right relationships within the earth community challenges the dominant and narrow view of ourselves as isolated consumers of resources out for personal advantage. A relational and interdependent view of personhood and *telos* of flourishing life also broadens the scope of what justice entails. All forms of injustice, not simply maldistribution of resources, must be addressed, and attention to nonhuman life on earth also matters.

While Christian feminists appreciate Rawls's concern for pluralistic conceptions of the good and do not advocate only one particular view of flourishing life, they nevertheless support a normative vision of the good life that includes the norm of "right relationships" with others as well as individual autonomy, bodily integrity, and freedom and opportunity to exercise one's capabilities. Someone supporting a Rawlsian perspective could find it perfectly "reasonable" to assume the family is just based on patriarchal understandings of gender, family, and women's fulfillment. Christian feminists argue, in contrast, that "conceptions of the good" which do not support the full dignity and moral worth of individuals and which ignore justice within our personal lives impede loving relations with ourselves, others, nature, and God, and they disrupt Divine vision/*telos* for all of creation. Rawls's claim to neutrality in respect to conceptions of the good leaves ample room for oppressive ideologies. A Christian feminist approach to justice is not impartial but always starts from the standpoint of, and in solidarity with, those who are marginalized and/or exploited.

Political liberalism: A virtue ethicist's response
Elizabeth Phillips

Daniel Dombrowski's essay on a Rawlsian approach to justice should be credited for his very interesting and important turn towards love. I was pleased to see his efforts to bring Rawlsian justice into conversation with the Christian virtue and norm of love. Dombrowski and I find some significant common ground when he says "the sense of justice and love are compatible. Indeed, they can easily work in tandem..." However, readers should carefully consider whether this is Dombrowski's own work within a Rawlsian framework (which in no way discredits it), or a truly clear trajectory already existing within Rawls's work. In other words, we have to ask, how Rawlsian is this common ground we have tentatively established between the Rawlsian and virtue approaches?

Regardless of your conclusion on that matter, the more substantial matter of teleology remains. Dombrowski has very succinctly shown how and why a Rawlsian approach to justice is directly at odds with the teleology of a virtue approach when he says "questions regarding the good have to be largely taken off the table in politics ... politics is not the place to debate ultimate questions regarding the purpose of human life..." As a Christian virtue ethicist I cannot imagine how or why Christian ethicists would attempt to conceive of political arrangements apart from a vision of the good or apart from an understanding of the purpose of human life in God. However, I cover the relationship between the right and the good, the differences between procedural and substantive approaches, and the commonalities between a virtue approach and the communitarian critiques of liberalism at length in my essay, so I will not repeat those points here.

If mine were the only word to be spoken in response to the Rawlsian approach, I would want to very seriously question the adequacy of the concepts of the original position, the veil of ignorance, and the difference principle (particularly Dombrowski's analogy between this principle and the liberationist preferential option for the poor), but Laura Stivers and Miguel De La Torre have covered these necessary critiques very well. In fact, this highlights very nicely how virtue ethicists such as myself are often in full agreement with and happy to be seen as dependent upon the important work done by liberationist and feminist scholars who raise critical questions (in both senses of criticizing and of urgent importance) about liberalism, as well as other establishment views (even when they believe this includes the virtue tradition).

However, I would like to use the remainder of my response to focus on an entirely different issue. In the opening pages of his essay, Dombrowski rightly identifies one of the central motivations in liberalism for tabling issues of the good and the ultimate, which is that people in a context of pluralism should be able to coexist without resorting to violence. This is indeed a noble motive which I share. However, tragically, the modern era gives us very little evidence that liberalism is preventing violence. One could argue that liberal democracies do not engage in modern warfare with one another, which may be largely true, yet liberal democracies have succumbed to civil wars and have been key players in all the most ravaging wars of the twentieth and now twenty-first centuries. In fact, it is difficult to see how the history of either the recent centuries or indeed the early modern centuries can still be interpreted by some liberals as supporting the narrative that liberalism prevents violence.

Central to the narrative of liberalism is the claim that the liberal approach of tabling questions of the good and the ultimate has saved the modern West from the atrocities of the so-called "wars of religion." Dombrowski resoundingly endorses this narrative when he says, "By ending both theoretically and practically the wars of religion that plagued Europe in the early modern period, it can be said without exaggeration that political liberalism can be seen as one of the great achievements of human civilization!" I must say that this is not only an exaggeration, it is a radical distortion, though one which Dombrowski is by no means alone in espousing.

In his excellent book *The Myth of Religious Violence*[1] William Cavanaugh drives several strong nails into the coffin of this narrative. In his title and the argument of the book, Cavanaugh is not suggesting that religious people are not violent, rather he calls into question a particular narrative which he calls "the myth of religious violence:"

> The idea that religion is a transhistorical and transcultural feature of human life, essentially distinct from "secular" features such as politics and economics, which has a peculiarly dangerous inclination to promote violence. Religion must therefore be tamed by restricting its access to public power.[2]

In other words, Cavanaugh questions three aspects of the narrative of

---

[1] William T. Cavanaugh, *The Myth of Religious Violence* (Oxford: Oxford University Press, 2009).

[2] Ibid., 3.

liberalism which Dombrowski has endorsed: 1) that there is such a thing as "religion" which exists across all times and cultures and can be adequately defined in such a way as to differentiate it from "secular" ideologies; 2) that "religion" is peculiarly violent and/or that most violence arises from religious disputes or religious impulses; and 3) that the modern, secular state is the antidote to "religious violence."

First, Cavanaugh shows that efforts to define "religion" all fail either to encompass everything we commonly think of as religion, or not to encompass many other things which are supposedly secular. Try it yourself. Can you conceive of a definition of religion that would, for examples, include something like Hinduism without including something like Marxism? Through his discussion of the difficulty of isolating something called "religion," Cavanaugh not only reveals that "the distinction between secular and religious violence is unhelpful, misleading, and mystifying,"[3] but also that the development of the concept of "religion" was intimately connected to the rise of colonialism and efforts to legitimize the power of the liberal state (which of course required violence against and domination of peoples outside the liberal West).

Dombrowski, to his credit, gestures towards an acknowledgment of this difficulty, along with Rawls, when he refers to "comprehensive doctrines (whether religious or non-religious)." In other words, Dombrowski shows an awareness that any worldview or philosophy of life can make the sorts of ultimate claims which "religions" make. However, he goes on to fully embrace the second and third aspects of the myth which Cavanaugh criticizes.

The central narrative of points 2) and 3) above is precisely the one which Dombrowski has echoed: that liberalism saved us from the madness of the wars of religion. Cavanaugh extensively examines these so-called "wars of religion" and demonstrates that in many cases the violence was not between groups with opposing religious views, and that where there were "religious" differences, these cannot be neatly separated from the political factors contributing to each specific dispute. In other words, calling these wars "religious" is just as problematic as identifying something called "religion" which causes violence but is different from any other "comprehensive doctrine."

Cavanaugh goes on to consider how, quite to the contrary of its claims to save us from "religious violence," liberalism in the modern era has actually served as its own form of absolute "us versus them" reasoning which is supposedly the problem with the absolute and ultimate claims which liberals like Rawls want to remove from political processes. In fact, the myth of

---

³ Ibid., 56.

religious violence is currently employed by many liberals not to save us from madness like the "religious wars" but to promote and justify the wars of the West.

> In foreign policy, the myth of religious violence serves to cast nonsecular social orders, especially Muslim societies, in the role of villain. *They* have not yet learned to remove the dangerous influence of religion from political life. *Their* violence is therefore irrational and fanatical. *Our* violence, being secular, is rational, peace making, and sometimes regrettably necessary to contain *their* violence. We find ourselves obliged to bomb them into liberal democracy.[4]

Let me be clear that I am not ascribing these views to Daniel Dombrowski; I do not know where he stands on current wars or on the current employments of violence by liberal states. However, he has been clear about his embrace of the narrative that liberalism saved the West from religious violence, and thus the connections between that narrative and current narratives of liberal Western states against Muslim, Middle Eastern states—and the violence legitimated by this narrative—has to be called into question, as does the mythology surrounding the genesis of liberalism as the answer to "religious" wars.

---

[4]   Ibid., 4.

3

Liberation Theology and Social Justice: A Defense

Miguel A. De La Torre

What is logical to the oppressor isn't logical to the oppressed. And what is reason to the oppressor isn't reason to the oppressed. The black people [and I would add all who are from the margins] in this country are beginning to realize that what sounds reasonable to those who exploit us doesn't sound reasonable to us. There just has to be a new system of reason and logic devised by us who are at the bottom.[1]

Malcolm X

As much as we may not want to admit it, both you and I approach justice from a specific social location—the cultural experiences which influence our identity. In spite of all the conversation concerning a post-racial America, the truth remains that being white is a vastly different experience than being black or Latino/a. We are all born into a society that shapes and forms who we are; it was constructed before we were born and it will continue to exist after our bodies become food for the worms. Our definition of justice has more to do with how our community modeled justice for us since our early childhood than any universal definition of justice. We may wish to deny our subjectivity, but the fact remains that our religious beliefs, interpretations of Holy Writ, spiritual traditions, and understandings of justice are mostly formed by our social location and the family we are born into; having more to do with how our identity was constructed rather than any ethereal form or universal truth.

What happens, then, when the community that bore and nurtured us has maintained oppressive and repressive social structures? For instance, those raised within a Eurocentric culture are a product of a society where white supremacy, class privilege, patriarchy, and homophobia have historically been interwoven with how Americans have been conditioned to normalize

---

[1] Malcolm X, "The Leverett House Forum of March 18, 1964," *The Speeches of Malcolm X at Harvard*, ed. Archie Epps (New York: William Morrow & Co., 1968), 133.

and legitimize how they see and organize the world around them. This subjective worldview becomes foundational for how the dominant culture constructs their understanding of justice. If indeed the concept of justice is a product of the social location of Euroamericans with the authority to make their subjective definition the acceptable objective societal norm, then the dominant culture's particularity of what justice means can prove damning to marginalized communities. Why? Because many from disenfranchised communities have been taught to define justice through the eyes of those in power, specifically through the eyes of white, middle- and upperclass heterosexual males. As alluring as a Eurocentric understanding of ethics in general and justice in particular may appeal to the marginalized, this understanding, influenced as it is by the idea of the American Empire, is incongruent with the Gospel message of liberation.

While some Eurocentric ethicists may challenge, critique, and even call for profound reform of this Empire, they still maintain the class, gender, racial, and ethnic assumptions that provided justification for the Empire in the first place. They fail to recognize their complicity with the overarching power structures that make empires possible. The Eurocentric understanding of justice fails to challenge the dominant culture's power and privilege. The underlying problem with Eurocentric ethical concepts is that moral reasoning is usually done from the realm of abstractions. It is less concerned with "what you do" than "how you think." So, why must the disenfranchised follow Euroamerican definitions of justice when engaging in moral reasoning? To engage in the Eurocentric ethical discourse, either conservative or liberal, will prove problematic for marginalized communities.

Failure of eurocentric understandings of justice

While the ethical positions held within the dominant culture are not monolithic, nevertheless, certain common denominators exist. These include a propensity toward hyper-individualism, a call for law and order, an emphasis on charity, an uncritical acceptance of the market economy, and an emphasis on orthodoxy and deductive ethical reasoning. While these ideas are congruent with the dominant culture, they are harmful to those residing on the margins of society because of how they reinforce the social structures responsible for their disenfranchisement. Eurocentric understandings of justice usually fail to grasp how the academic discipline we call "ethics" aids and abets the structures of Empire. The Eurocentric-driven culture maintains a status quo that privileges one group at the expense of the marginalized. It is a culture where the disenfranchised are the object, the problem, never the subject or the solution. In order for the privileged to reconcile the Empire that benefits them with their commitment to justice which demands liberation from oppressive structures, they must develop an abstract ethic that stimulates the mind without changing the structures responsible in maintaining and sustaining their privilege and power.

The ultimate failure of Eurocentric ethicists, as well as those ethicists or scholars of color who uncritically subscribe to the dominant culture's worldview, is in overlooking power analysis and their own location within the prevailing power structures. Their complicity with empire relieves them of any responsibility of actually establishing a justice that can be liberating for marginalized communities. Eurocentric ethics becomes a product of power held by those who benefit by making the dominant ethical perspectives of the privileged normative for everybody else. Eurocentric ethics is not finally about establishing justice. It is about justifying the status quo. The Euroamerican ethical discourse becomes a strategy for reconciling moral reasoning with the existing structures that remain detrimental to the dispossessed, without sacrificing the privilege amassed by the dominant culture.

Those seeking a liberative approach to justice begin with the realization that Eurocentric-based ethics will not bring justice to marginalized communities, mainly because Euroamericans do not know, nor do they need to know, the social location of the dispossessed. For an ethic to be liberative, it must move beyond the ethic of the dominant culture, even when it seems liberal and progressive. Why? Because most Euroamerican-based ethics either ignore the causes of or provide justification for the prevailing structures of oppression that remain detrimental to the marginalized.[2] If mainstream ethics fail to address oppressive structures, then the marginalized must construct new ethical paradigms for their communities that can lead to a liberative understanding of justice.

Constructing liberative approaches to justice

There is not one liberative ethical approach to justice upon which everyone can agree. All theologies, theories, and ethical paradigms are contextual; all are rooted in the social location of those seeking faith-based responses to injustice. Whatever liberation looks like, it can only be determined by those living under oppressive structures, not paternalistically by those who

---

[2] See Miguel De La Torre, *Latina/o Social Ethics: Moving Beyond Eurocentric Moral Thinking* (Waco, TX: Baylor University Press, 2010).

benefit from how society is organized. How rural blacks in Georgia understand God's response to their repressive conditions is different from how Latinas in Los Angeles understand God's presence within the urban jungle. Different ethnicities, geographical locations, and oppressive situations lead to different understandings about God and the praxis required for a more liberative social order; even though congruency can be found in the message of seeking an abundant life. Any attempt to provide a unified definition of liberative ethics or justice is therefore problematic. Although the common starting point of liberative theological and ethical reflection remains the existential experience of the marginalized, the ultimate goal remains liberation from the reality of societal misery. While the focus for the remainder of this chapter will be on a Christian-based liberative theory of justice, we should recognize that liberative perspectives can be found in many faith traditions (or lack thereof) which space prevents us from exploring.

Understanding the message of justice

Justice, for Christians, can be reduced to the purpose of Jesus Christ's ministry as articulated in the Gospel of John: "I have come that they might have life and have it more abundantly" (10.10). To experience life more abundantly is not limited to waiting for some eschatological future; the message of Christ is for the here and now. This abundant life, which Jesus claims to offer, reveals a God of life, not a God of death. Structures or individuals, whether they be interpersonal or corporate, that bring death are therefore anti-Christ. The gospel message of liberation stresses freedom from all forms of oppression: social, economic, political, racial, sexual, environmental, or religious. A liberative approach to justice becomes the process of integrating faith with the socio-political everyday (*lo cotidiano*) in which the oppressed find themselves.

In a very real sense, liberation is salvation. The Hebrew word *yāša'* and the Greek term *sōzō* appear in most English translations of the Bible as "save"; yet these words can also mean "liberate." Salvation is neither an abstract concept nor a personal emotional feeling; it is a state of being that encompasses rescue and deliverance. Hence the question: salvation/liberation from what? From what (or from whom) are the wretched of the earth rescued and delivered? To be liberated from sin, personal or corporate, is to be saved. Among liberationists, liberation and salvation are used interchangeably. Justice occurs when we are saved/liberated from sin, when sin is understood as the forces that bring oppression, enslavement, and death.

The ultimate goal of salvation/liberation is to break with sin through a new life in Christ. This is achieved through the process of consciousness-raising, learning how structures of oppression prevent the dispossessed from experiencing the abundant life promised by Christ. Hence, the evangelical goal of liberative thought is not to convince non-believers to believe doctrinal tenets; it is to convince non-persons of their personhood—their infinite worth—because they, regardless of what the world tells them, are created in the very image of God, the *imago Dei*.

The purpose of ethics is, therefore, the pursuit of justice, not to create, expand, or sustain doctrinal beliefs or abstract concepts. Ethics becomes the *physical* response in the here-and-now to the inhuman conditions to which the vast majority of the world is relegated. One of the phrases often repeated by Jesus is that the reign of God is at hand. For Jesus, God's reign was not a future event. Historically, the reward of a hereafter has been used to encourage submission to oppression as an earthly trial in preparation for heavenly riches. In contrast, the proclamation that God's reign is at hand signals that liberation/salvation is now. In a very real sense, theories concerning justice provide the disenfranchised with theological grounding for *actions* that can lead toward the rescue and deliverance of all who presently face socio-cultural and economic oppression.

Sin

According to the Brazilian liberation theologian Leonardo Boff, what social analysis calls "structural poverty" faith calls "structural sin." What analysis calls the "private accumulation of wealth" faith calls "the sin of selfishness."[3] Sin represents all that is wrong with the world. It is responsible for the enslavement of humanity, forcing individuals to act against their best interest and the best interest of others. While a Eurocentric culture, whose salient characteristic is hyper-individualism, understands sin as a personal failing or the outcome of individual choices, the marginalized, who often stress a more communal worldview, understand sin as the consequences and ramifications of the prevailing social structures.

Liberationists understand sin as communal. All sins, even those committed privately by individuals, have communal consequences. All too often, Eurocentric spirituality has made sin and its redemption personal. Sin becomes an act of commission or omission, while salvation from our sinfulness rests in a *personal* savior in the form of Jesus Christ, who has a plan for our *personal* life. What is missing from this kind of religious thought

---

[3] Leonardo Boff, "Salvation in Liberation: The Theological Meaning of Socio-Historical Liberation," in *Salvation and Liberation: In Search of a Balance Between Faith and Politics*, eds. Leonardo and Clodovis Boff, trans. by R. R. Barr (Maryknoll, NY: Orbis Books and Melbourne: Dove Communications, 1984 [1979]), 9.

is the structural nature of sin. Conversion is never personal; it must extend to social transformation. Oppression and poverty as expressions of sin are caused by societal structures that are designed to enrich the few at the expense of the many.

For example, it is the will of God for humanity to share the fruits of creation. In opposition to this is what has come to be known as the dependency theory. This theory maintains that the world's industrial nations of the global North have grown prosperous at the expense of the global South. Because the consequence of such socio-economic structures is death, they are understood to be sinful. A person can use a gun and kill a child. We have no difficulty in characterizing such a heinous act as sin. But death does not solely come from the barrel of a gun. Death is also caused by economic, social, and political structures. While all may feel horror at the brutal and violent death of a child shot in the head, most fail to notice the roughly 30,000 children who die of hunger and preventable diseases each and every day.[4]

Yet while these children are perishing, impoverished countries are spending three to five times more money paying off foreign debt than providing basic services that can alleviate this silent genocide. We are quick to label the brutal shooting of a child a sin, but we ignore the tens of thousands of children who die slowly, wasting away over a period of years. Liberationists see that the deaths of the least of these, caused by a global economic structure (neoliberalism) that is designed to benefit those located in the so-called first world, as much a sin as violently shooting a child. This form of sin has come to be known as institutional violence.

Justice's ultimate aim is to go beyond reform, for reform attempts to make sinful societal structures more bearable while still justifying the fact that they keep the vast majority of the world's resources in the hands of the few. Liberationists envision the hopeless utopia of a new creation free of injustices, where human dignity and the freedom to seek one's own destiny reign supreme. Envisioning the absurd leads liberationists to call for social revolution, a radical change of the structures that cause oppression, a move closer to Jesus' promise of an abundant life.

Solidarity with the marginalized

Theories of justice can never be reduced to collections of definitions and paradigms based on the past that were meaningful in different eras among different people facing different forms of oppression. This is not to say that a

---

[4] Sakiko Fukuda-Parr, ed., *United Nations Development Programme's Human Development Report 2003* (New York: Oxford University Press, 2003), 8.

concept of justice understood in a bygone context should be totally rejected because nothing can be gleaned. Nevertheless, if indeed all theories and theologies are contextual, then past understandings and definitions of justice must change and evolve with the new locations in which today's marginalized find themselves. Hence the quest for justice must be oriented toward the future. What must occur among the disenfranchised to usher in God's salvation, understood as liberation? How can the dispossessed discover a path toward their salvation and liberation?

Because most liberationists are more than simply academicians (many are pastoral agents working with and for the disinherited), their concern has less to do with developing a body of scholarly thought, and more to do with standing in solidarity with faith-based, grassroots movements whose ultimate goal is social justice. Consequently, liberative thought about justice is more concerned with engaging in an open dialogue with the world, rather than preserving the status quo. Far from repeating timeless principles, liberationists concentrate upon reflections that are connected to the daily experiences of the disenfranchised. For liberationists, all praxis is derived from the perspective of the oppressed. From the underside of power and privilege, a worldview is constructed from which to address the existing structural injustices.

Unfortunately, Christendom has historically been closely linked to the dominant culture, and the political structures designed to protect the interests of the privileged few. In contrast, liberationists believe the church can never be neutral in the face of injustice. When the church stands in solidarity with the marginalized, it ceases to be a mere extension of Christendom, instead becoming the church of the oppressed. In this way, the church fulfills the mission of Christ, who said: "The Spirit of the Lord is upon me, and anointed me to preach the good news to the poor, to heal the brokenhearted, to bring freedom to the enslaved, provide sight to those who cannot see, proclaim liberation to the oppressed, and announce the acceptable year of the Lord" (Lk. 4.18-19).

Those claiming to be disciples of Jesus are called to struggle with and for the oppressed, always willing to learn about God from them. It is crucial in the struggle for justice to break the tie between the privileged and Christianity so that the coming together of believers can occur. Latin American liberationist Pablo Richards argues that the church must live in solidarity with the poor, incarnated among the oppressed. Its mission is to serve the world, a witness to God's will for life.[5] The church not only

---

[5] See Pablo Richard, *Death of Christendoms, Birth of the Church: Historical Analysis and Theological Interpretation of the Church in Latin America*, trans. Phillip Berryman (Maryknoll, NY: Orbis Books, 1987).

evangelizes the oppressed but is in turn evangelized by the oppressed. Hence the church is not only called to signify liberation, but also to be an instrument by which liberation is achieved.

Although some of those engaged in liberative thought are scholars, many holding privileged PhDs, they attempt to root their academia within the faith community as "organic intellectuals," à la Antonio Gramsci. These scholar–activists connect the intellectual enterprise, which is informed by the grassroots, with popular movements where they participate in contributing to its consciousness-raising. Their scholarly contributions raise the consciousness of those who are unaware of their complicity with oppressive power structures, and those who may be aware but nevertheless are committed to working in and with disenfranchised communities during their struggle for salvation/liberation. These scholar–activists theorize and theologize for the express purpose of changing oppressive social structures, as opposed to simply better understanding said structures for the sake of scholarship alone.

God of the oppressed

Justice begins with the plight of the poor, the oppressed, the marginalized, the outcast, and the disenfranchised. To engage in justice is to do it with, and from, the perspective of those whom society considers (no)bodies. Incarnating liberative thought among those who are dispossessed roots the quest for justice in the material as opposed to the metaphysical. While many within the Eurocentric context question the existence of God; those on the margins are more likely to wrestle with the character of this God who supposedly exists. Whoever God is, God imparts and sustains life while opposing death. Wherever lives are threatened with poverty and oppression, God is present and offended by the dehumanizing conditions into which the marginalized are relegated. This is a God who acts in history, a God who hears the cries of the enslaved Hebrews, physically enters history, and leads his people toward a promised land. It is in the everyday—during trials and tribulations as well as joys and celebrations—where one encounters the Divine. And while God is present in history, the construction of a new society remains a human project. God may lead God's people to a promised land, but the people must commit to the praxis of walking there.

To enter history and stand in solidarity with the oppressed means that God takes sides over and against the rich and powerful; not because the marginalized are better Christians or somehow holier, but because they are the oppressed in need of justice. God makes a preferential option for the poor and oppressed, over and against the pharaohs of this world. This is the God whom the Hebrews called *Goèl*, the one who provides justice for the weak, makes a home for the alien, becomes a parent to the orphan, and comforts the widow—biblical euphemisms for the most vulnerable within society. The type of worship that best honors this God, where God finds pleasure, is in the doing of justice (Isa. 1.10-17).

Jesus, as God made flesh, chose poverty. He denied some heavenly abode to dwell among the least of these. The miracle of the incarnation is not that God became human, but rather that God became poor. Through Jesus, God learns what it means to suffer under unjust religious and political structures. The cross is meaningless except when viewed in fidelity to Christ's mission. For many liberationists, the crucifixion is less about atonement than it is about solidarity. Condemnation to death is the ultimate consequence faced by many who struggle against unjust oppressive structures. Jesus takes up his cross as the definitive act of solidarity with all crucified people, who continue to be crucified today. Often Christ's crucifixion is spiritualized, ignoring that this moment in history was both a political and religious act. Crucifixion recognizes that death-dealing actions are the usual response from authorities who protect the power and privilege of the few.

Jesus, in the ultimate act of solidarity with all who continue to be crucified today on the crosses of sexism, racism, ethnic discrimination, classism, and heterosexism, carries the wounds upon his feet, hands, and side. Thus God knows dispossession, discrimination, destitution, disinheritance, and disenfranchisement. Those who suffer under oppression have a God who personally understands their suffering through the incarnation. Because Jesus suffered oppression on the cross, a divine commitment to stand against injustices exists, a stance believers are called to emulate. In short, to know God is to do justice. To stand by while oppression occurs is to profess non-belief, regardless of any private or public confession, or any aisle walked to give one's heart to Jesus.

To be a Christian is to become a new creature in Christ. This transformation includes liberation for both those exploited and their exploiters. To seek liberation is to hopelessly strive toward a new society that establishes God's reign on earth. If a tree is known by its fruit, then social justice becomes the fruit by which Christianity is recognized. If there is no justice-based praxis, there is no fruit; thus the fruitless tree needs to be cut down and thrown into the fire. Faith becomes the manifestation of what is done to "the least of these"—the hungry, the thirsty, and the naked. As the Book of James reminds us, "faith without works is dead" (2.26). Only through praxis do we see the face of God. This is a religious perspective that enacts the Gospel rather than simply meditating on it.

Methodology

There is a tendency among many Eurocentric thinkers to reduce the Christian life to individual piety or virtue, thus limiting the liberative goal of changing social and political structures. Among those engaged in the Eurocentric project, the quest for justice is conducted deductively—from theory or truth comes action or praxis. First comes some conceptualized universal truth, such as the Bible, philosophy, or doctrine. Based on said truth, an action is determined and implemented. Thus orthopraxis (correct action) flows from orthodoxy (correct doctrine). Those engaged in the liberative quest for justice instead consider orthodoxy to be the second step flowing out of orthopraxis. Truth, beyond the historical experiences and the social location where individuals act as social agents, cannot be ascertained, whether it exists or not. Only through justice-based praxis, engaged in transforming society, can individuals come closer to understanding God's will and revelation.

The liberative approach to justice is praxis-centered. It recognizes that before we can construct truth, we must *do* liberation—connecting spiritual with material realities. Those implementing this ethical model as a spiritual response to material disenfranchisement follow a "see-judge-act" paradigm (borrowed from the Young Christian Workers of the 1930s), in which we must first do liberative praxis before we can do liberation theology.[6] Simply stated, believers "see" the oppression that is occurring. Through consciousness-raising, they "judge" the causes of oppression. Finally they commit themselves to "act." The praxis implemented is informed by considerations of social analysis, philosophy, and biblical hermeneutics. Therefore it is a reflective praxis rooted in the experience of the oppressed. It brings us back to "see" where the impact of the action can be evaluated.

A methodology that leads to praxis is crucial for any movement toward a more just social structure to take root. Recognizing that any approach toward justice is fallible rather than universal—a "roadmap" rather than a set of rigid principles—is important in ascertaining Christian praxis. And while the Catholic model of *seeing–judging–acting* is helpful, I propose an ethical paradigm that expands this model to five basic steps forming a wider hermeneutical circle [see Figure 1]. This five-step hermeneutical circle serves as the methodology for seeking justice.

---

6   See Pope Paul VI, "Pastoral Constitution on the Church in the Modern World: Gaudium et Spes," *The Vatican*, December 7, 1965, http://www.vatican.va/archive/hist_councils/ ii_vatican_council/documents/vat-ii_cons_19651207_gaudium-et-spes_en.html   and "Apostolic Letter: Octogesima Adveniens," *The Vatican*, May 14, 1971, http://www. vatican.va/holy_father/paul_vi/apost_letters/documents/hf_p-vi_apl_19710514_ octogesima-adveniens_en.html (accessed November 13, 2013).

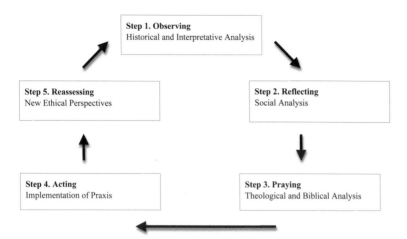

FIGURE 1: The Hermeneutical Circle for Ethics

The first step is observation—an attempt to understand why the present moral dilemma exists. To observe is to seriously consider the historical situation responsible for the oppressive circumstances where the marginalized are forced to live. Understanding the social location of the oppressed requires exploring why, how, and when the present oppressive structures were created as well as how they were maintained, normalized, and legitimized. To observe is consciously to seek the voices of the disenfranchised that are often excluded from history. An attempt is made to "see" through the eyes of the dispossessed who are poor, victimized, and made to suffer. To observe is to recover their voices so as to provide a critique of the prevailing powers.[7]

The second step is reflection: an attempt to understand how social structures contribute to and maintain oppression. Society cannot be transformed without first doing social analysis. The social sciences provide a means to collect raw data that can elucidate the reality faced by the marginalized. To point out how social mechanisms maintain institutionalized oppression is to point out the sin of the dominant culture. No adequate response to oppressive structures can be made if the disinherited fail to fully understand how society created and preserved the economic, social, and political subjugation of the world's marginalized.[8]

---

[7] Miguel A. De La Torre, *Doing Christian Ethics from the Margins* (Maryknoll, NY: Orbis Books, 2004), 58–61.

[8] Ibid., 62–3.

The third step is prayer as an attempt to understand what should be the responsibility of communities of faith. Prayer is not limited to holding a private conversation with the Creator of the universe. Prayer also encompasses a communal act by which the members of marginalized faith communities stand in solidarity during trials and tribulations. Prayer establishes community where the stories of the oppressed are critically listened to and where a commitment to work in solidarity for full liberation, both spiritual and physical, takes place. To pray is to discern God's will through a critical application of the biblical text to the moral dilemmas faced by those relegated to the underside of history. To read the Bible as a community of faith is to fuse the biblical narrative with the everyday, producing a biblical witness capable of addressing the marginalization of the oppressed.[9]

The fourth step is praxis; a response based on what Christians claim they believe. Regardless of how sincere and noble those from the dominant culture may appear to be, theorizing about justice changes nothing. To do ethics from the margins is *to do*, not simply to theorize. The praxis called for moves beyond paternalistic "charity" toward actions that dismantle the social structures that are detrimental to the vast majority of humanity.[10]

The fifth and final step is reassessment, an attempt to insure that the action taken is faithful to the gospel message of liberation/salvation. This final step asks if the implementation of praxis brought more abundant life to disenfranchised communities. If so, what additional praxis is required? If not, what should be done to replace the previous praxis with new and more effective actions? It is through the analysis of the effectiveness of the actions taken that the creation of theology occurs. Reflecting on praxis can lead to more correct doctrine. Praxis therefore forms doctrine, informs the interpretation of scripture, and transforms the system of ethics.[11]

Toward an indecent understanding of justice

To include the voices or perspectives of the outcast, specifically the sexual outcast, is usually considered inappropriate if not indecent. It is precisely this indecency that Marcella Althaus-Reid calls for, as she seeks a sexual theology that can challenge oppressive social structures. Those most likely to be considered indecent are usually poor women of color. Constructing acceptable theological perspectives of sexuality often ignores the complex set

---

9   Ibid., 63–6.
10 Ibid., 66–8.
11 Ibid., 68–9.

of sexual regulations and gender expectations placed on women. To counter this imposed "decency," she calls for the doing of theology with one's panties off. In other words, she calls for a move beyond what has been constructed as proper behavior, which in reality masks oppressive relationships. The "indecent theology" that she advocates is a perverse and subversive theology which starts with people's experiences without censorship. It is a theology that tells people to come as they are, by first coming out of the closets which constrain and domesticate them.[12]

In a similar way, I argue for an indecent approach to justice-based praxis. The global success of neoliberalism makes any real hope of liberation from global oppressive economic systems unrealistic. The marginalized occupy the liminal space between the crucifixion of Friday and the Resurrection of Sunday. To occupy Holy Saturday is a hopeless space where all that is known is the brutality and violence of Friday. Sunday remains uncertain, too far away for those suffering today. To live in the space of Holy Saturday is to embrace the hopelessness of the moment. It is a space where hopelessness becomes the companion of those who are used and abused. The problem with those who have middle-class privilege is that they are in a rush to get to Sunday. All too often the advocacy of hope gets in the way of listening and learning from the oppressed. To sit in the reality of Saturday is to discover that the semblance of hope becomes an obstacle when it serves as a mechanism to maintain rather than challenge the prevailing social structures.

What is needed is to sit with the disenfranchised in the uncertainty of Saturday, reflecting upon their crucifixion. Often those used to middle-class privilege confuse this with fatalism. But for the oppressed, they have no choice but to continue struggling for their basic necessities, regardless of whether they are going to win or not. The hopelessness in which the oppressed live propels them toward praxis, regardless of whether it leads to salvation/liberation, because they have so few options. Here is the true ethical question: do we engage in the fight for justice because we know we will win, or do we fight for justice, regardless of the outcome, solely for the sake of justice alone?

Eurocentric approaches to justice fail marginalized communities because they seldom consider their own complicity with Empire. The bourgeoisie ethics emanating from the Empire, with their concentration on idealized virtues, become problematic for marginalized communities dealing with the "messiness" of life. Virtues are hollow when the struggle for justice is absent. Those forced to choose, due to economic, social and political

---

[12] Marcella Althaus-Reid, *Indecent Theology: Theological Perversions in Sex, Gender and Politics* (London: Routledge, 2000), 1–9.

disenfranchisement, between the lesser of two moral evils appreciate the "ambiguity of how ethics is done" from the underside of privilege.[13]

Here, we can learn much from slave religion. The ethical assumption of an antebellum white America was (and still is) that stealing is immoral. So a slave who steals a chicken from the master's coop is being—by definition—unethical, immoral, and non-virtuous. And yet, the social structures constructed by the master are what define what is ethical and moral. The master ignores the fact that he or she stole black bodies for personal gain. Within this oppressive structure, slaves understood that they had a moral responsibility to their families not only to steal from the master, but also do as little work as possible, even if it meant being stereotyped as shiftless or lazy.[14] Stealing thus becomes a justice-based praxis. What marginalized communities understand is that at times they have a moral obligation to engage in ethical practices defined by those in power as unethical.

What the disenfranchised need is an indecent and vulgar ethic that reflects the indecent and vulgar conditions marginalized communities are forced to endure. The disenfranchised require a "disruptive" ethic which subverts the normative Eurocentric ethic designed to legitimize the bourgeois lifestyle. An ethic *para joder* (an ethic that "screws with") is a term I coined to illustrate how the prevailing social order can be de-centered. The word *joder* connotes an individual who is purposely a pain in the rear end, who intentionally causes trouble, who constantly disrupts the established norm, who shouts from the mountaintop what most prefer to be kept silent, who audaciously refuses to stay in his or her place.

While the majority of ethicists from the dominant culture insist on social order, marginalized communities must call for a subversive social disorder. This is a process achieved by *jodiendo*. An ethic *para joder* is an ethic that "screws" with the prevailing power structures.[15] Note that an ethic *para joder* does not mean to screw, but to screw with, an important semantic difference. Those who are among the disenfranchised, who stand before the vastness of neoliberalism, which offers little hope for radical change in their lifetimes,

---

[13] See Simone de Beauvoir, *The Ethics of Ambiguity*, trans. by Bernard Frechtman (Secaucus, NJ: The Citadel Press, 1948).

[14] Cheryl Sanders, *Empowerment Ethics for a Liberated People: A Path to African American Social Transformation* (Minneapolis: Fortress Press, 1995), 14–15.

[15] The *ethics para joder* I advocate that arises from the underside of society is an ethics which: 1) disrupts the social order and equilibrium; 2) employs the cultural Hispanic symbol of the trickster in the formation of praxis; 3) looks toward the biblical text for narratives of figures who played the role of trickster; 4) moves beyond the Civil Rights concept of civil disobedience toward the Sanctuary Movement's concept of civil initiative; and 5) roots itself in the pastoral which is linked to a communal, not individualistic ethos of the marginalized. A full elucidation of these components can be found in De La Torre, *Latina/o Social Ethics*, chapter 4.

have few ethical alternatives. Regardless of the good intentions of those who are privileged by society or the paternalistic praxis they employ to rescue the marginalized, the devastating consequences of Empire will worsen as the few get wealthier and the many sink deeper into the despair of stomach-wrenching poverty. The dominant culture, including progressive ethicists, may be willing to offer charity and even to stand in solidarity but few are willing or able to dismantle the global structures designed to privilege them at the expense of the world's majority. To *joder* refuses to play by the rules of orderly dissent, which pacifies the need to vent for the marginalized and is designed to preserve the political power relationships within the existing social structures. If the goal of justice is to bring about change then it is crucial to go beyond the rules created by the dominant culture and beyond what is expected according to their universalized experience.

There is a temptation to end this chapter on a hopeful note, but the fact remains that dispossession, disenfranchisement, destitution, and death await too many. The reality of reading our daily newspapers is that for far too many on the margins, there is little if no hope. Billions live in poverty and die due to its consequences so that you and I can enjoy the privileges of First World status. The marginalized offer up their lives as living sacrifices so that you and I can live, and live well. Praxis that promotes justice will occur when those of us with power and privilege learn how to stand in solidarity with the hopelessness of the marginalized and follow their lead in *jodiendo*. Then, maybe, we might discover and secure our own salvation/liberation.

Liberation theology: A libertarian response
Jason Jewell

> Do not pervert justice; do not show partiality to the poor or favoritism
> to the great, but judge your neighbor fairly.
>
> Leviticus 19.15

As best I can tell from Miguel De La Torre's presentation of liberation theology, there may be libertarian (non-aggressive) ways to advance the goal of "liberation from the reality of societal misery." I would like to outline these areas of common ground first before moving on to addressing what I think are likely areas of disagreement.

A major concern for De La Torre appears to be the problem of Empire. Moreover, he views Empire to be primarily a product of European action and Eurocentric ways of thinking. Although many non-European empires litter the pages of history, it is true that people of European ancestry have created the most far-reaching empires in the modern era. European states have been forced to wind down their imperial enterprises since World War II for economic reasons, but the *pax Americana* is alive and well.

Libertarians agree that Empire is a major problem in the world. If we look only at the United States' participation in this area, we see a long train of dubious policies, including but not limited to the often outrageous treatment of various Indian nations, the conquest of the Philippines from Spain and subsequent violent repression of the Filipino people, "Dollar Diplomacy" and occasional outright military intervention in Latin America, and frequent economic and military intervention in the Middle East to ensure the presence of US-friendly governments and American access to the region's oil. US entry into both world wars can also easily be interpreted as the result of imperial policies. Moreover, the US government funds problematic international organizations such as the World Bank and International Monetary Fund. Through their lending, these bodies enable profligate spending by the governments of developing countries, which then oppress their own populations by taxing them to repay the loans, leaving fewer resources to address those countries' challenges (De La Torre refers to this problem in his essay). Libertarians have produced a steady stream of scholarship criticizing the policies of Empire since at least the mid-1960s and have been some of the most outspoken antiwar voices in American society since before the end of the Cold War.[1]

---

[1] See for example, Leonard Liggio, "Early Anti-Imperialism," *Left and Right* 2.2 (Spring

I am doing my best here to find common ground with De La Torre on important issues relating to justice. However, his own testimony leaves me in doubt whether he thinks such a thing is possible. How can he and I come to agreement if our respective understandings of justice "are mostly formed by our social location and the family we are born into; having more to do with how our identity was constructed rather than any ethereal form or universal truth"? Is it even possible for us to have a constructive conversation?

This brings me to some problems I see with this presentation of liberative justice. De La Torre quotes approvingly Malcolm X's call for "a new system of reason and logic devised by us who are at the bottom." Such a statement is strongly reminiscent of the Marxist contention that the lower class (proletariat) employs a different logic than the upper class (bourgeoisie), and that arguments based on "bourgeois" logic need not be refuted, but simply dismissed out of hand. For Marx, Malcolm X, and (apparently) De La Torre, the invitation "Come, let us reason together" is replaced by the slogan "Revolution Now!" If it is indeed the case that each group is hopelessly stuck in its socially constructed understanding of justice, no reconciliation may be possible, and violent conflict might be the only way to resolve the tension.

I believe, on the other hand, that there is an objective truth—about justice as well as a great many other things—and that through the use of our God-given reason, our experiences, and divine revelation, we can apprehend enough of that truth to make our way through life and establish and maintain social institutions that reflect that truth. To take just one example, the laws of logic (e.g., the Law of Non-Contradiction[2]) are as valid in Brazil, South Africa, and Bangladesh as they are in North America and Europe. To deny this basic idea is to destroy any hope for fruitful exchange of ideas among people of differing viewpoints. Our *perspectives* may differ, a result of conflicting *assumptions* and *interpretations* of data we encounter, but our *logic* must be the same, or we will have no hope of even understanding one another's positions.

I find it difficult to reply to several of the specifics of De La Torre's argument because his language is often vague and imprecise, and I don't wish to attribute positions to him that he does not hold. For example, take the statement, "It is the will of God for humanity to share the fruits of creation."

1966): 39–57; Jonathan Marshall, "Empire or Liberty: The Antifederalists and Foreign Policy, 1787–1788," *Journal of Libertarian Studies* 4.3 (Summer 1980): 233–54; Joseph Stromberg, "The Role of State Monopoly Capitalism in the American Empire," *Journal of Libertarian Studies* 15.3 (Summer 2001): 57–93; Michael Rozeff, *Essays on American Empire: Liberty vs. Domination* (East Amherst, 2009). The influential website Antiwar.com has been operated by libertarians since the mid-1990s.

[2] No statement can be both true and false in the same way and in the same sense.

What exactly does this unsubstantiated assertion mean? Is it possible for a collective entity like humanity to "share" something with itself? Does De La Torre mean that the component parts of humanity (individuals, families, nations, etc.) should exchange goods with each other? That's what happens now.

But this apparently is not De La Torre's meaning, for in the next sentence, "In opposition to this is what has come to be known as the dependency theory..." he refers disapprovingly to the unequal wealth distribution between the global North and South.[3] So does he mean that God wants each region of the earth to be equally wealthy? Or is he simply condemning an alleged theft of wealth from the South by the North? I can't tell. The next sentence refers to "these socio-economic structures" that allegedly cause death and are thus sinful, but the context does not make clear which structures are in view: governments, multinational corporations, supra-national bureaucracies, all of these, or something else entirely (is a mere disparity in wealth a "structure"?). A similar problem exists with the phrases "structures of oppression" and "oppressive structures" which occur repeatedly throughout De La Torre's essay, but are nowhere defined beyond a reference to their causing death. Nearly every paragraph contains a passage that can be interpreted in multiple ways or is otherwise obscure. I find myself continually thinking, "If he means *this*, I agree with him at least to some extent, but if he means *that*, I disagree."

To say anything substantive, I'm afraid I will have to make some assumptions about De La Torre's position based on what others in the tradition of liberation theology have written. If I mischaracterize any of his beliefs, I trust he will correct me. Prominent liberationists such as Gustavo Gutiérrez and Desmond Tutu have openly advocated socialism as a preferable alternative to the market economy. De La Torre criticizes the "Eurocentric" "uncritical acceptance of the market economy," so I shall assume that he agrees with this advocacy of socialism, an ideology requiring enormous state interventions into the economy—classical socialism, indeed, calls for state ownership of all farms, factories, and other means of production. I oppose this prescription for the reasons I outlined in my foundational essay: it involves massive institutional aggression. Moreover, if I may borrow De La Torre's language, no institutional structures have caused more death in the past century than socialist ones through both violent purges of class enemies and the progressive decapitalization and impoverishment of their

---

[3]   I assume that De La Torre is criticizing the process which the dependency theory claims has taken place, not the dependency theory itself.

societies.[4] According to De La Torre's definition, these realities should lead us to condemn socialist structures as sinful. The results produced by sinful human beings in market economies, indeed, leave much to be desired, but do we have a better alternative in a fallen world? Liberationists, according to many commentators, are much better at critiquing markets than they are at describing persuasively what ought to replace them. It may be fair for us to ask, along with Michael Novak, "Institutionally, how will they [liberationists] protect human rights? Institutionally, how will they achieve the economic growth that raises up the poor?"[5]

Finally, I feel compelled to point out that De La Torre's argument appears to be in conflict with both scriptural injunctions and the most venerable traditions of the Christian church in certain places. Prohibitions on stealing, the meaning of the Incarnation, the Atonement—these are not products of "Eurocentric" logic, but rather doctrines and commands that have divine origins and that long predate anything that could conceivably be called "Euroamerican" civilization. I imagine that the Syrian and Egyptian bishops at the Council of Nicea (325), who had been under the threat of martyrdom a few years before, would be quite surprised to hear that their emphasis on the nature of Christ (orthodoxy) was the product of a Eurocentric reasoning that was not sufficiently concerned with the disenfranchised.

[4] For examples of violent purges, see R.J. Rummel, *Death by Government* (New Brunswick, NJ: Transaction Publishers, 1997), and Stephane Courtois, ed., *The Black Book of Communism* (Cambridge, MA: Harvard University Press, 1997). For a thorough discussion of the theoretical reasons why socialism results in social decapitalization, see Ludwig von Mises, *Socialism* (Chicago: Liberty Fund, 1981 [1922]).
[5] Michael Novak, *Will It Liberate?* (New York: Paulist Press, 1987), 35.

Liberation theology: A liberal response
Daniel A. Dombrowski

It is instructive to note the deep similarity between Miguel De La Torre's liberative approach to justice and political liberalism's concern (indeed, requirement) that the first priority in a just society is that the least advantaged and the historically marginalized be treated fairly. Their needs should be addressed first. That is, in both political liberalism and liberationism justice requires concern for the plight of the most vulnerable. However, there is also a deep difference between liberative theories of justice as articulated by De La Torre and political liberalism as articulated by John Rawls. The locus of this difference can be found in the meat cleaver dichotomy De La Torre cuts between abstract notions of objective justice on the one hand, and an understanding of justice informed by concrete social location on the other. De La Torre praises the latter and criticizes the former as being too ethereal and as either Eurocentric or embedded in the American Empire. Like Stivers, De La Torre is skeptical of theories of justice that are overly abstract (or even abstract). "Liberal" theories, as De La Torre uses the term, are problematic because of the tendency toward abstraction.

It is unfortunate that De La Torre's project is depicted as being so much at cross-purposes with that of Rawlsian political liberalism. I suspect that the difficulty lies in his equation of "liberalism" with "neo-liberalism" or "libertarianism." I would like to make it clear that political liberalism is very much at odds with libertarianism in that political liberalism is not committed to what De La Torre calls "hyper-individualism." The liberties that are defended by political liberals are those of groups (including churches) as well as those of individuals. Further, as I have argued in my essay above, the levels of taxation that would be required in a politically liberal society to fund equal liberty for all (including the material underpinnings that would make such liberty meaningful), would militate against any sort of hyper-individualism. Libertarian thinkers like Robert Nozick and Jason Jewell have always noticed the significant difference between their view and that of Rawlsian political liberalism.

In addition, Rawlsian political liberals do not view the priority of attention to be paid to the poor as an optional act of charity, as De La Torre implies. Rather it is viewed as a requirement of justice. In a related vein, there is no uncritical acceptance of market economics in political liberalism, as he alleges. Indeed, markets are subservient to, and must be framed by, principles of justice (in contrast to the libertarian view). And the Rawlsian method is not deduction, as De La Torre implies, but rather is based on dialectical exchange and mutual correction of various views that might initially seem to be in opposition. That is, the overall Rawlsian method is that of reflective equilibrium, which includes, but is not identical to, the hypothetical thinking found in the original position.

Nonetheless, De La Torre's concepts of structural sin and institutional violence are congenial to a politically liberal view. And political liberals can appreciate his emphasis on historical context in the development of a theory of justice that is defensible. Like Stivers, however, De La Torre does not address the problem that occurs when reasonable citizens from various historical contexts adhere to views that are at odds with each other. Here *some* sort of fair decision-making procedure is required, with Rawls's original position behind a veil of ignorance being the most prominent example since the development of the utilitarian impartial spectator in the eighteenth and nineteenth centuries. If one interprets Adam Smith as a utilitarian, as Rawls does, the fact that the Rawlsian original position is superior to Smith's impartial spectator is noteworthy and should recommend the Rawlsian method to De La Torre, given his presumed opposition to Smith's defense of capitalism.

It is to De La Torre's credit that he encourages us to be "organic intellectuals" who engage concretely with marginalized people, in contrast to a strictly theoretical approach to injustice. But this commendable exhortation on his part should not be seen as necessarily at odds with abstract theory. It only indicates that theory, although necessary, is not sufficient in the effort to achieve a society that approximates justice. I take it that Rawls's interest in fraternal/sororal bonds, in addition to an interest in liberty and equality, shows a family resemblance to the solidarity with the oppressed mentioned by De La Torre. I especially like the way that he deftly weaves this theme with incarnational theology by seeing racism, sexism, classism, heterosexism, and, I would add, speciesism, as types of contemporary crucifixions. It is not merely that God became human, on De La Torre's version of incarnational theology, but that God became *poor*, that is noteworthy.

I am not clear, however, regarding De La Torre's broad use of the term "Eurocentric." He seems to use this term to refer to the reduction of ethics to individual piety or virtue (in contrast to Rawls's version of Kantianism, which is explicitly social in character). I also think there are problems with the claim that the method of political liberals concentrates solely on deduction (in contrast to Rawls's dialectical or conversational method of reflective equilibrium), and reduces the intellectual life to a meaningless project in that, according to De La Torre, theory *about* justice changes nothing. I would like to indicate that, although I disagree with this last point from De La Torre, I nonetheless share his frustration. But I think that a better way to make his legitimate point is to say that there is a time lag that seems to be required for a powerful theory in political philosophy to take effect: John Locke's seventeenth-century views were not put into practice until the American Revolution in the eighteenth century; Adam Smith's eighteenth-century theory was not significantly implemented until the nineteenth and twentieth centuries; and Karl Marx's famous views from the mid-nineteenth century were not notably put into practice until the revolutions in his name took place in the twentieth century. The hope is that Rawls's powerful twentieth-century theory will more and more seep into twenty-first-century political reality. Concrete reality *does* change; indeed it improves, as a result of powerful theory, although it takes a patient view of time in order to appreciate this fact.

I am not sure what to think about the following question asked by De La Torre: Do we fight for justice because we know we will win or do we fight for justice solely for the sake of justice? I think I might agree with him here in that it makes sense to emphasize the idea that the whole point to developing a theory of justice is to contribute positively to a better world and to the divine everlasting whole of things. But I think that I am not alone in wanting to avoid the word "victory" if such is achieved through unjust means. For example, one pays quite a price for agreeing with De La Torre's rationalization for stealing and, presumably, for lying. Further, I am not sure of the referent when De La Torre speaks of bourgeois ethics. Does he have Kant, Mill, or Rawls in mind?

The hope is that through continued dialogue and mutual questioning the degree of rapprochement between Rawlsian political liberals and De La Torre-like liberationists could be enhanced. In this regard I would like to ask one final question: although I think I understand De La Torre's left-wing critique of contemporary society, I am not sure what sort of society he thinks should replace it. In what ways would a liberationist society be different from the highly egalitarian society defended by Rawls and labeled by him as a realistic utopia?

Liberation theology: A feminist response
Laura Stivers

Christian feminist approaches to justice as I have outlined them are liberative theories of justice; thus, I agree with much of what is said in this chapter. Liberative theories of justice that address *all* forms of oppression challenge reformist feminism that only serves certain groups of women. That is, some forms of feminism are content to leave oppressive structures in place as long as women are included (usually white, heterosexual, middle- to upper-class women). Miguel De La Torre is very clear that the dominant culture's American-empire understanding of justice (through the eyes of white, middle and upperclass heterosexual males) must be rejected, not simply reformed. In the first part of this response I will note how De La Torre's rejection of Eurocentric ethical concepts of justice can push white Christian feminists to be more aware of whose voices they listen to and more accountable for whose liberation they promote. I will, however, question the benefit of dualistically creating an "enemy" discourse of Eurocentric justice as De La Torre does. Many of us are simultaneously privileged and oppressed, are situated in complex ways in the "matrix of domination," and are usually complicit in empire even when we are consciously resisting and challenging its reach. Furthermore, while I agree that power analysis is generally weak if not absent in many Eurocentric approaches to justice, there might nevertheless be some aspects of the discourse that could be appropriated for liberative approaches. On a final note, I will argue that liberation of the marginalized is not possible without environmental justice. Liberative theories of justice must do more to incorporate perspectives from the environmental justice and ecofeminist movements.

Christian feminists would agree that much of Euroamerican ethical discourse has reconciled moral reasoning with existing structures that are detrimental to the dispossessed and keep privilege in place for the powerful. When women started entering the Academy they began to critique and challenge the androcentrism of Christian theology and ethics, but these primarily white women certainly did not acknowledge their Eurocentric bias until challenged by women of color. Over time Christian feminists of all races have become more sophisticated in their ethical analysis and theological reflection, including in addition to race and gender analysis, examination of the interconnections of heterosexism and sexism, the ways in which class shapes our thinking, how disability rights connects to justice, and the implications of globalization and environmental destruction. Long gone is the belief that feminism is solely about women being equal to men, although gender inequality remains a problem.

De La Torre's emphasis on social location and worldview is extremely important for conceptions of justice as there will always be a tendency for middle-class to upper-class white Christian feminists to accept existing systems as long as they have a secure place within them. It is also too easy for white Christian heterosexual feminists to narrowly confine their sources to familiar aspects of their identity, ignoring theological reflection from scholars in different racial groups or of varying sexual orientations or disabilities. For a feminist theory of justice to be liberative it must be revolutionary, not reformist. Feminist bell hooks is quite critical of what she calls "lifestyle feminism," that is, "the notion that there could be as many versions of feminism as there were women."[1] She argues that the politics have slowly been removed from feminism. Revolutionary feminism, in contrast, decries the assumption that women can be feminist without "fundamentally challenging and changing themselves or the culture."[2] A revolutionary feminist understanding of justice must include both resisting and changing all life-denying aspects of, and practices within, our culture, especially for the most marginalized. Connecting to all forms of liberative ethics keeps Christian feminists accountable for promoting justice and changing unjust structures for all groups of people (as well as other living beings and the earth) that are marginalized.

Christian feminists would agree with De La Torre's critique of dominant definitions of justice that emphasize individualism, law and order, charity, the free market economy, and abstract deductive reasoning. What Christian feminists might be wary of is his claim that all "Euroamerican definitions of justice," whether conservative or progressive, are necessarily oppressive. First of all, how do we clearly distinguish whether a definition of justice is Eurocentric or not, and how do we know whether we have "moved beyond the ethics of the dominant culture," especially when De La Torre is claiming even "progressive" definitions are suspect? Christian feminists would adamantly agree with De La Torre that ethical discourse complicit with empire, lacking sophisticated power analysis, and providing justification for structures of oppression must be jettisoned. But how will we know that our new paradigms do not also hold seeds of oppression? Christian feminists have found through experience that we all have blind

---

[1] bell hooks, *Feminism is for Everybody* (Cambridge, MA: South End Press, 2000), 5.
[2] Ibid., 6.

spots. Listening to and heeding the voices from marginalized communities has been a way to open up our vision, but we all have internalized societal constructions of knowledge and can never be sure we have fully dismantled oppressive thinking from our worldviews. This is why justice-making is a communal and ongoing process, and why the reassessment step in liberative methodology is so important.

Second, as we offer constructive liberative understandings of a just society, will we not be employing some principles or aspects of justice that are part of Eurocentric definitions of justice? Philosopher Martha Nussbaum notes that women in developing countries are appealing to liberal concepts such as autonomy, rights, equality, and freedom. They do so in spite of the fact that "Eurocentric" liberalism is not a culturally prevalent mode of thought. While Christian feminists have critiques of libertarian and liberal theories of justice (see my responses to the representative essays in this book), they would nevertheless hold that the freedom and equality of individuals is crucial to the liberation of women and other oppressed groups. Need these principles be rejected along with Eurocentric ethical discourse? Christian feminists advocate a methodology of "contextual response" and argue that ethical ideals must always be put into dialogue with concrete social problems. There might be aspects of Euroamerican-based ethics that can be appropriated for justice and liberation of women and other marginalized people. Christian feminists would argue that the important task is critical attention to each situation of injustice, its historical roots and complex array of factors. Christians must identify ways that justice might be realized for those who are routinely and systemically denied liberation.

Liberative theories of justice must address the flourishing of *all* of God's creation, not simply humans. De La Torre writes, "Justice begins with the plight of the poor, the oppressed, the marginalized, the outcast, and the disen-franchised. To engage in justice is to do it with, and from, the perspective of those whom society considers as (no)bodies." The earth and its other living inhabitants have also been treated as "(no)bodies" in our society. A Christian feminist approach to justice is relational. We are not simply in relationships with one another but with the natural world that we inhabit. We cannot be free, physically or spiritually, if we are not living sustainably with the earth and other living creatures. Christian ecofeminists have been critical of anthropocentric worldviews that deny the intrinsic value of nature, seeing it only as resource for human consumption. Furthermore, they have noted the similarities between the oppression of women and "Mother Nature," and have pointed out that overwhelmingly poor women bear the brunt of environmental destruction. Pragmatically, from an anthropocentric lens, liberation of the most marginalized humans (and all of us in the long-run) requires radical transformation of human living from overconsumption to sustainability, with the onus of change on those who consume the most. Environmental destruction like global warming is already having disastrous effects on the poor.

If the marginalized (and those who are in solidarity with them) are truly to construct new ethical paradigms for their communities and not adopt "Eurocentric worldviews," as De La Torre advocates, they must incorporate the flourishing and interconnection of the full web of life and land. This is not a paradigm shift for marginalized groups of people who have always been in relationship with their natural environs but it might be for others who have been forcibly removed from their land or alienated from their environmental connection through poverty, pollution, or other forms of oppression. Empire requires destruction and oppression of earth and all living beings. Christian ecofeminists advocate sustainable living as symbolic resistance to empire and practical action towards both environmental and human justice.

Liberation theology: A virtue ethicist's response
Elizabeth Phillips

Miguel De La Torre refers to my theological and philosophical approach as the "bourgeoisie ethics emanating from the Empire." Irrespective of his sentiment, it is impossible for me to be so categorically dismissive of his approach. Liberation theology is one of the most important Christian movements of the twentieth century, and indeed of the modern era. Christian theology has been transformed by its convictions about God's preferential option for the poor and the centrality of praxis, and rightly so.

As Miguel De La Torre aptly expresses, the preferential option for the poor does not simply encourage the privileged to paternalistically help "the needy." Rather it says that God is peculiarly incarnate in poverty and marginalization and that, as De La Torre writes, "Whatever liberation looks like, it can only be determined by those living under oppressive structures; not paternalistically by those who benefit from how society is organized." In other words, liberation is not a theology *for* the oppressed; it is a theology *of and with* the oppressed.

The liberationist focus on praxis has so permeated contemporary Christian theology that it is inexcusable in most circles to call what one does "theology" if it is intentionally without any connection to current practice in church and society. This is an important area of overlap between liberation and virtue approaches. Virtue ethicists would agree with De La Torre that ethical approaches to justice are fundamentally flawed if they are "less concerned with 'what you do' than 'how you think.'" This is one of the central motivations for the contemporary revival of virtue ethics: a conviction that learning how to think through difficult decisions is not the crux of morality; the crux is who we are and how we live our lives together every day. As De La Torre says of liberation, "This is a religious perspective that enacts the Gospel rather than simply meditates upon it."

However, a serious concern also arises with De La Torre's insistence on doing rather than merely thinking, or on being less concerned with "developing a scholarly body of thought, and more to do with standing in solidarity with faith-based grassroots movements…" There seems to be a persistent undertone throughout the essay of denigrating theological work that is meditative, theoretical, metaphysical, doctrinal, and/or orthodox. The reader begins to wonder whether the point he is making is that theologians should not focus on these aspects apart from/in isolation from/to the exclusion of liberative praxis (which I take to be a valid point), or that actually such work is of far less importance and is much more likely to be the vehicle of oppression and/or privilege than grassroots praxis. If indeed there are elements of the latter impulse in De La Torre's approach, this must be challenged. Theological inquiry and praxis must be pursued equally in an ongoing back-and-forth in which each continues to shape and revise the other. Praxis which is not examined in the light of careful theological inquiry is no less empty or capable of becoming dangerous and oppressive than theology which is disconnected from praxis. Only through robust and careful theological inquiry can we faithfully scrutinize our own and others' practices.[1]

Perhaps such scrutiny is required to address my next question: do liberative theologies cease to be liberative when they become so calcified that they seem incapable of granting any truth, sincerity, or good faith to perspectives other than their own? As a feminist, for example, I would argue that feminism ceases to be liberative in those fringe instances where it becomes a vehicle for the hatred and dismissal of men. The models of liberation with which I identify are those that recognize the need for all people to be liberated from the structures and cycles of domination and violence, the oppressed and oppressors alike. The actual praxis of such liberation requires the Christian practices of enemy love and of seeing God and the good in every other human being. I do not find these practices at work, nor the academic practices of open, honest analysis of arguments other than one's own, when theologians use terms like 'Eurocentric' in ways which paint all Christian theology of an entire global hemisphere across many centuries with the same broad and dismissive brush.

Let me be entirely clear: it is not my contention that terms like

---

[1] I am making a different point here than De La Torre makes in his five-step hermeneutical circle. While the proposed circle partially overcomes the errors of foundationalist, deductive reasoning by including praxis and by returning through the steps in a circle, this model does not overcome the error of foundationalist, deductive thought which assumes that human thought processes can progress in a single direction of movement in a specific order of steps. We cannot choose to begin from nowhere with a specific first step whether that is a universal concept or a particular observation, nor can we move from one step to the next as if untouched by the other steps in the process. Instead of a series of uni-directional steps (whether that is linear and deductive or cyclical and hermeneutical), human inquiry is more like a web, with all the elements of the process interconnected and influencing every other element. In a web we are not concerned with identifying a first step, but rather identifying the convictions and/or practices which are at the center and hold the rest together. See Nancey Murphy, *Beyond Liberalism and Fundamentalism* (Valley Forge, PA: Trinity Press, 1996), especially chapter 4, "Epistemological Holism and Theological Method."

"Eurocentric" should not be used, nor that there do not exist within the mainstream of Western theology both historical and contemporary strands of thought and practice which serve to benefit males of European descent and disadvantage or oppress all others. That tragic truth is absolutely undeniable, and thus we need words like "Eurocentric" and "sexist" and others to name and critique these strands and the ways in which they have pervaded our thought and lives. However, both the impact of this critique and its faithfulness to the way of Christ are hindered when its use is so blunt, indiscriminate, and categorical as to deny that anyone but a particular type of liberation theologian has any sincere interest in living the gospel or ability to elucidate any aspect of it for others.

De La Torre's undefined use of "Eurocentric" leaves me wondering whether he means theology and ethics which are exclusively from the perspective of and serve to benefit those of European descent, or if he means all Christian theology which has ever been done in Europe and North America by people of European descent. Critical questioning of the former is necessary; a categorical dismissal of the latter is absurd not only in its narrowness but in its denial of the history of liberation theology itself.

When Latin American liberation theology arose in the mid-twentieth century, it was in at least three different contexts: the grassroots communities of Latin America, the meetings and actions of Latin American Catholic bishops, and the academic work of priest-theologians. The most well-known priest–theologians who wrote the central texts of liberation theology's inception (including Gustavo Gutiérrez, Leonardo Boff, and Juan Luis Segundo), and who suffered great personal cost for both their activism and their thought, studied in Continental Europe, where they were immersed in the key traditional texts of orthodox Catholic Christianity, encountered the new philosophical perspectives of European critical theory, and became influenced by *la nouvelle theologie*, a stream within European Catholic theology which advocated the twin movements of *ressourcement* (returning to the scriptural and patristic sources) and *aggiornamento* (openness to modernity and to doing theology in dialogue with contemporary life). The central tenets of liberation theology were born in these scholar–priests' critical efforts both to learn from what these texts and movements (all traditional/orthodox or contemporary European) had to say to their Latin American contexts, and to consider what these texts and movements were not saying because of their situatedness in other contexts. How very strange if liberation theologians following them were to insist that these very sources and contemporary sources like them should be discounted today because of their "Eurocentrism."

Furthermore, I wonder how aware De La Torre is of the work that is actually being done today by those he seems to dismiss as "Eurocentric," whom he describes as hyperindividualistic lovers of capitalism who are wedded to "law and order" and "deductive ethical reasoning." While it is true that we must all be wary of the blind spots and complicities in oppression that may exist in our work and lives due to our positions of privilege (and I am sure De La Torre is aware that this is no less true of his own life and work, as he is himself a tenured professor in a mainline American Christian seminary and therefore a privileged member of society's elite), it is very obviously and demonstrably not true that the most prominent theologians outside of liberation circles today, including some of the most privileged white male professors, could be identified with all (or, in many cases, *any*) of those descriptors. While it seems that De La Torre is not willing to take their critiques of individualism, capitalism, and modernist philosophical approaches seriously, he should at least be aware of and honest about their existence, which negates his summary of their shared characteristics.

I hope that in his reply De La Torre will correct me and we will find he has not intended to be so dismissive of others as I have interpreted him to be. In a day when many theologians, philosophers, and ethicists are saying that liberation theology is a fad of the past, I have consistently affirmed its enduring influence and relevance (along with the necessity to be critical about its potential shortcomings). It is something of a bitter pill to be dismissed by an advocate of a perspective that I have been so intentionally unwilling to dismiss.

4

A Christian Feminist Theory of Justice

Laura Stivers

Introduction

Bra-burning lesbian man haters! Many of my female students come to my ethics classes wanting to distance themselves from this stereotypical feminist image and with a belief that while feminism was important historically, women in the United States are now liberated. They understand feminism to be solely about equality between women and men. Their experience from a young age is that they have equal opportunity with men and the freedom to define who they want to be. They see gender injustice as primarily an issue for women who live in patriarchal cultures, not in modern US culture. When we do critical analysis of social issues with attention to factors like gender, race, and class, they begin to see how oppression and privilege are deeply ingrained in our cultural norms and practices as well as our institutions and social policies. They find out that gender role expectations and the gendered division of labor both in the home and the workplace continue to limit women's empowerment; that women earn less, do not have as much say in policy-making, and are more likely to live in poverty; and that women have less autonomy over their bodies, from fear and experiences of sexual harassment and rape to lack of reproductive rights. Students also find out that movements for gender justice (sometimes labeled feminist but not always) are found in all corners of the globe. Not all of my students finish the semester calling themselves feminists but they do come away with a new-found understanding of what feminism entails and are more apt to advocate for a conception of justice that addresses oppression in all its forms.

While feminism has clearly opened up many new opportunities and freedoms for women, there continues to be a need for resistance to injustices women and other marginalized groups experience. The starting point for a feminist approach to justice is to begin with the lived experiences of injustice which people on the margins, especially women, face. Critical analysis of *essay structure*

the historical and current facets of systematic and structural oppression is a crucial second step of a feminist methodology. Third, a feminist approach advocates a vision of flourishing life and supports particular values such as inclusivity, right relations, and sustainability as normative foundations for policies and practices that promote justice. The fourth and most important feature of a feminist methodology is commitment to resisting and addressing systematic oppression that women and other marginalized groups face. A feminist vision of justice entails, at minimum, that all people have access to adequate resources to meet their basic needs, that they be given the opportunity and means to participate in meaningful ways in their communities, and that they be treated with dignity and respect. Feminists do not claim a neutral stance, and in fact are wary of theorists who claim universality without explicit acknowledgment of their assumptions, biases, and loyalties. They believe that preference to the oppressed and marginalized is necessary for justice to be achieved, and that policy-making ought to be in solidarity with those who routinely and systematically experience injustice.

✳ Christian feminists do not differ significantly from secular feminists in their methodological approach to justice, but they do frame their normative justifications for justice through a biblical and theological lens. Both their theological reflection and their participation in justice-making are a response to their understanding of the divine call to love one another and to do justice to themselves, others, and all of creation. Creating right relationships is central to their understanding of what it means to be connected to God. They are outraged at the many injustices in our world that thwart loving and just relationships. While suffering from injustice is the impetus for a Christian feminist approach, the hope and faith in the possibility of a sustainable, just, and compassionate world is what keeps the fire of justice-making alive. A deep joy in the wonder and goodness of life and an abiding faith in a good and compassionate God(dess) of liberation makes justice-making for the marginalized an imperative for Christian feminists. Justice-making for them is intricately connected to what it means to be fully human in relation to the Divine. And working collectively in solidarity with others in the ongoing practice of justice-making nourishes their joy and sustains the flame.

In this chapter I will outline key aspects of a Christian feminist methodology in relation to justice, drawing both on philosophical and Christian feminist thinkers. I am aware that there are multiple feminist methodologies and so I present this approach not as the definitive feminist voice but as one among several possibilities. There can also be various theological foundations for a feminist approach to justice. I will develop two in particular: right relationships/flourishing life and responsibility/discipleship.

Christian feminism

The feminist movement got its first impetus in the United States with the publication in 1792 of Mary Wollstonecraft's book *A Vindication of the Rights of Women*. The first wave of feminism did not begin, however, until the nineteenth century, when women advocated and organized for the right to vote. Feminists also organized during this time in support of Prohibition and against slavery and war. The concept of doing theology from a feminist perspective began in earnest after the second wave of feminism in the 1960s, when women were finally able to participate more fully as leaders in both the church and academy. The work of second-wave feminists in feminist theology, biblical scholarship, and ethics has transformed traditional Christian scholarship. For example, feminist theologians have challenged the exclusively male images for God, the concept of sin as being primarily one of pride, and an understanding of Jesus as only representing salvation for individuals. However, religious institutions have often been slow to adopt new feminist insights and some have even been outright hostile to them. Many denominations still prohibit the ordination of women and others do not reward pastors who express a feminist theological outlook.

Many Christian feminists, while fully aware of patriarchy and oppression in biblical times, draw sustenance for justice-making from biblical stories, especially the radical servanthood and justice-making that Jesus exhibited. New Testament scholar Sandra Schneiders writes:

> Jesus taught by world-subverting parables, challenging questions, insistent dialogue, by patient persuasion, repeated invitation, probing argument, and especially by his original and arresting interpretations of Scripture which were sometimes startling in their radicality because Jesus favored people and their needs over the requirements of even the most sacred laws (see, e.g., Mt. 12.1–8).[1]

Christian feminist biblical scholars and theologians have re-examined biblical stories from the standpoint of women and identified and envisioned the ways that women "survive in the wilderness," biblical scholar Delores William's concept to describe Hagar's struggle to liberate herself from oppressive power structures with God at her side.[2] Christian feminists do not gloss over the misogyny found in scripture. They interrogate and challenge

---

[1] Sandra Schneiders, "Acceptance Address for LCWR Leadership Award" (presentation, St. Louis, MO, August 12, 2012).

[2] Delores S. Williams, *Sisters in the Wilderness: The Challenge of Womanist God-Talk* (Maryknoll, NY: Orbis Books 1995).

the oppression and violence while also finding patterns and themes within scripture that support justice and empowerment for women. Even more importantly, they insist on a critical reading of biblical texts when they are related to ethical issues. Ethicist Michelle Tooley illustrates critical interrogation of the use of scripture in ethics:

> Because the Christian Gospels record names of twelve male apostles, some Christian groups forbid female clergy. Do these groups mention the role of Mary Magdalene in the early church or talk about Martha's confession in the Gospel of John? Should we assume that because these twelve men were from the Middle East and were Jewish that all clergy should be Middle Eastern Jews?[3]

Christian feminists interpret biblical texts in light of what they consider to be healthy religion, that is, religion that functions to empower, not harm or exploit.

Third-wave feminism emerged at the end of the twentieth century. These modern feminists appreciate the gains that early feminists achieved, such as the right to equal pay, reproductive rights, and a widening of career opportunities. They also critique the second wave's narrow definition of femininity and assumption of a universal female identity based on the experiences of upper-middle-class white women. Third-wave feminists are more aware of the intersections between different forms of oppression—racism, classism, heterosexism, and even environmental destruction. Some simply see the third wave as an extension of the second. The Christian feminist approach to justice in this chapter will draw on the work of both second- and third-wave Christian and philosophical feminists.

Also of note for an approach to justice are the different starting points and goals of various forms of feminism. First-wave feminists primarily subscribed to "liberal feminism," with the goal that women should have equal access to the privilege, power, and opportunities afforded men. This view did not challenge existing structures but instead supported the inclusion of women into them. Second wave feminism developed two different streams in response to liberal feminism. Marxist-inspired "radical feminism" sought to overthrow existing structures, institutions, and patterns that perpetuate oppression, with the end goal of an egalitarian social order. Radical feminists argued that inclusion into systems structured to protect the privilege of some and oppress or marginalize others does not support justice for all.

A second response was "essentialist feminism" that challenged the idea

---

[3] Michelle Tooley, "Feminist Liberative Ethics," in *Ethics: A Liberative Approach*, ed. Miguel De La Torre (Minneapolis: Fortress Press, 2013), 169.

that women needed to "act like men" or assimilate to masculine-defined structures and institutions for inclusion and success. Equality was a goal of justice but not through assimilation on male terms. Essentialist feminists argued that there are "women's ways of knowing" that are non-hierarchical, caring, intuitive, and collaborative, and that practices, roles, and values associated with the "feminine" are routinely devalued. Furthermore, they argued that emphasizing the "feminine" challenges the so-called neutrality and universality of "masculine-defined" practices, institutions, and structures within the dominant culture. More recently, "postmodern feminism" has challenged the idea that there are essentially feminine and masculine values and traits, and shown that these meanings are socially constructed within cultures.

Many feminists today celebrate a "politics of difference" in relation to gender, race, class, disability, and sexuality. They argue that asserting the value of specific cultures and attributes of oppressed groups highlights the particularity of the dominant culture. Universally formulated standards and policies have often presumed the values and behavior of dominant groups (e.g., white, male, middle-class, able-bodied, heterosexual), thus disadvantaging those who do not exhibit these traits. For example, women who work collaboratively in a non-hierarchical way have often not been promoted to powerful leadership positions in organizations because of an "unstated" understanding of leadership as assertive, top-down, and competitive—all socially constructed masculine attributes. Some worry that affirming different, group-conscious policies might reinstate exclusion. For example, claiming women are more collaborative and caring can result in female leaders or managers being critiqued when they do not exhibit "feminine" behavior (the "dragon lady boss"), whereas men are simply seen as competent and efficient when they "behave like men." Advocates of a politics of difference, however, claim that denial of difference has been even more oppressive because it hides the ways in which particular groups are privileged even under formal policies of equality. We all lose out when the talent of people in oppressed groups is overlooked because they are deemed "inferior" by dominant norms.

Christian feminist ethical method

Christian feminists have found that simply following the call to love our neighbor is not adequate. An understanding of the multiple intersections of varying oppressions is necessary to identify what remedies to injustice might actually promote love of neighbor. Also crucial is a sophisticated understanding of the ways that injustice is structurally rooted, rather than simply a matter of individual discrimination or violence. Thus, social analysis of injustice, especially women's experiences of it, with attention to the complex practices, policies, and ideologies that support injustice, will be a key task in any Christian feminist approach to justice. An important step in this process of social analysis is listening to people who are marginalized and/or oppressed and taking seriously the insights gained from their stories. Recognition that their experiences are crucial for knowledge is not only necessary for adequately addressing injustices but is important for promoting the norm of participation, a central aspect of justice-making. Identifying how women and other oppressed groups have already been resisting injustice and constructing alternatives is also important for identifying both the oppressions particular people face and the agency they exhibit in responding to oppression.

Addressing inequality and unequal distribution of power and resources (distributive justice) must be central to any Christian feminist approach to justice, but respecting the dignity of people (justice of recognition) and promoting right relations is equally important to the material and spiritual wholeness of people. We all need a sense of belonging in a community, and we need acknowledgment by those we are close to and by society as a whole that we are valued and of intrinsic worth, fully created in the image of God. Justice of recognition and communal right relations are only possible, however, if there is distributive justice. Inequality thwarts solidarity and the lack of basic necessities keeps people powerless and sends the message that they are of no value. Furthermore, promoting right relations extends beyond the human species as we are but one species in the entire universe of God's creation. While Christian feminists start by understanding particular injustices, they never end there. Instead they always advocate the collective responsibility we have for justice-making in light of what God is calling us to do.

Women as the subject of analysis

The empowerment of women is central to a conception of feminist justice. Feminist theorists today are aware that they face a dilemma when they posit women as a social collective. Whenever they aim to identify the attributes of the collective "women," invariably some women are left out. This problem has plagued the feminist movement. For example, when the middle-to-upper-class white women of liberal feminism argued for inclusion and equal pay in the workplace they assumed that their needs mirrored the primary needs of all women. They were blind to the ways race and class, not simply gender, shaped women's experiences. Without naming women as a social collective, however, there is no feminist politics or place for identifying specific forms of gender injustice. Naming women as a collective makes feminism a political movement and brings awareness to women that their particular sufferings are often not natural or simply personal.[4] While there can be many groupings of women and particular gender injustices will vary, the gender structure, like race or class, names certain aspects of the lives of women with which they must deal.[5] All women face a general commonality of patriarchal oppression and the consequent denigration of values and attributes considered "feminine."

This commonality of patriarchy and the devaluing of the feminine are experienced in multiple ways by different women, however. Women of different classes, races, sexual orientations, and physical abilities are treated according to different understandings of femininity, and therefore their experience of the devalued feminine varies widely. For example, welfare for white women who had lost husbands due to death or divorce was first instituted in our country based on the belief that these women should be able to remain in the home as homemakers. After Civil Rights when women of color finally got access to welfare benefits, the ideological message was that women on welfare were lazy and should not get something for nothing but should instead be forced to work.[6] Neither group was particularly empowered in the welfare system and both suffered from a devaluation of the feminine, but a protective paternalism was extended to white women while a spirit of punishment was meted out to women of color. White feminists in their discussions of patriarchy have historically been blind to these differences; furthermore, they have often failed to talk about women's oppression of women through classist and racist value systems. For example, middle-to-upper-class white women railed against the injustice of unequal pay for equal work, the glass ceiling, and traditional gender roles while simultaneously sustaining their privilege through exploitation of poor women of all races.

To keep such privileged standpoints from becoming the dominant feminist perspective, Christian feminist theologians and ethicists hold that we must listen to the experiences of all women who suffer injustice,

---

[4]   Iris Marion Young, "Gender as Seriality: Thinking About Women as a Social Collective," *Signs* (The University of Chicago, Spring 1994), 718.

[5]   Ibid.

[6]   See Elizabeth M. Bounds, Pamela K. Brubaker, and Mary E. Hobgood, eds., *Welfare Policy: Feminist Critiques* (Eugene, OR: Wipf & Stock, 2010); Mimi Abramovitz, *Regulating the Lives of Women: Social Welfare Policy from Colonial Times to the Present*, revised edition (Cambridge, MA: South End Press, 1999).

with special attention to the most marginalized because their voices bring forth a different and valuable perspective that is often ignored. Democratizing power is crucial so that those who are most marginalized and/or exploited may participate in envisioning and planning what justice entails. Without their participation, problems that most affect them are often misaddressed, at times due to overt discrimination but equally due to ignorance. Many Christian and non-Christian feminist approaches to justice advocate narrative method, that is, listening to the experiences and stories of women. While we must critically assess all narratives, hearing each other's stories with a disposition of openness to challenging our worldviews will give us a more complex understanding of the injustices women face. Active listening also broadens the possibilities for collective solidarity in challenging and addressing injustices. For example, most citizens are unaware of the experiences and stories of women who are homeless, and policy-makers rarely seek out their expertise. Most of these women are simply trying to survive, often with children in tow. They are not in City Hall advocating for subsidized childcare or housing, yet understanding both the internal and external obstacles they face is important if efforts at justice-making are to aid them. We need to consciously make a way for their stories to be heard, not simply assume that we understand what assistance or structural changes would be most beneficial to them.

Critical analysis of oppression

1) A contextual response

Feminist Christian ethicists are critical of theories of justice that assume standards can be ahistorically applied and deduced from a few assumptions. Attention to cultural context and analysis of historical and present forms of oppression in particular situations are necessary. Karen Lebacqz writes, "The task of justice and a theory of justice will be different depending on which forms of injustice are primary."[7] Rather than basing the distribution of goods on Aristotle's formal definition of justice—"equals should be treated equally and unequals unequally"—Lebacqz starts instead with the realities of injustice. She claims that injustices are not random events but are interrelated. Thus, addressing each form of injustice separately according to such criteria as "need," "merit," or "effort" is inadequate to righting disordered relationships.

---

[7] Karen Lebacqz, *Justice in an Unjust World* (Minneapolis: Augsburg Publishing House, 1987), 150.

The prior question in a radical notion of justice is not the question of what is our due, but whether the status or station into which we are born is itself just.[8]

Distributing goods to the slave Hagar to meet her needs, for example, would not have challenged the unjust structure into which she was born. Both understanding the historical roots and the cultural policies and ideologies that supported her oppression and listening to her story would have been necessary starting points for envisioning a just response. A Christian feminist approach would also advocate solidarity with her in a way that recognizes and honors her actions of justice-making in relation to oppressive forces.

While ideal visions and norms are crucial for defining the ends of justice-making, they cannot be applied to situations of injustice in a universal manner. Each instance of injustice has different historical roots and encompasses a complex array of factors. As ethicist Traci West points out, ethical ideals must always be put into dialogue with concrete social problems. For example, in her work on sexual violation, she explores whether human dignity is a genuine social value in our society.[9] While Christian theology holds that we are all "created in God's image" and therefore, human dignity ought to be central to any vision of human flourishing, the reality of what it means to actually accord each individual full human dignity is only discovered through relationships, and in particular, through engagement in struggles for justice. Often we are not even aware of the ways we have assaulted the dignity of others until we are working in solidarity for justice and called to account for our own blind spots and limitations. According to Harrison, only when we make an effort to step outside our comfort zones and join with others to support human dignity do we begin to see what "rightly ordered community and God's transcendence may mean."[10]

Although addressing injustice is contextual, it is not relative. While Christian feminists might not all have identical visions of flourishing life and they might advocate different paths for achieving justice depending on the circumstances, they do believe that humans are created as relational beings and our purpose (or *telos* in Greek) is to be in right relationship (which includes care and justice) with the entire earth community. Right relationship includes both human and environmental flourishing, and will

[8] Beverly Wildung Harrison, *Justice in the Making: Feminist Social Ethics*, (Louisville: Westminster John Knox Press, 2004), 23.

[9] Traci C. West, *Disruptive Christian Ethics: When Racism and Women's Lives Matter* (Louisville, KY: Westminster John Knox Press, 2006), 38.

[10] Beverly Wildung Harrison, *Justice in the Making* (Louisville: Westminster John Knox Press, 2004), 23.

require more democratic forms of power and participation in local and national political realms. The norms of right relationship, flourishing life, empowerment, and participation serve as plumb line and guide for ascertaining what justice entails in any particular situation.

Last of all, the context for a Christian feminist approach to justice must include both the private and public realms of women's lives. Beverly Harrison once said that justice begins in the bedroom.[11] In other words, what happens in the personal and familial realm affects women in the work and community realm. So-called private issues such as domestic violence, access to abortion, and responsibility for dependent care affect how women fare in the workplace and in society in general.

2) Intersecting oppressions and structural analysis

Christian feminists must do more than simply address sexism and patriarchy if their goal is to truly empower all women. Contemporary feminist theory has shown that different forms of oppression intersect and affect people in multiple ways. Critical theorists Margaret Andersen and Patricia Hill Collins use a structural framework that they call a "matrix of domination" to analyze race, class, and gender oppression. This framework allows them to examine the structural patterns that join these forms of oppression together rather than comparing them as separate systems of power. They argue that studying the interconnections within the context of social structure can highlight how people can be simultaneously privileged and oppressed and how the manifestations of these systems of power can vary widely. For example, while all women share the risk of rape, they do not share it equally; Hillary Clinton does not experience the same risk as a poor single woman of color who works at night and commutes by bus.[12]

Andersen and Collins also argue that the matrix of domination approach to race, class, and gender oppression must be historically grounded, and therefore intersect with other categories of experience, such as sexuality, age, ability, and religion. They contend that this model is a better tool for analyzing structural systems of power and inequality than a "difference framework" that treats oppressions separately or "diversity initiatives" that aim to help people understand differences with no attention to power inequalities (e.g., programs that emphasize multiculturalism).[13] Achieving

---

[11] From a posting by Nancy Richardson on the *Feminist Studies in Religion* blog: "In Memory of Beverly Wildung Harrison," http://www.fsrinc.org/blog/memory-beverly-wildung-harrison (accessed November 20, 2013).

[12] Samantha Brennan, "Feminist Ethics and Everyday Inequality," *Hypatia* 24.1 (Winter 2009): 152–3.

[13] Margaret L. Andersen and Patricia Hill Collins, *Race, Class, and Gender: An Anthology* (Belmont, CA: Wadsworth Publishing, 2009), 4–9.

justice will require analyzing the hierarchies and systems of domination within a society, not simply appreciating differences and cultural diversity.

Theorists studying forms of oppression distinguish between individual and institutional forms. Individual forms of oppression, that is, overt acts of prejudice of one individual against someone from a targeted social group, are more often the focus of societal attention. Institutional forms that are found in policies, laws, and norms of organizations and social institutions (e.g., religion, government, education, law, media) are not as easily identifiable, especially since they are historically and culturally embedded in institutions and not the result of any one identifiable act of discrimination by a prejudiced culprit. Feminists increasingly advocate changing institutional forms of oppression since they are usually more detrimental on the whole to women than individual acts of prejudice.

Philosopher Iris Marion Young suggests an even more complex analysis of oppression. She argues that to think adequately about justice, an emphasis on structure beyond individual institutions is required. To illustrate her conception, Young uses an example of Sandy, a divorced mother of two who must move as her apartment building is being converted into condominiums. She hopes to find a place to rent closer to her sales clerk job at a suburban mall so that she does not have to take two buses to work, but she finds that the rents are out of her price range. The places she can afford are unsafe for her children, and the bus commute is even more arduous. Sandy's story illustrates structural injustice that is not tied to individual actions of prejudice or even specific institutional policies; nor is it due, in this case, to unvirtuous behavior on Sandy's part. Her vulnerability to homelessness is not simply a situation of bad luck either; many people are in similar circumstances. She simply earns a wage that is insufficient to pay rent. Young refers to these kinds of injustices as "social-structural processes."

Many of the constraints that Sandy experiences are a result of "social policies, investment decisions, cultural preferences, and racial hegemonies" that no one person put in place to directly coerce others but which nevertheless constrain some people and enable others. Yet the actions of individuals created and sustained these structures, even if the participating groups of people did not necessarily intend the outcomes. For example, the phenomenon of middle-to-upper-middle class white families choosing where to live based on good schools for their children has led to racially segregated neighborhoods despite the current illegality of redlining (keeping people of color out of white neighborhoods by not giving them bank loans for houses in those neighborhoods). While the decisions these families made might not have been about racial prejudice, the result is racial inequality. Justice-making requires that we study the structures and understand the power differentials and relations in a broad way so that we can collectively address injustice. To address the inequality and oppression that Sandy experiences, groups might organize for jobs with higher wages and benefits, more equitable educational opportunities, and mixed-income neighborhoods with excellent public transportation.

An emphasis on structure is different than a focus on institutional oppression. Social structure is much more difficult to identify because it is not a specific part of society but rather a series of patterns and positions that become visible only when one takes a broad look at the actions of individuals. It is also different than a focus on individual oppression. We often base accountability on a "virtue model" by examining individual actions. That is, we judge whether people have treated other individuals with dignity and respect and not intentionally excluded or discriminated against them. We rarely note whether our everyday actions "contribute to structural processes that produce vulnerabilities to deprivation and domination for some people."[14] Young argues that responsibility through solidarity and collective action is the only remedy for bringing about more just structures. Christian values of hospitality and love of neighbor on an individual level will be useless, and in the form of paternalistic charity even detrimental for women like Sandy unless each is connected to justice in the form of structural change.

3) Attention to different forms of justice

Christian feminist ethicists are very concerned about just distribution of resources and power, but they also believe that narrowly focusing on distribution will not address all forms of oppression that women and others face. Two philosophical theorists, Iris Marion Young and Nancy Fraser, have addressed this problem. Both argue that oppression clearly has distributive aspects but is not limited to the distribution of social goods. Fraser argues that subordination by misrecognition, which she illustrates with an example of a black Wall Street banker who cannot get a cab, also prevents people from participation as peers in social life. All adult members of society have a right to interact with one another as peers. Young identifies injustices that limit participation: powerlessness, cultural erasure, and marginalization. Fraser claims that misrecognition is wrong because it is a form of institutionalized subordination that violates justice.[15] In contrast, Young says it is wrong because it thwarts human access to a good life that includes "satisfying work,

---

[14] Iris Marion Young, *Responsibility for Justice* (Oxford: Oxford University Press, 2011), 73.
[15] Nancy Fraser, "Recognition Without Ethics?" *Theory, Culture & Society* 18.2–3 (June 2001): 21–42.

social participation, and expression."[16] She holds that these limits to participation can impede people from exercising their capacities and determining their own actions for the end goal of living a good life.

Christian feminists agree with Fraser that the principle of justice is important, but they do not generally separate justice from a conception of the good life. While they would be wary of claiming there is only one conception of the good life, they clearly have some specific visions of what it means to promote a flourishing life (or an "abundant life" in the words of Jesus [John 10.10]). They believe that meeting the basic needs of all persons is a minimal standard for a good life.[17] They also want social arrangements that permit all members of society to participate and be treated with dignity and respect. Both the way social goods are distributed and what social constructs and attributes we value (e.g. whiteness versus blackness, masculine versus feminine, independence versus dependence) have implications for the degree to which people can participate in public life, the amount of autonomy they have in decision-making, and their ability to enact a life plan that allows them to exercise their particular capabilities. For Christian feminists, maldistribution, subordination, and misrecognition are also wrong because they impede loving relations with one's self, others, nature, and God.

Care for the earth and all its inhabitants must also be included in a Christian feminist approach to justice. The goal of environmental sustainability in our world is intricately linked to gender justice and justice of equitable distribution and recognition. When 17 percent of the world's population is consuming 80 percent of the world's resources, there is clearly a problem of maldistribution.[18] The minority's overconsumption is destroying our planet and causing untold misery and injustice for large numbers of people (overwhelmingly women and children), other species, and the earth. There are many interconnections between human oppression, of poor women of color in particular, and the destruction of the environment. For example, the issues of deforestation, pollution of water sources, depletion of natural resources, and global warming result in poor women in developing countries having to walk twice as far to get firewood, to tend to their children who have pollution-induced illnesses, and to struggle to keep their

---

[16] Iris Marion Young, *Justice and the Politics of Difference* (Princeton: Princeton University Press, 1990), 91.

[17] See Cathrin Jarl, *In Justice: Women and Global Economics* (Minneapolis, MN: Augsburg Fortress Press, 2003).

[18] "Social and Economic Injustice," *World Centric*, http://worldcentric.org/conscious-living/social-and-economic-injustice (accessed October 15, 2012).

families fed.[19] Environmental destruction, even global warming, does not affect everyone equally. Those with power and privilege are better able to ameliorate the effects of such destruction, but even they will not be immune. Justice will require a radical switch from growth-centered to sustainability-centered economies and lifestyles, most notably for those who are affluent.

Vision of right relationships and flourishing life

The Christian feminist emphasis on empowering women usually entails the norm of "right relationships" with others (one-on-one and in community) as well as individual autonomy, bodily integrity, and freedom and opportunity to exercise one's capabilities. Many feminists have been wary of Western culture's overemphasis on individual autonomy since it often ignores the many relational responsibilities that women have for children, aging parents, and others. All humans are relational beings, but women have especially deep relational connections that can limit full autonomy. Christian feminists value interrelatedness and the deep connections that women have; they claim that relationality is how we are connected to the Divine and how we are most spiritually whole. Yet feminists are also aware that bodily integrity and autonomy are often not granted to women (e.g., rape laws, restrictive abortion laws), and that women still do not have equal opportunity in many arenas. Thus a continued emphasis on granting women autonomy, freedom, and opportunity is imperative if there are to be right relations.

An emphasis on right relation is connected to the feminist insight that God(dess) is at heart relational and immanent/transcendent and not a "wholly other" God. Feminist theologian Sallie McFague, for example, critiques the sole use of metaphors for God that depict distance and "power over," such as king, lord, and father. She instead envisions metaphors for God(dess) that suggest "power with" and deep relationality, such as mother, lover, and embodied earth.[20] She argues if we imaged the earth as God's body we would not consider nature as simply a resource for human use, but as sacred and part of God(dess) with intrinsic value. The Christian feminist premise that we are created as relational beings implies that our *telos* is to be in right relation and harmony with all of creation. Humans are but one species and we ought to see ourselves as one strand in the web of life, not

---

[19] See Rosemary Radford Ruether, ed., *Women Healing Earth: Third World Women on Ecology, Feminism, and Religion* (Maryknoll, NY: Orbis Books, 2000), and Heather Eaton and Lois Ann Lorentzen, *Ecofeminism and Globalization: Exploring Culture, Context and Religion* (Oxford: Rowman & Littlefield Publishers, Inc., 2003).

[20] See Sallie McFague, *Models of God: Theology for an Ecological, Nuclear Age* (Minneapolis, MN: Augsburg Fortress Press, 1987) and *The Body of God: An Ecological Theology* (Minneapolis, MN: Augsburg Fortress Press, 1993).

as the pinnacle of a pyramid. Being created in the "image of God" does not mean humans are superior or have license to dominate nature. Instead it implies a need for relationship. In fact, humans are dependent for survival on all of creation, whereas ecosystems would be fine without humans.

Most Christian feminists assume relatedness as our ethical and cosmic reality and believe that spiritual wholeness entails working towards a world that supports relationships of respect and reciprocity between humans and the earth's ecosystems. For them, spirituality is connected to the ethical task of challenging life-denying factors in our world and promoting sustainable and life-affirming practices. Christian feminists uplift a relational Jesus who was extremely sensitive to human suffering and proclaimed abundant life for all. Their emphases on interdependence and the relational incarnate Jesus stem from their beliefs that all of life is sacred, has the ability of creation and destruction, and is intricately interconnected with God/dess as the energy and presence within all of creation.

Commitment to justice-making

Beverly Harrison once said, "Love is not a way of feeling, but a mode of action."[21] While Christian feminists start by understanding particular injustices, they never end there but always advocate the collective responsibility we have for justice-making in light of what God is calling us to do. Their understanding of justice is based on a vision of abundant/flourishing life that includes values of love, compassion, sustainability, and participation. While this vision serves as background for what justice entails, there is no single standard of justice applicable to all situations because each injustice has historical and cultural particularities. Christian feminists take seriously Christian discipleship, but realize that we all fall short in our call to justice-making. Thus we tread humbly in our discernment of what God is calling us to do and in our actions towards justice, knowing that justice-making is always an ongoing process. Sometimes our efforts are in error and new expressions of injustice will always unfold.

Taking seriously Young's complex understanding of the structures that we all participate in through our everyday actions means that while change on an individual level is important, the only way for larger structural change to occur is for groups of individuals to change their actions collectively. One person boycotting the buses in Birmingham during the Civil Rights movement would not have brought change, but the whole black community

---

[21] From a posting by Nancy Richardson on the *Feminist Studies in Religion* blog: "In Memory of Beverly Wildung Harrison," http://www.fsrinc.org/blog/memory-beverly-wildung-harrison (accessed November 20, 2013).

boycotting collectively was able to force change. While Christian feminists have an ideal vision of flourishing/abundant life, they are not naïve in thinking that changing a capitalist-structured economy that benefits and gives immense power to an elite few is going to be easy. The biggest hurdle is getting the majority to see that the status quo of inequality and injustice is not inevitable and that we do not need to acquiesce to it.

Many people think they have too much to lose (e.g., power, privilege, material wealth) to be concerned about poverty, inequality, and justice for people on the margins. The truth is that we all lose when we do not have a collective vision of a common good for all and do not promote justice for those most negatively affected. Our communities are divided and segregated, people are scapegoating others out of fear, we are putting more money towards prisons than public education, and, most of all, our children are suffering from our lack of a collective vision of justice.[22] Christian feminists know that an embodied and relational self is only spiritually whole and related to the Divine through involvement in creating right relationships in solidarity with others. The process of justice-making, while never easy or clear, is "profoundly spiritual."[23] God(dess) is calling us to such discipleship.

---

[22] Sharon Welch, *A Feminist Ethic of Risk*, revised edition (Minneapolis: Fortress Press, 2000), 165.

[23] Ibid., 172.

Christian feminism: A libertarian response
Jason Jewell

Laura Stivers writes early in her foundational essay, "A feminist vision of justice entails, at minimum, that all people have access to adequate resources to meet their basic needs, that they be given the opportunity and means to participate in meaningful ways in their communities, and that they be treated with dignity and respect." This claim provides a good starting point for discussion, and I suspect most readers (including myself) would affirm that these are desirable social goals.

However, I fear that Stivers has presented us, intentionally or not, with a "fuzzy" set of criteria that may prevent constructive exchange. What exactly constitutes access to adequate resources, meaningful community participation, and respectful treatment? I suspect answers to this question will differ radically from one reader to the next. Thus I encourage Stivers to get a little more specific on these points in her summation. What are "basic needs"? Are they a roof over one's head, clothes on one's back, and 2,000 calories per day? Saint Paul believed these were sufficient (1 Tim. 6.8). If more is required, how much more and why? Is there any obligation on the part of the recipient of these resources to work to produce their equivalent economic value? If access to resources is a right, who has the obligation to provide this access to everyone, and where will this entity procure these resources?

Does being a stay-at-home mom constitute meaningful participation in the community? What about other activities traditionally located in the "domestic sphere" (extending hospitality in one's home, involvement in church and other non-profit benevolence work, etc.)? If these activities are in fact meaningful, has any traditional society failed this requirement of feminist justice? If they are not, why not? Who is to provide everyone the opportunity and means to perform these meaningful activities? Why?

What exactly constitutes being "treated with dignity and respect"? Does this simply mean we should expect good manners from our fellow citizens? Should we sue and expect to win a judgment against anyone who insults us? Do we have a right to a job pursuant to the realization of our human dignity? If we have jobs, are we entitled to demand annual pay increases from our employers? Or can we demand jobs we find more fulfilling? Once we decide what it means to be treated respectfully, is someone supposed to enforce this standard? If so, how?

The above questions are not rhetorical. Various social and political thinkers have answered them in radically different ways. Stivers must give us a clearer picture of what her vision of feminism entails before we can even begin to identify "the lived experiences of injustice that people on the margins, especially women, deal with."

As I noted in my foundational essay, many libertarians identify themselves as feminists.[1] Libertarian feminists generally see themselves as heirs to the "first-wave" feminism Stivers identifies in her essay. They all agree that women should be free of government coercion to the same extent men are; for example, they oppose legal prohibitions on women's participation in certain occupations or restrictions on the right of women to own property apart from their husbands or fathers. They also call for an end to ways in which the state privileges women over men, as in, for example, the presumption of most courts that a mother should have primary or sole custody of her children in the aftermath of a divorce. Many so-called "equity feminists" view their goals as having been largely, though not completely, accomplished in countries such as the United States.

Other libertarian feminists go beyond arguing for legal equality of women and assert that patriarchy, even when voluntarily adopted, oppresses women. For example, Charles Johnson and Roderick Long write:

> State power is always part of an interlocking system of mutually reinforcing social practices and structures, not all of which are violations of the nonaggression axiom. There is nothing un-libertarian, then, in recognizing the existence of economic and/or cultural forms of oppression which, while they may draw *sustenance* from the state (and vice versa), are not *reducible* to state power. One can see statism and patriarchy as mutually reinforcing systems.[2]

On this view, libertarians can and should participate in social activism to reduce the influence of patriarchy in society. Such activism, however, should not be political (once legal equality between men and women has been achieved). Rather, it should focus on initiatives such as voluntary programs to help make women more independent and the development of more deeply consensual relationships and institutions. These "cultural libertarian feminists" view the use of the state—not a consensual institution!—to reduce

---

[1]   See Amy R. Baehr, "Liberal Feminism," *Stanford Encyclopedia of Philosophy*, ed. Edward N. Zalta (Winter 2013), http://plato.stanford.edu/archives/win2013/entries/feminism-liberal/ (accessed November 13, 2013).

[2]   Roderick Long and Charles Johnson, "Libertarian Feminism: Can This Marriage Be Saved?" *Charles W. Johnson*, May 1, 2005, http://charleswjohnson.name/essays/libertarian-feminism/ (accessed January 21, 2014).

cultural patriarchy as simply the substitution of one form of oppression for another. Clearly libertarianism is compatible with at least some forms of feminism, although I do not know whether Stivers will find it to her liking. Stivers offers Iris Marion Young's story of Sandy, a divorced mother of two who suffers economic hardship, as a paradigmatic instance of "structural injustice." According to Young and Stivers, Sandy's plight is not the result of anyone's "unvirtuous behavior." Rather, it's because our society simply doesn't function as it should; we have "unjust structures." Apart from the vagueness of this concept, which can seemingly be stretched to encompass any social outcome an author dislikes, libertarians in general (whether feminist or not), and Christian libertarians in particular, are likely to challenge the premises of this narrative.

For example, abundant evidence indicates that married couples are much more financially secure than divorced people. Christians also know that Jesus condemned divorce in most circumstances (Mt. 19.1-12). Thus if we want to understand Sandy's financial situation from a Christian perspective, it seems we need to know more about the facts surrounding her divorce. Why did it happen, and who was at fault? If the divorce occurred because Sandy's husband committed adultery or left her and the children, her situation is the result of his "unvirtuous behavior," and justice demands that he make restitution to her *via* alimony and child support payments. The court system ought to impose such payments at a level that will, at least, guarantee subsistence for the family he betrayed. There is no need to make a sweeping indictment of the socio-economic system.

On the other hand, what if Sandy's divorce occurred because of her misconduct? In this case, her economic plight is the direct result of her own actions. Attempts to blame "the system" or "structural injustice" are likely to be a deflection from the need for repentance. It is not just to demand that others clean up messes we have made ourselves. In this case, Sandy needs to seek reconciliation with those she has wronged and ask for help where appropriate from family, a local church, or some other nonprofit organiz-ation. Through such venues she could either lower her monthly expenses or secure training enabling her to find employment at a higher wage. If others assist Sandy in her attempts to repair the damage she herself caused, we have an instance of *mercy*, not one of *justice*. If all else fails, Sandy may need to make the painful decision to move to a different city with a lower cost of living.

Of course, both Sandy and her ex-husband may share in the blame of the divorce and the responsibility for her subsequent economic plight. In that case the remedy is likely to be some combination of the actions mentioned above. I have treated this example at some length in order to point out the frequent necessity, contrary to Stivers and Young, of examining the particulars of individual cases to understand the causes of people's suffering and what the just response to them is. Too often the rhetoric of "structural injustice" or "structural oppression" allows individuals to escape responsibility for their actions. It presents us with the counter-intuitive and dubious picture of millions of innocent individual actions that collectively add up to giant injustices and oppressions. Such an understanding of justice is foreign to scripture and to the traditions of Christianity. However, it is quite conducive to calls for state action to "fix" things through regulation and redistribution of wealth. Needless to say, libertarian Christians find these calls problematic.

Space prevents me from discussing other portions of Stivers's essay that deserve comment. I will simply conclude by expressing the hope that she will prove willing to explore nonviolent means to achieve her stated goals of providing all members of society with access to resources that meet their basic needs, opportunities and means to contribute meaningfully to their communities, and respect.

Christian feminism: A liberal response
Daniel A. Dombrowski

The view that I defend in this volume has much in common with the approach taken by Laura Stivers. The reason for this is that in a fair decision-making procedure, no rational person would agree to sexist principles or sexist practices. That is, in reality some people hold sexist views, but if one were to think about the possibility behind the veil of ignorance that one were to live in society as a female, it would be rational to insist that sexist principles and practices be abandoned.

It makes sense for Stivers to say that justice-making for the marginalized is an imperative for Christian feminists. Political liberals say the same. It should be remembered that Rawlsian political liberalism is not to be confused with what is often called neo-liberalism or libertarianism. In fact, the greatest libertarian philosopher, Robert Nozick, was an early and energetic opponent to Rawls's thought. Although in reality some people defend libertarianism, it would not be rational to choose this view behind a veil of ignorance.

It would be a mistake to assume that political liberals are advocating a "trickle-down" theory whereby if we look after the interests of the fortunate, then the less than fortunate will be indirectly benefitted through the creation of wealth brought about by the fortunate. By contrast, political liberals advocate a "suffuse-up" view wherein the first order of business in a just society is to make sure that the demands of the equal liberty principle are met for *everyone* in society, including the material underpinnings that make liberty meaningful. As Stivers correctly notes, addressing unequal distribution of wealth and power that is unfair is central to any Christian feminist approach to justice; indeed, it is central to *any* defensible theory of justice.

If there are any differences of opinion between the politically liberal approach that I defend and the position that Stivers defends, these can largely be explained in terms of some terminological matters or in terms of differences of method in that Rawls is a philosopher and Stivers is a theologian. Stivers frames the normative justifications for her views in terms of a biblical and theological lens. A political liberal cannot use this lens if he or she wants to develop a concept of justice that will be fair to all religious believers as well as to all non-believers. Further, it should be noted that what Stivers calls "liberal feminism" is *a* version of liberal feminism, not the only approach that is compatible with, or that does the most justice to, political liberalism.

It will be helpful at this point to discuss Stivers's narrative method so that it becomes clear how this method can be fruitfully supplemented by Rawls's own method of reflective equilibrium, which includes deliberation about a just society from behind a veil of ignorance. Stivers's approach to justice involves listening to the various stories told by people in society, especially the narratives told by those who belong to groups that have historically been marginalized or oppressed. This understandably forces us to stay close to the ground by paying attention to what concretely matters to people and by highlighting what those who tell these stories think is unjust about the society in which we live. So far, so good. This narrative method involves a bit of suspicion regarding any method that is ahistorical and that deduces conclusions regarding justice from a minimal set of assumptions. Once again, so far, so good.

Conceptual difficulties arise when it is realized that in contemporary societies characterized by pervasive pluralism, narratives collide among otherwise reasonable people. Thus, a key question arises: how are we to discover which principles of justice are to guide our decisions when the principles embedded in conflicting narratives collide? It is at this point that the Rawlsian original position, with its veil of ignorance, makes its most significant contribution in that it enables us to see that reasonable people who have quite different stories to tell nonetheless would agree to the equal liberty principle, the opportunity principle, and the difference principle, and in precisely this order.

Stivers is surely correct that when addressing injustice, context is crucial. But it is equally correct to say that the effort to discover the principles of justice that would be fair to everyone in society, regardless of the narrative structure of their lives, both individually and in terms of the group identities that they share, requires some sort of vantage point that is at least partially above the fray. And Stivers is also astute in noting that norms of justice serve as plumb lines to guide us. But it is also crucial to pay attention to how these norms are justified and what biases might have informed the discovery of these norms.

It makes sense for Stivers to be wary of any political theory that overemphasizes individual autonomy in that such an approach would be at the expense of social forces that are necessary conditions for any society that is just. But it is not clear to me that the political liberalism that I have outlined is vulnerable to this criticism in that in a just liberal society it is not only individual autonomy that is protected, but also associational liberty. That is, what is appealing about a liberal democratic society is not only that it protects the rights of individuals to freely choose if they want to worship God and in which institutional setting they want to do so, but it also protects the group rights of associations like the Catholic Church, Assembly of God churches, atheist clubs, etc. In fact, the realistic utopia that is political liberalism's goal involves the flourishing of as many associations as possible given the many religious (or non-religious) beliefs defended by reasonable citizens.

There is much room for productive dialogue between political liberals and feminist theorists. Both the Rawlsian revolution in political philosophy and the feminist revolution in ethical thought happened in the same time span, but unfortunately very often independently of each other. If these two intellectual currents joined I could imagine many benefits, both theoretical and practical. For example, it seems to me that a national program for not only subsidized healthcare but also for childcare is needed in order to fulfill the demands of the equal liberty principle; otherwise there are pressures put on women with children that prevent them from obtaining both the social basis for self-respect as well as real equality of opportunity. In this regard Rawls's view is very much compatible with the best in the new ethics of care tradition that dominates some versions of feminist theory. Further, there are politically liberal reasons to be still concerned about equal employment opportunities for women, equal pay for equal work, and the continued presence of glass ceilings. But none of these goals should occlude the obvious need for economic justice for women who live in grinding poverty, both in "advanced" societies and especially in "developing" ones. Here political liberals and feminists can work as one.

Stivers would be correct to be suspicious of the decision-making procedure in the original position if it were to be identified as *the* method on which political liberalism depended. However, the hypothetical, abstract character of the reasoning behind the veil of ignorance is only part of Rawls's overall method of reflective equilibrium or dialectic. That is, it is concrete, historical beings who engage in the hypothetical reasoning in the original position. After this hypothetical thought experiment is completed, they then "return" (the scare quotes are needed because they never really left their concrete existences) to their concrete, embodied, historical existences and they then try to reach equilibrium or fit among the historical conditions within which they live, their own conceptions of justice, and what they would agree to behind the veil of ignorance. None of these is fixed and each is subject to modification. It is crucial to notice, however, that if there is disequilibrium or a poor fit between one's own actual views on justice and what would be agreed to behind a veil of ignorance, then more conceptual work needs to be done so as to approximate equilibrium or fit among the relevant parts.

Of course, some thorny theoretical problems remain. For example, more work needs to be done by both feminist thinkers and political liberals on the role of families in a just society. The work that is required is framed by a certain tension that is not easily relieved. On the one hand, there is a tendency to think that in a just society characterized by reasonable pluralism, the government should largely stay out of family life so that citizens can lead the lives they wish to lead, regardless of their religious beliefs or lack thereof and regardless of their sex or sexual orientation. On the other hand, the state has a legitimate interest in insuring that the family and educational institutions act as schools for citizenship so that children grow up to be responsible members of society. This means, at the very least, that the state can legitimately intervene in family life if wives or children are the victims of abuse *or*, more controversially, if women or girls are encouraged to view themselves as less than equal when compared with men or boys. These matters are notoriously difficult and often involve prudential judgments that require more than theoretical wisdom.

Christian feminism: A liberationist response
Miguel A. De La Torre

There is no question that Stivers's feminist approach *is* a liberative theory of justice. Her assertion that "the starting point for a feminist approach to justice is to begin with the lived experiences of injustice that people on the margins, especially women, deal with," means there exists much agreement and overlap between her work and my own. Hence, I find myself providing less of a response than a clarification to some of the insightful points Stivers raises.

Before elaborating on Stivers's comments, allow me to make an important disclaimer. I am a recovering sexist. Because I was raised in a misogynist Euroamerican and Hispanic culture, sexism is interwoven into the very fabric of my being. Regardless of how much of a feminist I consider myself to be; I can easily "fall off the wagon." I have the privilege to remain silent, and thus complicit, in the face of sexist structures whenever I do not wish to pay the price for speaking out. Even when I do choose to speak out, I can rest assured that at the end of the day the social structures will be sexist for me. More than likely, regardless of my liberative pronouncements, I will be hired before a woman, and more definitely be paid a higher salary.[1]

Feminists, as Stivers points out, also struggle with complicity to oppressive structures. She reminds us: "middle-to-upper-class white women railed against the injustice of unequal pay for equal work, the glass ceiling, and traditional gender roles while simultaneously sustaining their privilege through exploitation of poor women of all races." While the liberative type of feminism Stivers argues for is more aware of the interconnectivity of oppressive structures, I would argue that third-wave feminists are "recovering racists," struggling like me not to fall off the wagon. Hence, our

---

[1] A white woman made on average 77 cents for every dollar paid to a man in 2013. See Ariane Hegewisch and Maxwell Matite, *Fact Sheet: America's Women and the Wage Gap* (Washington DC: National Partnership for Women & Family, 2013), 1. Not surprisingly, women of color fared worse, with African American women making 64 cents for every dollar paid to a white man, and Latinas making 55 cents. See National Partnership for Women & Family, *Fact Sheet: African American Women and the Wage Gap* (Washington DC: National Partnership for Women & Family, January 2013), 1; and *idem, Fact Sheet: Latinas and the Wage Gap* (Washington DC: National Partnership for Women & Family, April 2013), 1.

conversations with different marginalized communities are crucial as we learn from each other and as we strive toward a more just social order.

Latina feminist thought is a response to the sexism existing within the Latina/o community and the racial, ethnic, and class prejudice existing within the Euroamerican feminist community, which ignores the fundamental ways white women benefit from the oppression of women of color. These Latinas are attempting to find liberation as members of the Hispanic community by obliterating those institutions which cause suffering so that all, women and men, can find fullness of life, or as Stivers would say "a flourishing life." However, at times the Latino/a community can detect the same paternalism among white feminists who seek to "save us." Assuming that *machismo* is somehow more barbaric than Anglo misogyny (hence the use of the Spanish term when wanting to describe a worse form of sexism even though both manifestations are equally horrific), some white feminists have felt a messianic calling to save and/or defend Latina women from Latino men. To avoid such detrimental paternalism we must employ, as Stivers points out, a narrative methodology that listens to the stories of Latinas. Such a method can lead sisters with race and class privilege to stand in solidarity with those relegated to their underside.

For those engaged in liberative ethics, such as the one advocated by Stivers, "creating right relationships is central to their understanding of what it means to be connected to God." Right relationship, however, is not limited to humankind. Stivers correctly points out the issue of environmental justice and the oppression of the earth as part of the relational quest of feminists. She is correct in ensuring that attention to the earth is part of liberative ethics, for as award-winning poet Alice Walker reminds us:

> Earth itself has become the nigger of the world. It is perceived, ironically, as other, as alien, evil, and threatening by those who are finding they cannot draw a healthful breath without its cooperation. While the Earth is poisoned, everything it supports is poisoned. While the earth is enslaved, none of us is free. While the Earth is a "nigger," it has no choice but to think of us as all as Wasichus. While it is "treated like dirt," so are we.[2]

There is no question that a prominent Eurocentric thread within Christianity, as practiced by the powerful and privileged, has been to create a faith with little connection to or understanding of a collective or communal spirituality

---

[2]   Alice Walker, *Living by the Word* (San Diego: Harcourt Brace & Company, 1981), 147.

linked to the land. Nor has much attention been given to the relationship between humans and creaturekind.[3]

I have no doubt that Stivers and I would agree with the Native American spiritual concept that within the circle of creation all are equal in value to the Creator. George "Tink" Tinker expresses this view when he writes: "A chief is not valued above the people; nor are two-legged valued above the animal nations, the birds, or even trees and rocks."[4] The relationship of human beings to creation becomes a matter of life and death, balancing one's needs and place within the world with preserving the world for one's descendants who will live "seven generations from now." While one takes from the plenty of creation, something must always be returned to maintain balance.[5]

While ecofeminism does unmask the interconnectedness between the oppression of women and the oppression of nature (i.e., taming virgin land), some white feminists fail to see the need to expand the paradigm to encompass marginalized groups of color. Environmental racism, defined as the link between the degradation of the environment and the racial composition of the areas where degradation takes place, is prevalent among communities of color. Race and ethnicity, according to a growing body of empirical evidence, continues to be the most significant variable in determining the location of commercial, industrial, and military hazardous-waste sites.[6]

Some Euroamerican feminists, with the privilege of not living in toxic, infested neighborhoods, fail to consider how race and ethnicity, more so than gender, remain the main indicators of who lives in ecologically hazardous areas and who does not. While environmentalists from the dominant culture concern themselves mainly with issues of clean air and water and the protection of the habitats of endangered species, Robert Bullard correctly observes:

---

[3] I am influenced by Carter Heyward, who uses the term "creaturekind" to refer to all that God has created that is other than human, meaning animals, plants, and minerals. While the term encompasses humans, Heyward struggles for language that avoids defining all God created that is not human as "other-than-human." See Carter Heyward, "Jesus Christ," *Handbook of U.S. Theologies of Liberation*, ed. Miguel A. De La Torre (St. Louis: Chalice Press, 2004), 18, 20.

[4] George Tinker, "Spirituality, Native American Personhood, Sovereignty and Solidarity." *Spirituality of the Third World: A Cry for Life*, eds. K. C. Abraham and B. Mbuy-Beya (Maryknoll, NY: Orbis Books, 1994), 126.

[5] Clara Sue Kidwell, Homer Noley, and George E. "Tink" Tinker, *A Native American Theology* (Maryknoll, NY: Orbis Books, 2001), 33.

[6] For a detailed exploration of the connection between environmental degradation and the racial/ethnic make-up of those most affected, see Miguel A. De La Torre, "Environment," *Doing Christian Ethics from the Margins* (2nd Edition) (Maryknoll, NY: Orbis Books, 2014), 126–46.

The environmental-equity movement is an extension of the social justice movement. Environmentalists may be concerned about clean air, but may have opposing views on the construction of low-income housing in white, middle-class, suburban neighborhoods... It is not surprising that mainstream environmental organizations have not been active on issues that disproportionately impact minority communities... Yet, minorities are the ones accused of being ill-informed, unconcerned, and inactive on environmental issues.[7]

Environmentalists benefitting from white privilege cannot continue to isolate ecological concerns from environmental racism. Continuing to mask environmental racism limits and frustrates any attempt or hope for the liberation of both humanity and creaturekind. Fortunately, some liberative feminist thinkers, like Stivers, recognize this connection.[8]

Finally, it should be noted that the focus of this response on these issues of clarification does not diminish from my total agreement with Stivers's essay. Instead, as I mentioned from the start, I have simply raised questions for further discussion so that those of us engaged in the reassessing step of the hermeneutical circle for ethics that I describe in my essay can learn from the praxis already employed and together move toward newer liberative praxis that brings us closer to a more just society.

---

[7] Robert D. Bullard, *Dumping in Dixie: Race, Class, and Environmental Quality* (Boulder, CO: Westview Press, 1994), 128–9.

[8] Another excellent example of an effort to understand environmental problems at the margins can be found in Rosemary Radford Ruether's book *Women Healing Earth* (New York: Orbis Books, 1996).

Christian feminism: A virtue ethicist's response

Elizabeth Phillips

In her response to my essay, Laura Stivers gives an excellent summary of the ways in which our approaches to justice resonate well with one another. Because I am also a feminist, it is not surprising that Stivers and I share much in common. I will not repeat here the commonalities which she discusses, rather I will highlight two important concepts in her essay, as well as one possible area of difference between us.

According to Stivers, a feminist understanding of justice "must include both the private and public realms of women's lives," and in fact "there really is no private arena that is not subject to the norms related to justice." This has been one of the most important contributions of feminism to questions of justice. Since the second wave of feminism, the phrase "the personal is political" has been both a rallying cry of activists and a focus of sustained philosophical attention. Feminism has called into question the divisions between "public" and "private" which have been central to modern, liberal understandings of politics, society, and morality, noting how these divisions tend to favor men and disadvantage women.

One of the most pronounced examples is the inability of most capitalist, post-industrial, liberal states to account for the raising of children and the management of households as *work* that is central to the functioning and wellbeing of societies. The industrial revolution created stark separations between homes and "workplaces." These newly formed "workplaces" became locations where men went and earned money for their labors while women stayed home and worked without pay. The inclusion of women in contemporary workforces has not yet begun to address the lingering injustices which arise from the persisting categorization of childrearing and housekeeping as private matters which are rarely subjects of political or economic policy (except insofar as it relates to the ability of wealthy people to pay others to help with or do the majority of this work).

These insights about the interrelatedness of the so-called "private" and "public" or "personal" and "political" are shared by virtue ethics. The cultivation of virtue is not for the good maintenance of individual character alone, but for the flourishing of human beings together, for the common good. Christian virtue ethics says that virtuous societies cannot arise without virtuous individuals, but equally that individual virtue, in order to be virtue at all, must issue forth in rightly ordered relationships and political life. The virtue, or lack thereof, of the "personal" and the "political" cannot be separated from one another.

Another commonality between feminism and virtue ethics is found in Stivers's emphasis on relationality. While Stivers maintains an important role for certain aspects of autonomy, she and I share with many feminists a suspicion of modern, liberal understandings of autonomy which neglect the relationality of human life. I would like to expand on the importance of relationality in contrast to some modern and masculine understandings of autonomy with a brief discussion of interdependence. "Dependence" is a word which can make feminists and liberationists nervous, and with good reason. Women, people of color, people with disabilities, the poor, and others at the margins have long been encouraged or forced to live in relationships of unjust dependence upon those in power. However, I believe that emphasizing the common interdependence of all human beings, and indeed all life on earth, does not affirm or collude with unjust dependencies, rather it calls into question the self-understandings of those who are privileged and powerful.

In *Dependent Rational Animals*[1] Alasdair MacIntyre criticizes moral philosophy for having assumed a "continuously rational, healthy and untroubled" self as the moral agent,[2] and he credits feminism with bringing dependence and nurture to the forefront of discussions of the self.[3] According to MacIntyre, we all exist on a continuum of dependence. We are all born and most of us die in utter dependence upon others. Those with certain severe disabilities may be equally dependent throughout life, while all others move back and forth across the spectrum due to injury, poor health (physical or mental), or tragedy, as well as happier circumstances such as childbirth and childrearing. Thus we find that dependence is central to the human experience and to a more accurate vision of the moral agent.[4] MacIntyre thus identifies "virtues of acknowledged dependence" as necessary complements to the "virtues of independent rational agency" which have often been the focus of the virtue tradition.

MacIntyre discusses these virtues in relation to justice, acknowledging that Aristotelian–Thomistic understandings of justice as desert and reciprocity

---

[1] Alasdair MacIntyre, *Dependent Rational Animals: Why Human Beings Need the Virtues* (Chicago: Open Court, 1999).

[2] Ibid., 2.

[3] Ibid., 3.

[4] One result of this shift is that "the disabled" are no longer thought of as "'them', as other than 'us', as a separate class"; instead those with disabilities are "ourselves as we have been, sometimes are now and may well be in the future." Ibid., 2.

are insufficient. As members of community we may be called on to give and nurture in a measure much different from the measure in which we were nurtured and received from others in the community, and the virtue of such a community is "just generosity" which both engages our affections in identification with the most needful, and pays critical attention to potentially dominant power structures. Justice involves the community's responsibility to those who have not received or been nurtured to an appropriate measure, which may be due either to individual failings of character or to the failure of social systems.

> The virtues which we need in order to achieve both our own goods and the goods of others through participation in such networks [of communal giving and receiving] only function as genuine virtues when their exercise is informed by an awareness of how power is distributed and of the corruptions to which its use is liable. Here as elsewhere in our lives we have to learn how to live both with and against the realities of power.[5]

MacIntyre's work in *Dependent Rational Animals* not only points to important insights about human dependence, but also shows the inaccuracy of many critics' assumptions about virtue ethics being bound to the inadequacies of Aristotle and/or Thomas Aquinas, and as ignoring social structures and the need for critical analysis of power.

Finally, there is a particular passage in Stivers's piece that worries me, but I wonder—based on other passages in her essay—if she perhaps does not intend it as I interpret it. Stivers says that, "Christian feminists do not differ significantly from secular feminists in their methodological approach to justice, but they frame their normative justifications for justice from a biblical and theological lens," and that, "While the suffering from injustice is the impetus for a Christian feminist approach to justice, the hope, and faith in the possibility of a sustainable, just, and compassionate world, is what keeps the fire of justice-making alive."

I am uncomfortable with the implication that our reasons for seeking justice, our understandings of justice, and our methods for approaching justice come from sources external to Christianity, and we simply take them up and reframe them in terms of biblical and theological materials. Indeed it sounds as if our hope is the same as non-Christian forms of feminism if our only horizon is the possibilities of justice and compassion in this world. I want to articulate Christian feminism as a much more resolutely and robustly theological perspective. Christian feminism can and must

---

[5] Ibid., 102.

learn much from non-Christian feminisms and other perspectives that critically analyze the realities of our world. While we must be honest about the fact that such perspectives have usually been the impetus for awakening feminism and other liberative movements within Christianity, it is not the case that Christian feminism is therefore merely a repetition of these perspectives baptized in Christian language and concepts. Instead, perspectives from outside of Christianity have awakened many Christians to all that was already within our tradition but had been denied or neglected, including the realities that we all equally share in the image of our Creator, that in Christ there is no longer male or female, that Jesus of Nazareth attended most carefully to those at the margins of society and those most disadvantaged by structures of power. Furthermore, our hope does not lie in the possibility that we may convince others to be more just and compassionate (though that is most certainly one of our aims; we must persist towards this goal all the while recognizing that it will be an ongoing, never-finished work until Christ returns); our hope is in God, in whose liberating life we have been given the grace to participate.

It may be that Stivers and I actually agree here, as she goes on to say, "A deep joy in the wonder and goodness of life and an abiding faith in a good and compassionate God(dess) of liberation makes justice-making for the marginalized an imperative for Christian feminists. Justice-making for them is intricately connected to what it means to be fully human in relation to the Divine." She later notes that, "For Christian feminists, maldistribution, subordination, and misrecognition are wrong not simply according to a principle of justice but because they impede loving relations with one's self, others, nature, and God, and they disrupt Divine vision/*telos* for all of creation."

5

Virtue Ethics and Social Justice

Elizabeth Phillips

Consider the following scenario. You enroll in a course to learn an art, like painting, piano, or theatre. You find that all the course content relates to the principles, rules, and theories of the art. After years of studying you realize that you have never actually picked up a paintbrush or sat at the piano or stood on the stage. At this point, would you not know something was wrong? Would it not be obvious to you that you were learning how to think about art, but not how to be an artist? You would have at least two problems. First, if a moment came when it was actually required of you to paint or play piano or act, you would be full of ideas and knowledge but entirely without the practices, habit, instincts, and skills required. Knowing how to think about something does not give you the ability to do that thing. Second, you would not have been able to experience and enjoy what it means to be an artist; you are not living the artistic life. Your study will have changed what you know and how you perceive things, but it will not have changed the shape or the meaning of your life. There is a similar danger in approaches to ethics in general and justice in particular which ignore the long moral tradition of virtue. Such approaches can lead to endless fine-tuning of theories of justice which neglect both the big-picture questions of what it means to *be* people of justice—central to which is the question of the ultimate end or goal of justice—and the practical questions of what practices and habits will cultivate in us the instincts and skills we need in order to act justly in our day-to-day dealings with one another. A virtue approach says that justice is not only about our duties in relation to specific political and social issues; rather justice is about the kinds of relationships we are created to have with one another, and thus the sorts of people we are meant to be.

Why virtue?

Classical virtue

Since the mid-1980s there has been something of a revival of the virtue tradition within the discipline of Christian Ethics. We will return to this revival shortly, but first we should briefly explore the origins of the tradition. The virtue approach to ethics did not begin in the twentieth century, or even within the Christian faith; it began in classical philosophy. D. Stephen Long has summarized the classical approach to virtue well: "Virtue is a power or potential in the human creature that is repeatedly exercised until it becomes part of who the person is."[1]

Plato taught that the human soul is threefold, and that three virtues govern the three aspects of the human being: courage is the virtue of the spirit, temperance for the appetite, and prudence (or practical wisdom) for the intellect. Above these three is the virtue of justice, which ensures the proper ordering of the other virtues. According to Plato, true virtue also requires knowledge of the good.

As in many aspects of their philosophies, Aristotle was indebted to Plato and followed his theory in some regards, but also came to understand virtue rather differently. For both Plato and Aristotle, the aim of morality is *eudaimonia*, which has often been translated as "happiness" but many agree is more accurately translated "flourishing." The *telos*, meaning "end" in terms of both goal and fulfilment, of human life is the flourishing of each individual and of the common good in our social and political orders. Thus the purpose of the virtues is to guide and shape the human life towards the end of flourishing. This emphasis on the ultimate end of morality is known as teleology.

The three components of the soul in Aristotle are the passions (including our desires and feelings), the faculties (our natural capacities and abilities), and states of character (how we are disposed to act in specific circumstances). Virtue resides in human character, governing how we live. Aristotle also distinguished between intellectual and moral virtues, but emphasized that both sorts of virtues require specific practices for their development. In other words, virtue is not gained by an act of decision, will, or contemplation alone; virtue must be cultivated through habits which affirm the good.

Aristotle is also known for the "doctrine of the mean," or the idea that each virtue is a mean between two vices, one of deficiency and one of excess. For examples, the virtue of courage is the mean between fear (the deficiency of courage) and recklessness (the excess of courage); the virtue of temperance

---

[1]   D. Stephen Long, *Christian Ethics: A Very Short Introduction* (Oxford: Oxford University Press, 2010), 15.

or self-control is the mean between the deficiency of being insensitive to life's pleasures on the one hand or simply indulging oneself on the other. It is important to understand that the mean is not simply the mid-point on a spectrum, nor is it a compromise or synthesis between two opposites. Instead, each virtue describes the proper ordering of a specific aspect of our character and behavior, while the two sorts of vices describe two ways in which that aspect can be wrongly ordered. Again, we are speaking in terms of teleology: as virtue in general aims towards the end of flourishing, so does each particular virtue order some aspect of our humanity towards the character traits and practical habits which will promote a particular aspect of the flourishing life. To take the virtue of temperance as an example again, that aspect of my character may be wrongly ordered by a type of self-denial which arises from not valuing myself or the world around me. It may also be wrongly ordered through selfishness. Neither self-denial nor selfishness will contribute to my flourishing, but self-control, properly understood and exercised, will.

While many virtues were discussed in the classical tradition, four were understood to be the cardinal virtues: wisdom, courage, temperance, and justice. Wisdom is both theoretical (having to do with knowing the truth), and practical (having to do with the ability to discern how to live in accordance with the good). Justice is that virtue which sums up and orders all the other virtues. In the classical tradition, virtues were not taught through lists of what one should and should not do in order to be virtuous, rather they were taught through telling the life stories of virtuous people (or, to be more accurate about how virtue was understood in the classics, virtuous *men*).

Virtue in the Christian tradition

Like many aspects of classical philosophy, the virtue tradition was taken into the Christian tradition and reinterpreted in light of the Christ event. Early and medieval theologians sought to relate the virtue tradition to Christian scripture and theology, some following Plato and others developing more Aristotelian approaches. Both retained the classical emphasis on teleology, but they differed between Plato's emphasis on the desires and Aristotle's emphasis on practice and habit. Christians also used stories to teach Christian virtue, and this was one of the functions of learning the lives of the saints.

Most well known in their adaptations of the virtue tradition were Saints Ambrose, Augustine, and Aquinas. They considered the cardinal virtues to be those which are acquired through good habits, while the theological virtues of faith, hope, and love (1 Cor. 13.13) were understood to be infused by divine grace. Saint Augustine, who was particularly critical of the short-comings of the "pagan" (classical) virtue tradition, taught that Christian virtue is the right ordering of our loves, and that the cardinal virtues are each forms of love for God. Saint Thomas Aquinas also connected the gifts of the Spirit in Isaiah 11.2-3, the Beatitudes in Matthew 5.3-11, and the fruit of the Spirit in Galatians 5.22-3 with the infused virtues of faith, hope, and love. He taught that the "pagan" or acquired virtues were not ultimate, in that their end was only found in more virtuous action. In contrast the end of the theological or infused virtues was found in the ultimate *telos* of humanity: beatitude, or the joyful worship of and sharing in the life of God. Thus, what is morally ultimate will always be more a matter of receiving gifts of grace from God rather than sheer determination of our own will, though Aquinas emphasized that through our will we must cooperate with the gift.

The fall and renewal of virtue

After the Enlightenment, the virtue tradition fell out of popularity, especially in Protestant theology. New approaches following various types of Enlightenment philosophy became the norm for philosophers and theologians alike. However, by the late twentieth century, many were becoming unsatisfied with the options available to them in modern ethics. This dissatisfaction can be described in at least two ways: a sense that the Enlightenment project had failed in relation to ethics, and a sense that ethical approaches should have a focus wider than the making of decisions.

In 1981, Alasdair MacIntyre published *After Virtue*,[2] a book which is considered by many to be a watershed moment in the renewal of virtue ethics in both philosophical and theological circles. MacIntyre argued that one result of the Enlightenment was that ethics had become a matter of rival forms of moral assertion between which there could be no rational settlement. People with opposing views on moral issues were not expressing rational truth; they were merely asserting their feelings in opposition to one another, and there is no rational way to settle a dispute between mere assertions of emotion. According to MacIntyre, this dilemma was the result of Enlightenment efforts to sever morality from tradition and theology in order to create objective and universal forms of moral reasoning. When morality was severed from its roots in particular traditions, we were left with sets of concepts and terms which we continued to use, including "justice,"

---

[2] Alasdair MacIntyre, *After Virtue* (Notre Dame: University of Notre Dame Press). The first edition was published in 1981, and subsequent editions followed in 1984 and 2007.

although they had been stripped of their meaning by being cut off from their roots.[3]

Consider ethical disagreements concerning war and abortion, two discourses in which rival parties claim justice as the core of their opposing convictions. Some say that justice sometimes demands acts of war, while others argue that no modern war can be just. Some say that justice demands reproductive freedom for all women, while others claim to demand justice for the unborn. All parties are using "justice" as their byword, yet making claims which are directly opposed to one another. There is no rational way to arbitrate between the rival claims. We are left not with rational, moral discourse, but with interminable assertions and counter assertions by rival groups.

The remedy to this impasse, according to MacIntyre, is the retrieval of virtue. Importantly, MacIntyre emphasized that virtue is not merely a list of things which are not vices; rather, in the Aristotelian sense, there are four main components of morality, which form a complex, interdependent web of concepts:

1) Tradition

Human life and society are formed by and take the shape of traditions. Each tradition is a "historically extended, socially embodied argument, and an argument precisely in part about the goods which constitute that tradition."[4] There is no form of human existence or ability for humans to reason apart from rootedness in particular social, rational, and moral traditions.

2) Narrative

Each tradition and each individual life possesses a narrative structure, a way of understanding its own story in the greater scheme of things. Crucial to such a narrative is the understanding of the *telos* of human life.

3) Practices

Traditions and narrative are not merely theoretical constructs. Particular practices (social, co-operative activities) arise from narrative and give shape to the life of a community embodying a particular tradition. Good practices promote virtue in individuals and the common good in society.

---

[3] See Alasdair MacIntyre, *Whose Justice? Which Rationality?* (Notre Dame: University of Notre Dame Press, 1988), and *Dependent Rational Animals: Why Human Beings Need the Virtues* (Chicago: Carus Publishing Company, 1999).

[4] MacIntyre, *After Virtue* (2nd edition), 222.

4) *Virtue*

There is a reciprocal relationship between virtues and practices; practices shape virtue in the members of practicing communities, and virtues are required in order to achieve excellence within a given practice. Virtues are also required for achieving the goods related to the *telos* of life, and for the good ordering of particular traditions.[5]

Following MacIntyre, it became clear to some Christian ethicists that one of the impasses of twentieth-century ethics created by the failure of the Enlightenment project was the assumption that ethicists must choose between two types of ethical approaches: deontological and consequentialist. While Christian ethicists generally agree that the sources of their discipline are scripture, tradition, reason, and experience (though serious disagreements exist about the relationship between, relative authority of, and interpretations of these sources), deontologists and consequentialists ask different questions of these sources.

The deontologist goes to the sources with the question, "What is the right thing for an individual to do?" According to this approach, the task of ethics is to determine things like laws, duties, and obligations and decide how each individual should make decisions based on these. (The word "deontology" is derived from a Greek root, meaning duty.) As is readily evident from the name, the consequentialist approach is more concerned with the consequences of actions than with duties which determine actions. A consequentialist goes to the sources with the question, "How does an individual achieve the best outcome?" According to this approach, the task of ethics is to determine what is ultimately desirable or good, and to determine how each individual should make decisions based on consequences. What these two approaches share in common is a focus on trying to figure out how an individual should make good decisions.

According to MacIntyre, the severing of ethics from teleology and virtue, which was seen in both deontological and consequentialist approaches, has led to the failure of modern ethics to engage in rational moral enquiry. One of the most important reasons for the shift away from deontology and consequentialism is a broadening of the concerns of ethics beyond the making of decisions. Virtue ethics is different from these approaches because it does not begin and end in a moment of individual decision. Instead ethics is about who we are and how we live our lives in relation to one another and to what

---

[5] See Alasdair MacIntyre, "The Claims of After Virtue," in *The MacIntyre Reader*, ed. Kelvin Knight (Notre Dame: University of Notre Dame Press, 1998), 69–72.

is ultimate. A virtue ethicist goes to the sources with the question, "Who are we and what sort of life should we be living?"

Many of the Christian ethicists who have called for the retrieval of the virtue tradition have been working within Protestant churches where the virtue tradition was most neglected in the modern era. The most well-known advocate of the renewal of virtue in Christian ethics has been Stanley Hauerwas. However, although virtue was never removed from the conversation so decisively within Catholic moral theology, there have been calls for the renewal of virtue there as well.[6]

Think back to the hypothetical art course with which we began this chapter. What I described there was precisely the quandary of modernist approaches to morality: ethics is all about how to think about decisions instead of about who we are and how we live our lives together, just as the hypothetical art course only taught how to think about an art instead of transforming its students into artists. Just as the person with years of learning about art could not actually paint or play piano or act, no matter how much you know about deontology or consequentialism as a way to make decisions, this knowledge cannot turn you into the kind of person who makes good decisions at crucial moments. Even more importantly, approaching ethics that way may make you a person who understands ethical theory, but it cannot make you an ethical person (just as the hypothetical art course could not make you an artist).

Justice as virtue

What then are the implications if justice is approached as a virtue, instead of from deontological or consequentialist perspectives? First, we will not be interested in a universal and timeless definition of justice. Instead of seeking to establish thin and abstract principles, we will turn to the thick descriptions of justice in Christian scripture and tradition which, as with all good theology, will be read through and in relation to reason and experience. This does not imply that Christians have always been in the right about justice–not by any stretch of the imagination! Delving into the thickness of justice within the Christian tradition requires us to be aware of and honest about the ways in which the Christian tradition has not been faithful to the visions of justice set out by Jesus and the prophets. Social practices which attend to

---

[6]   See Bernard Häring, *The Virtues of an Authentic Life* (Ligouri, MO: Ligouri Publications, 1997), and Jean Porter, *The Recovery of Virtue: The Relevance of Aquinas for Christian Ethics* (Louisville: Westminster/John Knox Press, 1990).

the needs and inclusion of those at the margins (widows, orphans, aliens), and which affirm peace rather than retaliation (turning the other cheek, going the extra mile) are at the heart of these visions.

Justice as virtue does not reject the abstract universalism of modernity because it is believed that there is no such thing as the universal. On the contrary, universality is key to Christian virtue ethics, but it is a universality of the particular. Is there not in Christology a claim about what universal humanity is meant to be? On this view, the universal is found in the particular person of Jesus Christ, not in supposedly timeless abstractions.

Second, an approach to justice as virtue will not begin and end with procedural questions about what duties justice entails or how to make societies "work" in terms of justice. Instead, we begin with questions about the ultimate realities to which justice points, the vices which justice stands against, and the practices required for our formation as people and communities of justice. The practical decisions, duties, and requirements of justice must then be worked out in more *ad hoc* ways. By "*ad hoc*" I do not mean in ways which are insufficiently intentional, which ignore systemic and structural realities, or are haphazard. Rather, just as the content of justice is particular, so must the practices of justice be fitted to particular times and places.

Following from the first two implications is a third: that we will not be able to offer a unified and universal "theory of justice," which has been the preoccupation of most modern approaches to justice. If the content of justice is particular and the practices of justice are *ad hoc*, no such universal theory is warranted or viable. I would suggest that the virtue ethicist's approach to justice is much like the approach to the state advocated by John Howard Yoder. He argued that when Christians are preoccupied with describing and establishing the ideal form of government, we have a false illusion that our work can and will be finished when this ideal government comes to power. Instead, we should have a constant prophetic and pioneering function in society, regardless of the form of government, seeking out and creatively addressing those places where our societies most need to be called into conformity with the kingdom of Christ.[7] Such a role is always shifting throughout history, and such work is never completed until Christ returns. Likewise, justice is something we must always keep doing—in the ways it most needs to be done in our particular time and place—rather than an abstract theory we need to keep perfecting.

Finally, justice as virtue must be thoughtfully and practically related to

---

[7]   See especially John Howard Yoder, *The Christian Witness to the State* (Scottdale, PA: Herald Press, 2002).

the theological virtues of faith, hope, and love—primarily the guiding virtue of love. The relationship between love and justice has always been a central question of Christian ethics. Some ethicists have defined love and justice in ways which set them in opposition to one another. This tension may be resolved by arguing either that love or justice is the primary guiding norm for Christian ethics, or that the task of Christian ethics is to hold the two in tension, always allowing them to challenge and interrogate each other. Those who would place love above justice tend to view justice as too tied to duties and rules, while love gives more freedom to do whatever is the most loving thing in a given situation.[8] Those who would place justice above love tend to view love as entirely self-sacrificial and non-resistant—an attitude of passive selflessness which cannot be the norm for social or political realities where the coercive enforcement of rights through justice must be the norm.[9]

Others argue, however, that love and justice, especially understood in light of narratives of love and justice in scripture, are complementary norms; they both function to deliver the oppressed and marginalized, to confront selfishness and injustice, and to create inclusive communities of peace.[10] This way of relating love and justice resonates well with the virtue approach, where virtues are understood as both complementary to and dependent upon one another, and where both love and justice are seen to have special roles in ordering and guiding all other virtues.

Communitarianism and/or virtue?

Some scholars would identify the virtue approach to justice as described here as a "communitarian" approach, though I would resist this label. "Communitarianism" is a term most often used by proponents of liberal approaches to politics and ethics to describe approaches which are critiques of their own. You are not likely to meet a Christian ethicist who would label herself "communitarian." While some political theorists and policy specialists have embraced this label, this was much more common in the 1980s and 1990s than it is today. In fact, the flurry of publications on the communitarianism versus liberalism debate, which was at its height between

---

[8] See Joseph Fletcher, *Situation Ethics: The New Morality* (Philadelphia: Westminster Press, 1966).

[9] This sort of argument was central to the work of Reinhold Niebuhr. See especially the essays collected in *Love and Justice: Selections from the Shorter Writings of Reinhold Niebuhr*, ed. D. B. Robertson (Louisville, KY: Westminster/John Knox Press, 1957).

[10] This argument is made in Glen H. Stassen and David P. Gushee, *Kingdom Ethics: Following Jesus in Contemporary Context* (Downers Grove, IL: InterVarsity Press, 2003).

the mid-1980s and the mid-1990s, has largely dissipated. It is telling that the self-proclaimed journal of the communitarian movement in America, *The Responsive Community*, ceased publication in 2004.

What was this flurry of publication about? What did the two sides of this debate mean by "liberalism" in contrast to "communitarianism"? First, it is important to note that we are not talking about liberal versus conservative, as in political parties such as Democrats versus Republicans or Labour versus Tories. Instead, "liberalism" in this sense refers to the central political philosophy of the modern era, from the Enlightenment until today, though it has come under increasing criticism since the mid-to-late twentieth century. America, the United Kingdom, France, indeed all Western, so-called "first-world" nations, are liberal states.

Robert Song distinguishes between three different types of liberalism: constitutional liberalism, which has to do with the political structuring of a nation; economic liberalism, which has to do with markets and private ownership; and welfare liberalism, which has to do with social safety nets and redistribution, or the sharing of resources more equally throughout society.[11] Across these differences, however, liberalism has the following key aspects in common:

a) An understanding of how humans think and behave which views each person as detached from others, making his or her own choices freely.
b) An approach to ethics which focuses on individual moral autonomy, or the right of individuals to govern and decide for themselves.
c) A way of reasoning which is individualist (focused on the individual instead of the society as a whole), universalist (broadening of what and who is relevant, as well as making generalizations which are believed to be true in all times and places), and abstract (this is necessary because that which is broadened and generalized in order to be universal will always be more abstract, less specific and particular).
d) An understanding of human rationality which emphasizes that
   1) disputes should be settled through reason instead of violence, and
   2) reason is an instrument to be used for the pursuit of individual advantage.
e) A conviction that history has been and will continue to be a story of human progress; humanity keeps improving and doing things better as time progresses.[12]

---

[11] Robert Song, *Christianity and Liberal Society* (Oxford: Oxford University Press, 1997), 37–9.

[12] This list is a summary of a more extensive treatment of the "family resemblances" of liberalisms in ibid., 40–47.

The critics of modern liberalism who have been grouped together under the heading of "communitarianism" tend to share:

a) A rejection of liberal approaches to ethics, which tend to be influenced primarily by Immanuel Kant and focus on procedural questions (how to fulfil one's duties morally) instead of substantive questions (about the meaning and ends of morality). Liberal, procedural ethics contends that the duties of justice must be determined and executed without reference to any theory of what is ultimately good, while substantive approaches (which tend to follow Hegel and/or Aristotle philosophically) contend that we must know the good toward which justice ultimately points in order to know what justice is and how to do justice.

b) A rejection of the modern, liberal notion of the self. Those called "communitarians" characterize the liberal self as an individual who is not bound to or by others, whose reality is not determined by history or context, and who may choose as he or she freely wills. They insist that this is a false notion of the self because as humans we are all conditioned by where, when, and how we live; we all have obligations to the communities of which we are a part, and both our knowledge and our abilities are necessarily limited.

c) A rejection of liberal, atomist individualism. This means that liberals are characterized as those who believe that ethics and politics in general, and theories of justice in particular, must begin with and be determined by the components of society (individual people) instead of the whole, while communitarians insist that individuals can only be understood as parts of the whole, as people necessarily situated within communities.

d) A rejection of modernist universalism. This may be in relation either to epistemology, theories of how we know things (thus denying that there are universal truths which can be the foundation of all human knowledge), or in relation to theories of social policy (thus denying that there are universal norms for all societies). Regarding justice, this means that so-called communitarians will question the idea that there is a universal reality called "justice," that we all mean the same thing when we say "justice," and that there can be a theory of justice which can be applied in all times and places.

Early in the liberalism/communitarianism debates of the 1980s, Michael Sandel summarized the differences at stake succinctly:

> Recalling the arguments of Hegel against Kant, the communitarian critics of modern liberalism question the claim for the priority of the right over the good, and the picture of the freely-choosing individual

it embodies. Following Aristotle, they argue that we cannot justify political arrangements without reference to common purposes and ends, and that we cannot conceive our personhood without reference to our role as citizens, and as participants in a common life.[13]

The approach to justice introduced in this chapter certainly has much in common with the approaches of those political philosophers and ethicists who have been called communitarians; it definitely stands in distinct contrast to liberal understandings of human personhood and morality. Yet there are several reasons why many of us who may be called communitarians by others reject the label for ourselves.

Some reject it because it does too little: "communitarianism" seems only to be a critique of liberalism, and not a constructive approach of its own. In fact, some say it only functions as a critique *within* liberalism, and does not go far enough in rejecting the model of the liberal nation-state altogether.

Others reject it because it does too much: many scholars who have been called communitarians intend only to describe how human beings are (situated, conditioned, parts of a whole), not to prescribe how societies should be ordered in ways which exalt the community over the individual, or which assume that a modern nation can be considered a community (in other words, they do not want to be understood as offering a communitarian theory for social policy). Charles Taylor has very helpfully made the distinction between communitarianisms of "ontology" (which describe how human beings are) and communitarianisms of "advocacy"" (which intend to shape social policy). Proponents of the advocacy type tend to own the label of "communitarian," while those of the ontological type tend to reject it.[14]

Alasdair MacIntyre has often been identified by others as a leading communitarian. However, he has always resisted this label. He has stated and written repeatedly that his theories of community are not to be confused with those which see the modern nation-state as the community in question. In fact, he agrees with the critics of communitarianism about the potential dangers of what Taylor has called advocacy communitarianism.

> Contemporary communitarians, from whom I have strongly dissociated myself whenever I have had an opportunity to do so, advance their proposals as a contribution to the politics of the nation-state ... [but]

---

[13] Michael Sandel, "Introduction," in Michael Sandel, ed., *Liberalism and its Critics* (New York: New York University Press, 1984), 7.

[14] Charles Taylor, "Cross-Purposes: The Liberal-Communitarian Debate," in *Philosophical Arguments* (Cambridge, MA: Harvard University Press, 1995), 181–203.

when practice-based forms of Aristotelian community are generated in the modern world, they are always, and could not but be, small-scale and local... The confusion of the Romantic vision with the Aristotelian conception did indeed lead some German thinkers to frame just that view of the nation-state as all-embracing community which liberals have rightly resisted, understanding how it generates totalitarian and other evils.[15]

Like Taylor and MacIntyre, I am presenting an approach which has some commonalities with the communitarian critique of liberalism, but in no way intends to offer a communitarian theory of justice to be implemented within the status quo of the modern, liberal nation-state, as if the nation-state could be the virtuous community. For this reason, the approach presented here is more accurately identified with virtue ethics than with communitarianism.

Why not virtue?

Apart from confusing virtue with communitarianism, there are several other reasons why a virtue approach may be criticized. Some critics of virtue ethics believe that the concept of virtue is too individualistic; it addresses each person's character instead of social structures and political realities. This criticism tends to arise most where "character" is a strong emphasis in virtue ethics, as in Stanley Hauerwas's early work.[16] However, the criticism that virtue is too individualistic betrays a basic misunderstanding of the reason so many ethicists have returned to the virtue tradition: virtue overcomes the individualism of modern ethics. Moral agency in virtue ethics is not only ascribed to individuals, but to communities. Thus, while it is entirely possible for particular virtue ethicists to be inattentive to structural and political issues, this is not due to the virtue approach necessarily focusing too narrowly on individual character.

   Some critics insist that virtue is a concept which is too internal; it only addresses moral inclinations and aptitudes, not actual praxis. Again, I would argue that such critics have misunderstood the virtue tradition. The cardinal virtue of wisdom includes practical wisdom; the virtues are always

---

[15] Alasdair MacIntyre, "A Partial Response to my Critics," in *After MacIntyre*, eds. John Horton and Susan Mendus (Notre Dame: University of Notre Dame Press, 1994), 302–3.
[16] It should be noted that Hauerwas himself is critical of numerous aspects of his early work on "character." See Stanley Hauerwas, "A Retrospective Assessment of an 'Ethics of Character': The Development of Hauerwas's Theological Project," in *The Hauerwas Reader* (Durham, NC: Duke University Press, 2001), 75–89.

about doing, not only about contemplation or formation. And moral traditions necessarily engage in practices, not only conversations and debates. Remember, one of the reasons for the renewal of virtue in Christian ethics was a dissatisfaction with the concept of ethics as how to make a decision in a moment of crisis, instead of how to live our lives together day to day, which is the business of virtue.

Critics of virtue ethics may also misunderstand all the talk of "tradition" within this approach. These critics assume that when one speaks positively of tradition, he must be longing for the good old days of the past when things were more "traditional"; he must be saying that the old ways are best, that change is bad, and that critical theories like feminism and liberation are necessarily threatening.[17] This is simply a fundamental misunderstanding of the word "tradition." To say that human beings exist and learn how to be rational and moral within particular traditions is to argue that traditions are constitutive—they constitute who we are and how we think and live—*for good or ill*. Tradition-constitutiveness should not be confused with traditional*ism*, which is the harkening back to an established status quo as the best reality.

Finally, some critics are convinced that virtue ethics is inherently and necessarily oppressive. This line of criticism usually begins with Aristotle's definition of justice as desert (giving people what they deserve) and his defense of slavery, then moves to criticize concepts of hierarchy and order in Aquinas and his views on women, and ends with the suggestion that ethicists such as MacIntyre and Hauerwas who emphasize virtue and community in line with the Aristotelian–Thomist tradition are simply affirming the status quo of traditional forms of structural and societal injustice. Some go so far as to suggest that virtue ethics and approaches to justice which some call "communitarian" are precisely the forms of ethics and politics that lead to totalitarianism.

First, we should note that reasoning within the Aristotelian–Thomist tradition does not require us to agree with everything Aristotle or Thomas Aquinas wrote. Remember that traditions are ongoing, socially embodied debates; they are not static affirmations of the status quo. Christian virtue ethicists today do not draw on Aquinas alone or unquestioningly. We agree with our critics about the unacceptable elements in the Aristotelian–Thomist tradition; we do not agree that it makes the tradition unusable or any more prone to be used oppressively than other traditions. Even a cursory knowledge of modern history reveals that Enlightenment philosophy and

---

[17] A striking example of this is found in Susan Moller Okin, *Justice, Gender, and the Family* (New York: Basic Books, 1989), especially chapter 3.

modern liberalism did not save us from totalitarianism. In fact, while liberals insist that reasoning about justice must be universal, it is this very aspect of liberalism itself which is so prone to injustice. As MacIntyre put it, "When men and women identify what are in fact their partial and particular causes too easily and too completely with the cause of some universal principle, they usually behave worse than they otherwise do."[18]

Virtue and other approaches to justice

A virtue approach to justice has the possibility of resonating with and/or incorporating aspects of some other approaches, while some approaches to justice are necessarily at odds with and cannot be reconciled to the virtue approach. The approach represented in this volume which is most at odds with virtue is the Rawlsian. Any theory of justice which assumes the liberal perspective that convictions about the good must be ignored or at least bracketed and excluded from conversations about justice cannot be reconciled to the deeply teleological nature of virtue ethics. Similarly, justice as virtue is difficult to reconcile with libertarianism, for at least two reasons: libertarianism is more about the freedom of the individual than the common good of the society, and like the Rawlsian approach libertarianism is a non-teleological, procedural approach.

However, feminism and liberation theology are different. While certain specific forms of feminism and liberation may be opposed to virtue ethics, and certain specific forms of virtue ethics can be inattentive to the questions raised by feminists and liberationists, there is no *necessary* opposition between these approaches. Feminist and liberationist virtue ethicists argue that equality of all people and liberation from oppression are central features of the Christian narrative and tradition and that practices of equality and liberation are necessary aspects of the formation of just and virtuous people and communities. Again, embracing tradition does not mean accepting every aspect of a tradition without question. Every healthy, viable tradition has both contested claims within it which must be weighed and discerned in relation to the tradition as a whole, and contesting claims from other traditions which pose external challenges and potentially refocus, renew, or lead to reinterpretation within the tradition. Feminism and liberation represent both kinds of challenges: to some degree the claims of oppressed and marginalized people arose in political discourses outside of Christianity and posed external challenges to the Christian tradition. Equally, some

---

[18] MacIntyre, *After Virtue*, 221.

have responded by retrieving the claims of equality and liberation already intrinsic to Christianity which had been denied, diluted, or drowned out by contesting claims which conformed to the status quo of societal oppression and marginalization.

Towards a more just justice system

Perhaps a good example of differences between approaches to justice can be found if we consider what is itself called "the justice system," that system through which crimes are prosecuted and punished. Procedural approaches would be concerned with aspects of how the system is (or is not) working. A Rawlsian approach would focus on the fairness of the system, and whether the system was equally fair to different sorts of people. A Rawlsian might want to analyze conviction and incarceration rates, for example. A libertarian approach would focus the freedom of individuals in relation to the system, which could take very different shape depending upon whether the individuals in question were the accused and incarcerated whose civil liberties may be violated by the justice system, or the victims of crime and other non-criminal civilians whose freedom may be seen to be violated if criminals are not duly punished.

Feminist and liberationist approaches would be more concerned with the relationship between the system and certain populations. They would likely critique the system's impact on the most vulnerable members of society: women, minors, people of color, and those who are socio-economically disadvantaged and/or disabled.

It is entirely possible that a virtue ethicist could find common cause with many of these analyses of the justice system. However, a virtue approach would not begin or end in the same place. The virtue ethicist would begin by asking, "What is the *telos* of a truly just justice system?" It would suggest that this *telos* must include more than prosecuting and punishing guilty individuals, and more than protecting innocent individuals from those who are guilty. The *telos* must also include, for example, virtuous reform of criminals, which may include restitution and/or reconciliation with the individuals and communities they have wronged. The concepts of restitution and reconciliation signal that what should be at stake in criminal justice is not only the punishment of individual wrongs and the protection of individuals against wrongdoing, but also the ways in which crimes rupture the relationships we are meant to enjoy with our fellow humans and the common good we are meant to promote in our lives together. In addition to beginning with the question of *telos*, the virtue approach would also go beyond (while by no means excluding) questions about how the system is functioning and is meant to function, to questions about how we, in our local communities and in our larger societies, become people of justice, cultivating communal virtue which prevents crime, points towards reform instead of punishment only, and seeks the restoration of both victims and offenders into positions which enable them to participate in the common good.

We see here that justice as virtue is not punctiliar; it is not only something that happens or fails to happen at a certain point in time in the process of prosecution and sentencing. Instead it is something which must be cultivated throughout communities and societies from prevention and the roots of crime through to the aftercare of victims and criminals beyond sentences served. This is not to say, of course, that these are the only implications of a virtue perspective for criminal justice, nor that these goals are possible in all criminal cases. However, at the core of virtue is the desire to lean towards that which is best in us, and the good for which we were created, and to build communities in which such flourishing is possible.

Virtue ethics: A libertarian response

Jason Jewell

Elizabeth Phillips appears to anticipate sharp opposition from me. In the conclusion of her foundational essay, she writes: "Justice as virtue is difficult to reconcile with libertarian approaches, for at least two reasons: libertarianism is more about the freedom of the individual than the common good of the society, and like the Rawlsian approach, libertarianism is a non-teleological, procedural approach." I hope to persuade her and readers that the differences between our positions, at least as stated in our respective foundational essays, are not as great as she seems to think.

Phillips devotes the first part of her essay to contrasting the modern liberal and communitarian frameworks. It is true that libertarianism is in many respects incompatible with the policy recommendations of communitarians. From the libertarian perspective, the latter often appear to be top-down attempts to micromanage the lives of citizens and further the centralization of political power, removing the accountability of state officials to the public they ostensibly serve. For example, news of several Washington scandals broke in quick succession in the spring of 2013: an alleged state Department cover-up of events surrounding the 2012 attack on the US diplomatic mission in Benghazi, Libya; the Internal Revenue Service's targeting of conservative political groups; and the Department of Justice's seizure of the Associated Press's phone records on national security grounds. Amitai Etzioni, long considered one of the leading voices of communitarianism, responded to this string of events by opining in *The Atlantic* that the United States needed measures to make impeachment of the President more difficult, some version of a state secrets act to restrict freedom of the press, and more restrictions on the activities of politically active non-profit organizations.[1] Libertarians fail to see how proposals like these, which can only further insulate the political class from public scrutiny and influence, are supposed to further justice or strengthen community.

Other major thinkers often associated with communitarianism, such as Alasdair MacIntyre and Marvin Olasky, are more palatable to libertarians because they recognize many of the failures of the modern, centralized state,

---

[1]   Amitai Etzioni, "Why it Should Be Harder to Impeach a President," *The Atlantic*, May 16, 2013, http://www.theatlantic.com/politics/archive/2013/05/why-it-should-be-harder-to-impeach-a-president/275929/ (accessed October 27, 2013).

and their proposals are designed to shift power and influence away from it to localities and voluntary associations. Phillips quotes MacIntyre to that effect, and in my own foundational essay I cite Olasky's work on the welfare state approvingly. From the libertarian point of view, though, communitarian proposals to empower civil society are often faulty because they may still rely on the state as the agency of supervision and funding.

One example of this phenomenon is found in the federal funding of the charitable work of faith-based organizations. This policy, which began in the presidency of George W. Bush, was shaped to a great extent by communitarian John Dilulio, although Dilulio later resigned in protest over the details of its implementation. Christian libertarians oppose this policy both because it attempts to promote the end of charity through the means of aggression and because the funded organizations (including many churches) run the very real risk of becoming dependent on federal funding and vulnerable to the undermining of their missions in the future. The libertarian insists that restoring churches and similar organizations to their central role in the provision of social welfare requires the removal of the state from that sphere.

However, I need not necessarily argue with Phillips about much of this, because she declares that she is not putting forward a comprehensive communitarian theory of justice, but rather a case in favor of virtue ethics. If she restricts herself to this more modest end, we may not find any necessary conflict between her position and libertarianism.

Let's begin with Phillips's first claim quoted above, that "libertarianism is more about the freedom of the individual than the common good of the society." Obviously this statement assumes a tension between individual freedom and the common good. This tension does indeed exist if one defines "individual freedom" as "the freedom of individuals to do whatever they want, including ways that damage the community, without any sort of restraint." However, this is not libertarianism's definition of individual freedom. Libertarianism insists only that restraints on individuals' actions and promotion of the common good do not include *aggression*. Other forms of restraint on individuals' actions rightly exist, such as contracts, covenants, and social pressure from voluntary associations.

We only need to reflect on the prevalence of homeowners' associations (HOAs) in neighborhoods across America to grasp how non-aggressive institutions can and do regulate people's behavior in the direction of the common good on a daily basis. These organizations already promulgate and enforce rules—with the consent of each homeowner, who has signed an agreement with the HOA—dealing with a variety of neighborhood issues, such as standards of lawn maintenance and noise pollution. However, from a libertarian perspective, nothing prevents a homeowners' association from instituting rules going well beyond what commonly exist today. As long as existing homeowners had agreed to the changes, the HOA could (for instance) mandate residents' weekly church attendance, charitable giving equivalent to a certain percentage of their net income, abstinence from recreational drug use, and a host of other behaviors. Prospective home buyers would weigh the costs and benefits of living under the HOA rules (including any impact of those rules on home prices in the neighborhood) when deciding where to live. Any homebuyer who disregarded the HOA's rules after signing an agreement to abide by them would be subject to whatever penalties were stipulated in that agreement.

Similarly, from a libertarian perspective, nothing prevents non-aggressive institutions (or networks of non-aggressive institutions) from operating on a scale beyond that of a single neighborhood with the goal of regulating people's behavior in the name of the common good. Community-, region-, and nation-wide organizations that grant credentials, accredited status, and designations of quality, e.g., the Good Housekeeping Seal of Approval, already flourish and would grow in importance in an environment of less regulation by the state. Think, for example, of organizations like the Better Business Bureau or the many "watchdog" groups that call attention to misconduct wherever they find it.

If Phillips insists that only the state can perform this task of advancing the common good, and that it must employ aggression to do so, then certainly the libertarian will find her position unacceptable. However, if we are willing to think outside the ideological straitjacket the modern state and certain classical thinkers impose on us, we can discover both in theory and history alternative methods of accomplishing that end.

Phillips also sees the fact that "libertarianism is a non-teleological, procedural approach" as a strike against it. My understanding, to the contrary, is that this procedural approach, if anything, makes libertarianism more, not less, compatible with virtue ethics. I noted more than once in my foundational essay that libertarianism is neither a comprehensive theory of justice nor one of ethics. To complete one's theories of justice and ethics, the libertarian must integrate a separate set of ideas that provides a teleology. The only requirement is that this complementary set of ideas be compatible with non-aggression. Does the virtue ethics tradition fulfill this requirement? Can we have a society characterized by virtue without having the state "see to it"? I say yes.

I may need to establish some credibility for making this claim. For many years I have taught courses in the Great Books to both undergraduate and graduate students. At my personal blog I am currently tracking a multi-year project of reading through more than 40,000 pages of the *Great Books of the*

Western World series.[2] The outstanding thinkers of the virtue ethics tradition Phillips cites—Plato, Aristotle, Saint Augustine, Saint Thomas Aquinas, in addition to many others—form part of my regular reading each week, as do Enlightenment thinkers such as Immanuel Kant. I have a deep appreciation for the insights of the classical and Christian virtue ethicists and agree with Phillips that something went wrong in the Enlightenment when it came to the study of ethics, despite whatever achievements the era may have enjoyed. To a great extent, I believe the virtue ethics thinkers "got it right" and the moderns "got it wrong."

It's true that most of the classical and Christian virtue ethicists envisioned a role for the state in the cultivation of virtue in its citizens, and this element of their thinking is largely incompatible with libertarianism. However, as Phillips notes, an advocate of virtue ethics need not endorse every position of these thinkers. I believe we can do without some of Aristotle's assumptions about the state,[3] just as we can do without his assumptions about the naturalness of slavery, while still keeping his insights regarding virtue as the result of habituation, as a mean between extremes, etc.

I should remind readers in closing that an endorsement of virtue ethics is not necessary for one to be a consistent libertarian. However, I hope that Elizabeth Phillips will concede that it is *possible* for someone who favors virtue ethics to be a libertarian as well.

---

[2] "Great Books Project," *The Western Tradition,* http://westerntradition.wordpress.com/great-books-project/ (accessed October 28, 2013).

[3] Early in his *Politics,* Aristotle proposes what I consider a faulty analogy and/or a fallacy of composition (treating the *polis* as a man) and continues to employ it/them throughout the work. Many later thinkers in the virtue ethics tradition repeated this error, which attributes thinking and acting to the state rather than to the individuals who control the state. This in turn encourages a glossing over of the oppression the state visits on its own subjects.

Virtue ethics: A liberal response

Daniel A. Dombrowski

Elizabeth Phillips is to be thanked for offering a clear and insightful summary of the relationship between the traditions of Christian justice and virtue ethics. However, I do not detect, as Phillips does, a necessary opposition between virtue ethics and liberal justice. Rather, the relationship between the two should be seen as one of inclusion wherein the two can be seen as quite compatible. In short, citizens in liberal democracies should be encouraged to live virtuous lives, but at two quite different levels that will be discussed momentarily.

As described above in my essay, there is an important distinction between a theory regarding the *comprehensive* autonomy of human beings, wherein human beings are viewed as essentially autonomous beings, and a theory regarding *political* autonomy, wherein human beings are seen as deserving the right to make up their own minds regarding political matters free from oppression, but who may not be autonomous in some more general sense. Phillips does not seem to notice this distinction, hence she seems to equate autonomy with comprehensive autonomy. By contrast, in political as opposed to comprehensive liberalism, one should be politically autonomous even if one believes via his or her comprehensive doctrine that one is subservient to divine love. Political autonomy, I contend, is a good thing even if comprehensive autonomy is an aggressive view that ought to be resisted. I think that this distinction could help to make Phillips's view more defensible.

I think that Phillips is premature in claiming that liberal political philosophy is essentially and problematically individualist in character. From the time of Locke's seventeenth-century classic, "An Open Letter Concerning Toleration," until the present, liberal freedoms have been seen as individual *as well as* associational in character. In a liberal society we would want not only individuals to flourish, but also groups of individuals: the Catholic Church, the Southern Baptists, atheist organizations, bowling clubs, Little League teams, etc. Nor is there an assurance that liberal societies will always progress. There is the possibility that liberal societies could regress as well as progress, despite what Phillips says. Political liberals agree with Phillips that human beings are conditioned by where and when they live. However, if they live in a society characterized by pluralism (which societies are not so characterized?), and if the human beings in question are capable of reasonableness and rationality (as described above in my initial essay), then there may very well be a need to temporarily engage in the sort of abstract reasoning found in a Rawlsian original position behind a veil of ignorance.

It is unfortunate that Phillips, along with some of the other contributors to the present volume, disparages the liberal attempt to articulate and defend the concept of universal human rights and, presumably, the praiseworthy organizations established in order to monitor the violation of universal human rights like Amnesty International and Transparency International. Who knows how many more people would have been murdered by governments around the world if it were not for liberal universalism? Who knows how many more people would still be living under political tyranny if it were not for the universal human rights movement? I think that we should be very skittish about any effort to slow down or dismantle the movement toward universal human rights, especially toward universal recognition of rights for women.

But perhaps I am being unfair at this point. Let us assume that Phillips and other critics of universal human rights agree that Amnesty International and Transparency International are doing good work. I am asking why we should value organizations such as these, which are, after all, motivated by a commitment to universal human rights. Political liberalism offers a philosophical basis that explains why these commitments are very important. When virtue theorists (and other contributors to this volume) disparage the concept of universal human rights it becomes unclear on what grounds they would affirm the sort of justice work done by these organizations.

Phillips wonders why liberals (she does not distinguish between comprehensive and political liberals) prioritize the right to the good. The proper response to this question is to ask in return: which view of the good? That of the agnostics/atheists or that of the theists? That of Catholics or that of Protestants? The reason why the right has priority to the good is that in contemporary liberal democracies there is no fair way to determine which of the competing conceptions of the good is *the* good. Of course there is a thin conception of the good that adherents to all reasonable comprehensive doctrines could affirm. This thin view of the good would deal with all of the basic goods (both material and formal) that any rational person would want, no matter which comprehensive doctrine is affirmed.

Despite these quibbles with Phillips's view, I think that rapprochement with her view can be achieved if we viewed communitarianism and virtue ethics as components of (or perhaps as friendly criticisms of) liberalism. On this view, a just society is one where members of various communities, with their various lists of virtues, could flourish as long as they respected members of other communities with their various virtues. Communities are, as Phillips notices, necessarily relatively small scale and local, as are the virtues embedded in practices that drive these communities. For example, the theological virtue of faith in theistic communities looms much larger than it does in communities of non-believers. Nonetheless, there are *some* virtues that one would hope to find in, indeed that should be required in, all reasonable citizens. Primary among these is tolerance of reasonable differences.

Here we can see the fruitful ways in which the relationship between virtue ethics and a liberal society can be understood. The Rawlsian assumption is that *all* citizens will be members of one or more communities (each with its own traditions, narratives, practices, and set of virtues), but not necessarily the *same* communities. Members of religious communities will be inculcated in, and expected to practice, the theological virtue of faith, but not all communities will take faith to be crucial. This is what I meant at the top of the present essay in saying that liberal political philosophy *includes* the best insights of communitarianism and/or virtue ethics. As before, however, there are also liberal virtues that should be practiced by all reasonable citizens, as in the toleration of reasonable differences among citizens. Another liberal virtue is the willingness to translate one's own comprehensive doctrine for all reasonable citizens when one's comprehensive doctrine is being used to justify the coercive apparatus of the state to restrict the freedom of others. These translation efforts are especially needed regarding the diminishment of liberty that is particularly controversial, as in restrictive abortion laws. Further, it should not escape our notice that justice itself is a liberal virtue toward which all citizens should strive.

I agree with Phillips that our approach to justice should not "begin and end" with procedural questions, but I think that such questions may very well be crucial. In our individual/associational lives we may begin with a concern with ultimate reality, but in political philosophy it makes sense to me, for both theoretical and practical reasons, to take such a concern off the table so as to talk about these later on and in a different context. One's response to ultimate questions may very well enable one to gain a prophetic voice that can benefit everyone in society, but only if such a prophetic voice meets the demands of the translation proviso wherein one's own comprehensive doctrine is made intelligible in public terms that any reasonable citizen might understand. This does not mean that we need to divorce love and justice. For example, in my above essay I have tried to make clear that a just society as designed by reasonable/rational agents in an original position behind a veil of ignorance is very close to the one that would be designed by purely benevolent agents. As Phillips rightly puts the point, love and justice are complementary norms.

In short, I am not convinced that communitarianism and/or virtue ethics are necessarily at odds with liberal justice. Indeed, the latter *includes* the best insights of the former at the associational level rather than at the level of pervasively pluralistic society as a whole. In different terms that allow for rapprochement with Phillips, the understandably teleological nature of virtue ethics, wherein human beings are directed to pursue their proper ends as human persons, should not be pushed so far as to say the virtue ethics is teleological in the sense that one set of virtues should be used to denigrate others from different traditions that involve different sets of virtues. Virtue ethics is, as Phillips herself rightly notes, deep, but it is not wide.

Virtue ethics: A libertarian response

Miguel A. De La Torre

If history is any guide, the virtues of Euroamericans have been at best damning, and at worst deadly to people of color. Marginalized communities have lived a history and continue to live a life of suffering, oppression, and death due to the social structures created by and for privileged Christians with virtuous characters. Not surprisingly, I feel a certain apprehension when virtue ethics is advocated. Seriously, how can communities of color trust Eurocentric virtues that have historically been anti-Semitic, racist, sexist and colonialist, and in many cases continue to be so?

No doubt Elizabeth Phillips does a superb job in elucidating what justice is from the perspective of virtue ethics. Phillips proposes that "while certain specific forms of feminism and liberation may be opposed to virtue ethics, and certain specific forms of virtue ethics can be inattentive to the questions raised by feminists and liberationists, there is no *necessary* opposition between these approaches." As seductive as her plea for a non-oppositional approach may be, still, I find liberative ethics and virtue ethics to be fundamentally irreconcilable—not because of the principles articulated, but because of how those principles have historically been implemented to mask injustice.

Yes, there are aspects of virtue ethics where agreement can be found, for example a suspicion of the Enlightenment project, a critique of liberal individualism, an emphasis on community, and recognition of the importance of narrative. Nevertheless, the lack of a prophetic ethic that challenges injustice is troublesome. One of the ethicists to whom Phillips refers, Stanley Hauerwas, makes it clear that "the current emphasis on justice and rights as the primary norms guiding the social witness of Christians is in fact a mistake."[1]

Phillips claims: "some critics insist that virtue is a concept which is too internal; it only addresses moral inclinations and aptitudes, not actual praxis." In spite of her protestation, Hauerwas writes: "Christian social ethics is not first of all principles or policies for social action, but rather the story of God's calling of Israel and the life of Jesus."[2] The primary task of Christian

---

[1]   Stanley Hauerwas, *After Christendom? How the Church is to Behave if Freedom, Justice, and a Christian Nation are Bad Ideas* (Nashville: Abingdon, 1991), 45.
[2]   Stanley Hauerwas, "The Gesture of a Truthful Story," *Theology Today* 42.2 (July 1985): 181–2.

social ethics "is not to make the 'world' better or more just, but to help Christian people form their community consistent with their conviction that the story of Christ is a truthful account of our existence."[3] No misunderstanding exists; there is a lack of praxes in Hauerwas's recovery of virtue ethics and there is an antipathy in establishing justice-based principles upon which to foster praxis.

For the liberationist, virtues are hollow whenever the struggle for justice is absent. Those forced to choose, due to their economic, social and political marginalization, between an ethically bad choice and ethically worse choices appreciate the ambiguity of liberative ethics. At times stealing may be the best ethical response even though those advocating virtues may construe stealing as a vice.

The liberationist's primary task in Christian ethics is societal change! Simply stated, if praxis is not emphasized, then ethics is not taking place. Although it is noble to envision how character ought to be formed and intended, and how this might influence behavior that might bring about change, it is only through praxis geared at dismantling the power and privilege bestowed upon Euroamericans and their churches that character develops. For what good is a virtuous character if oppressive structures remain? Just as faith without works is dead (James 2.20), so too are right virtues without right praxis meaningless.

It is interesting that Phillips claims that "while some political theorists and policy specialists have embraced the label of communitarianism, this was much more common in the 1980s and 1990s than it is today." One can only assume that she is speaking about Euroamericans, for among most communities of color engaged in the ethical discourse, the primary context from which analysis occurs is communitarian. Phillips indicates that her position "has some commonalities with the communitarian critique of liberalism," but she "in no way intends to offer a communitarian theory of justice to be implemented within the modern, liberal nation-state." Here then is the fundamental difference between the virtue ethics Phillips advocates and liberationist thought. Liberative ethics does offer a communitarian theory of justice rooted in the lives of the disenfranchised to be implemented within the modern state.

As much as Phillips insists that "virtue overcomes the individualism of modern ethics," those relegated to her underside would disagree. For virtue ethicists, personal piety or the demonstration of virtues is equated with ethics; yet, for disenfranchised communities, ethics can never be reduced

---

[3] Stanley Hauerwas, *A Community of Character: Toward a Constructive Christian Social Ethics* (Notre Dame, IN: University of Notre Dame Press, 1981), 112.

to such individual traits. No matter how personal we wish to make ethics, it always has a collective dimension. Ignoring or minimizing this dimension is the root of all injustice. While the state of individualistic being constitutes the basis of most Eurocentric ethical paradigms, for most US communities of color, the group is the cornerstone upon which they begin praxis, that is, begin to do ethics.

The danger of virtue ethics to marginalized communities is that Eurocentric moral visions often provide a virtuous way of conduct that ignores the complicity of the virtuous with the social structures that cause oppression. Regardless of the virtues expounded by the dominant culture, there exist self-perpetuating mechanisms of oppression that normalize and legitimize subjugation in the customs, language, traditions, values, and laws of the United States. Our political systems, our policing authorities, our judicial institutions, and our military forces conspire to maintain a status quo designed to secure and protect the power and wealth of the privileged few. In some cases, the virtue ethics advanced by the dominant culture appears to rationalize these present structures, protecting and masking the political and economic interest of those whom the structures privilege. In effect, it is a virtue ethics driven by the self-interest of Euroamericans.

Even though Phillips and other virtue ethicists recognize that complicity with these structures of privilege exists, they underestimate the extent of said complicity. Virtue ethics lacks a thorough analysis of how the power relationships within society construct and define what Euroamericans consider virtuous. Virtues, whether they be beneficial or detrimental to communities of color, are in the final analysis a construct of what the dominant culture deems to be morally good or evil. Confusing Eurocentric virtues with some set of universal virtues adoptable by communities of color creates a facade which masks power and reinforces Eurocentric Christian dominance in the discourse as well as the culture. Through the construction of virtues, employing the myth of objectivity, injustice within society is masked through legitimization and normalization.

Not surprisingly, a Eurocentric culture based on individualistic capitalism would label sloth as non-virtuous and "the Protestant work ethic" as virtuous. While it may be beneficial to be industrial rather than lazy, this so-called "virtue" has more to do with the economic good of society then Christian ethics. Being industrial may indeed be a good virtue for those residing in the dominant culture; sloth, at times, might prove more virtuous for oppressed groups. For example, antebellum slave masters preached against the vice of laziness in favor of the virtues of hard work, but the slave understood that sloth was an act of resistance against societal injustice and as such there was a moral obligation to do the least amount of work possible as a means of preserving her/his life and the lives of the rest of the slave community, even at the risk of being stereotyped.

In order for the dominant Euroamerican culture to reconcile the Empire that benefits them with their commitment to Christianity, Euramericans must construct an abstract ethic. As such, virtue ethics becomes a Eurocentric theory which is part of a larger metanarrative that privileges the vision and virtues of Euroamericans. As desirable as cultivating certain virtues may be, their implementation can ignore, and even justify, unjust social structures. Rather than effectively challenging these structures, virtues can lead individuals to create a false sense of righteousness. While liberationists agree that the language of virtues may lead to desirable behavior and that personal piety is good and should be pursued by all humans, such language has historically marginalized communities of color and continues to do so. For this reason, an uncritical adoption of the virtues of the dominant culture is detrimental to the marginalized specifically because they are constructed by those who benefit if all groups assimilate their moral standards.

Virtue ethics: A feminist response

Laura Stivers

According to Elizabeth Phillips, there is no *necessary* opposition between a virtue and feminist approach to justice. I would agree that the feminist approach I have described and the nuanced virtue approach that Phillips presents do indeed have many points of agreement. Of particular note are the following: our shared belief that a just procedure is not adequate and that a notion of the good (in particular flourishing lives for individuals and the common good) is necessary; our understanding of humans as intrinsically relational selves within community; our claim that justice-making is a never-ending process; and our understanding that justice is contextual and cannot simply be determined by a universal deontological or consequential formula valid for all situations. Justice theorists who take a Christian feminist approach would not take issue so much with what was said in this essay but rather with what was not emphasized. I will focus on four areas in which I think this virtue approach to justice pays insufficient attention.

First, while Phillips is aware that cultural worldviews shape who our society considers virtuous, she does not adequately deconstruct how people are currently marginalized by dominant understandings of virtue. She critiques Aristotle's defense of slavery and the Greek emphasis on the virtuous male citizen of the Athenian city-state. She notes that Aquinas and other Christian theologians from the past also had biases that limited their vision of virtue and justice. Phillips, in paying attention to the ways tradition shapes our character and practices, is not advocating for a static oppressive reality. She writes, "Tradition-constitutiveness should not be confused with traditional*ism*, or the harkening back to an established status quo as the best reality." In fact, she critiques some of what feminists have considered "masculine" ways of applying justice that include an emphasis on universalist generalizations, humans as detached and autonomous moral agents, and abstract rationality.

Despite these critiques, she does not emphasize how people today are routinely considered virtuous or unvirtuous based on what social group(s) define their identity. For example, would a teen prostitute, a transvestite, or a homeless addict ever be considered virtuous within our society? Women who "stay in their place" are considered virtuous (e.g. powerless), but derided for their uppityness or bitchiness if they display "masculine" traits of aggressiveness, especially in the workplace. And low-income single mothers, especially women of color, are routinely depicted as lazy and unable to raise children with good character (e.g., the welfare mom) despite actual reality. Almost everyone, including feminists, judge people by their character and make decisions based on these considerations of worthiness. Without a sophisticated deconstruction of the cultural meanings given to race, gender, class, sexual orientation, and other aspects of identity, a virtue theory of justice will contribute to keeping in place systems of privilege and oppression.

Not only are individuals considered virtuous or unvirtuous based on social identity, but areas of study and social practices are as well. Phillips argues that virtue ethics is not simply about having knowledge but about embodying the "practices, habit, instincts, and skills" required of any particular practice. She uses the example of being an artist (e.g. painting or playing piano), or "living the artistic life." In my youth I was taught in piano lessons that an artistic pianist played European classical music from male composers such as Bach, Beethoven, or Mozart. Similarly, revered painters in the Western world have overwhelmingly been European males. Generally, our understandings of the "cultured" or virtuous artistic life have not included art or artists from the margins. Aristotle's dictum that we know what is virtuous by noting what virtuous people do does not account for the ways we have structured virtue and vice in ways that privilege some and exclude others.

Second, Phillips fails to couple her defense of virtue with a full commitment to doing sophisticated analysis of how social structures and systems of power contribute to oppression. Phillips opts for a virtue approach to overcome the individualism of modern ethics and argues that virtue ethics is not only "ascribed to individuals, but to communities." Thus, a virtue approach to justice can be attentive to structural and political issues, not simply about individual character. Feminists who advocate for an "ethic of care" would agree. For example, Joan Tronto argues for a virtue ethic of care in relation to political life, claiming that care as a political idea "describes the qualities necessary for democratic citizens to live together well in a pluralistic society."[1] Phillips addresses both individual character and structural/political issues by relying on the traditional Christian dialectic between love and justice; love as the self-sacrificial and non-resistant personal virtue and justice as the public and coercive enforcement of rights. For her, these two

---

[1] Joan C. Tronto, "Care and Political Theory," in *The Canon and its Critics*, eds. Todd Furman and Mitchell Avila (New York City: McGraw Hill Publishers), 458.

values or virtues together will challenge oppression and bring forth inclusive communities of peace.

Christian feminists are not necessarily opposed to the dialectic of love and justice or even an emphasis on care as a political idea. They would caution, however, that without sophisticated structural analysis of power, privilege, and oppression in society, what is considered the "loving" or "just" action, policy, or practice might not in fact be so for those with the least power and privilege. Furthermore, they would contend that an explicit claim of justice for those on the underside is imperative. For example, what does a virtue-oriented approach to love and justice mean in relation to abortion policies and practices? Christian feminists would advocate a structural analysis of abortion with attention to power in deciding what justice entails, and while they would not assume that all women are of one mind as to what is empowering, they would give preference to the right of women to make choices about their own bodies based on historical and current policies and practices that serve to control and disempower women.

Third, Phillips's virtue approach to justice does not take the experience of those on the "underside" of history as the proper starting point for reflections about justice. Christian feminists argue that without an explicit emphasis on justice for those on the underside, virtue ethics will tend to favor the status quo. Aristotle's doctrine of the mean does not really encompass the prophetic radicality of people like Sojourner Truth, Dorothy Day, Cesar Chavez, Malcolm X, Martin Luther King Jr., and more central for the Christian tradition, Jesus. The extreme courage these people exhibited would not be a virtuous and moderate mean under Aristotle's theory but a vice. Feminist and liberationist approaches to justice will by necessity be disruptive of the status quo, and disruption is rarely seen as virtuous within society (except after prophets die and we turn them into Messiahs or Saints, or perhaps name a street after them). Phillips argues that "peace not retaliation" is one criterion for justice, but peace apart from disruption of oppression and privilege (e.g., justice-making) is not true peace. Phillips is concerned that her virtue approach to justice avoid the trap of hegemonic universalism, but the downside to this emphasis is that she does not stand up as strongly as she could for justice on the margins. She retrieves the values of equality and liberation from the biblical tradition and argues that the prophets and Jesus emphasized the needs and inclusion of those at the margins, yet the starting point for her virtue approach to justice is not primarily one of prophetic disruption.

Fourth, Phillips's virtue approach lacks the gender analysis necessary to ensure that the common good supports gender justice. Christian feminists agree with the emphasis within the virtue approach on flourishing lives and a common good. However, this emphasis is not enough. Without more explicit gender analysis (as well as analysis of race, class, sexuality and more) the so-called "common good" will not be fully inclusive. Feminists would clearly not support Yoder's vision of the "kingdom of Christ." Women have never fared well in a kingdom. While steering clear of universalism throughout her essay, Phillips nevertheless argues that in Christology there is a claim about universal humanity and that the universal is found in the particular person of Jesus Christ, not timeless abstractions. Christian feminists would argue, however, that our particular theological understandings of Christology are not universal but culturally constructed and that oppressive constructions based on a patriarchal worldview (or other oppressive ideologies) must be deconstructed and reimagined in empowering ways.

Clearly the worldview one brings and the standpoint one takes shape one's vision of flourishing life and the common good. Christian feminists would argue that not all visions or practices and policies are equally empowering for all. Thus, critical social analysis is crucial for justice-making. Christian feminists start from the particular reality of injustice, listen to what people identify as sources that thwart them from living flourishing lives, and work in solidarity with one another to promote justice. This labor is essential for knowing what actually promotes flourishing lives and the common good. Christian feminists do agree with the virtue approach to justice, however, that the process of justice-making will be on-going and will never by fully realized in our lifetime.

Libertarianism: A Concluding Response

Jason Jewell

I have learned several valuable things in the process of contributing to this volume. Not only have I become better acquainted with the perspectives of Rawlsian liberalism, feminism, liberation theology, and virtue ethics, but I have also realized that inaccurate preconceptions are difficult to overcome. In the individual responses I wrote to my colleagues, I strove to limit my points to the arguments they themselves made, but even so, I fear I may have misattributed certain beliefs, positions, or motives to them. Upon reading their responses to me, I can see that they experienced the same difficulty, whether or not they realized it.

In several places they have misstated or otherwise reached faulty conclusions about the libertarian position. Several times they rebutted positions I had not advanced or, in a few cases, had explicitly disavowed. Indeed, one contributor's response to me addressed almost none of the arguments I actually made, and instead offered a string of inaccurate statements about the history and content of libertarianism before digressing into a lengthy instance of the genetic fallacy[1] with an attack on the personal character of a seventeenth-century figure I had not relied on in my essay and had mentioned only once in passing. Another contributor mistakes my opening anecdote, intended merely to illustrate the difference between political activism and participation in civil society, to be a philosophical starting point for reasoning about justice and pronounces it gravely flawed. With so many misunderstandings and mischaracterizations in view, the task before me is thus challenging. I can correct only a few of these misapprehensions in the space allotted for this summation essay in the hopes that future dialogue might proceed on a sounder footing. I hope they will do the same.

However, before I reply to specific passages in the various replies to my foundational essay, I must point out that none of my colleagues has addressed certain key points I have advanced in support of the libertarian position. They have not seriously attempted to refute the characterization of the state as an institution based on the exercise of aggression. They offer no arguments from scripture or reason why Christians should have a benign

---

[1] The *genetic fallacy* is a fallacy of distraction in which the writer attempts to dismiss an argument, not on its merits, but on the basis of its alleged origin.

view of the state or why aggression is justifiable from a Christian perspective. They have not answered my objections to the supposed feasibility of actually bringing about their various visions of the just society through reliance on the state. To that extent, the rebuttals to my foundational essay leave much to be desired.

It seems I have been insufficiently clear in at least one area. Elizabeth Phillips writes of my "indiscriminately interchangeable uses of 'aggression,' 'coercion,' 'violence,' and 'force.'" She believes that libertarianism is about "freedom from aggression, coercion, and violence." This is not correct. Libertarianism seeks freedom from aggression only, the *initiation* (or threat of initiation) of physical violence against others' persons and property. Violent acts committed in self-defense are not aggression (so long as they are proportional). One may also come to the physical defense of a third party without being guilty of aggression. Thus all aggression is violence, although not all violence is aggression.[2] Phillips is simply equivocating in her depiction of Jesus as "aggressive," as she herself seems to recognize ("depending on how you define the term"). Similarly, she seems to employ a curious definition of "violence," claiming to be a pacifist who "categorically rejects the use of violence" while endorsing the collection of taxes (presumably at gunpoint, if necessary) to fund programs that advance her definition of the common good. From the libertarian perspective, this is a contradiction, a wish to aggress against others using the state as a proxy while trying to maintain a nonviolent stance.

Phillips and Daniel Dombrowski resist the characterization of welfare programs and public education as "institutionalized aggression" or as "equally coercive forms of force exerted by the state which are equivalent to violence"; for Phillips, "the mind boggles." Here again a clarification may be in order. I did not claim that these programs are institutionalized aggression. My references to the "coercive nature" of public education and social welfare programs were a reference to the means used to fund them (taxation), not to the programs' functions. Were the state to announce that henceforth these programs were to have their tax funding phased out and were to be funded in the future *via* subscription, lottery, or some other non-aggressive means, libertarians would no longer have any objections to them.[3]

Dombrowski appears to believe he has caught me in an inconsistency

---

[2] I confess to having used "violence," "coercion," and "force" more or less synonymously in my foundational essay to avoid monotony. The important thing to remember is that they all involve actual physical violence; nagging someone or driving a hard bargain in negotiating does not qualify as "force" or "coercion" in the sense I have used these words.

[3] For evidence of how privately funded education can serve the poor, see James Tooley, *The Beautiful Tree* (Washington: Cato, 2013).

when I did not refer to taxation as "theft" throughout my essay. Libertarians actually disagree on this question. Philosophical anarchists do believe that all taxation is morally equivalent to theft, but minarchists believe that limited taxation solely to fund the protection of citizens from aggression—what they consider the only legitimate state function—is philosophically justifiable and not aggressive. I have attempted to sketch libertarianism in a way that both camps will see as a reasonable representation of their views.

Laura Stivers and Daniel Dombrowski acknowledge my point that the state enables Big Business's oppression of ordinary people. However, they think we can reform this tendency out of the state and adopt, in Stivers's words, "public policies that limit corporate influence on the state so that democracy has a chance." The history of the relationship between Big Business and governments worldwide over the last 150 years offers little justification for such a hope. The phenomenon of "regulatory capture," of large firms gaining indirect control of the government agencies that regulate their respective industries, is pervasive and well known to political and economic historians. The captured agencies then set about, through regulation, erecting barriers to entry in those industries. The large, established companies can bear the cost of the regulations, but smaller companies cannot. The results are protection from competition for the large companies and higher prices for consumers. This pattern has played out with the major railroad companies and the Interstate Commerce Commission, pharmaceutical companies and the Food and Drug Administration, banks and the Federal Reserve, and investment banks and the Securities and Exchange Commission, to name just a few examples. More recently, Big Business has upped the ante and used the state directly against the consumer in attempts to force people to purchase their products.[4]

Dombrowski appears to misunderstand the libertarian position when he writes that I would "be willing to use state power to solidify property rights and to enforce anti-monopoly law." A minarchist would agree with the first part of this statement, but no libertarian would agree with the second. Antitrust and similar laws are part of the same network of cronyism I have just described. From the time they were passed early in the twentieth century, their primary function has been to allow private companies to wield state power against their more competent competitors, firms that did not actually enjoy monopolies. The only real monopolies that exist today result from positive grants the state confers by statute, such as those to the Post Office and the Federal Reserve. Revoking those grants would not be

---

[4] I refer here to the Affordable Care Act of 2010, which requires individuals to purchase health insurance or face substantial fines.

enforcing anti-monopoly law, but rather a withdrawal of an illegitimate privilege.[5]

Thus, when Stivers asks why libertarians "disregard… the dominating, and fast-growing power of multinational corporations," the short answer is, "They don't." Perhaps Stivers overlooked the passage in my foundational essay where I referenced the voluminous writings of libertarians that deal with the various problems caused by corporations, or the passage where I noted that many libertarians are opposed to the corporate model. Her equivocations on "theft" and "violence" may be clever, but I fear they obscure more than they illuminate. Her sweeping indictment of the "inherent violence of capitalism" in particular is problematic and needs a great deal of elaboration. I have no idea what she means by "capitalism," a term I intentionally avoided in my foundational essay because it is often employed by various authors to refer to radically different things.

Dombrowski and Stivers believe a libertarian environmental policy would be disastrous; Dombrowski inaccurately holds that libertarian principle demands an auctioning off of all national parks to the highest bidder. The reality is that pollution, erosion, and other environmental problems are nearly always more acute on state-owned land than on privately owned land. state ownership (or heavy regulation) of land actually brings with it poor incentives for land stewardship and use, and the "tragedy of the commons" is often the result.[6]

All four of my colleagues condemn libertarianism on the grounds that it will benefit a relatively few people. Elizabeth Phillips asks "*Cui bono?*" and answers "Those who are already the most free." Laura Stivers claims that libertarianism reinforces "societal structures that benefit only a minority." Daniel Dombrowski asserts that no rational person would choose libertarianism behind a veil of ignorance. Miguel De La Torre, pulling no punches, accuses libertarians of creating a "preferential option" for society's oppressors. In taking this line of attack, it seems to me that all four of them have shown their consequentialist colors, although some of them may resist that characterization. Christian libertarians say we must pursue visions of the just society through just (non-aggressive) means. My four interlocutors say with one voice: "We don't think those means will get us the results we want. Therefore we want the state to step in."

The truth is that I don't know exactly what would result from a libertarian

---

[5] See Dominick Armentano, *Antitrust and Monopoly: Anatomy of a Policy Failure* (Oakland, CA: Independent Institute, 1996).

[6] See Richard L. Stroup, "Free-Market Environmentalism," *The Concise Encyclopedia of Economics*, http://www.econlib.org/library/Enc/FreeMarketEnvironmentalism.html (accessed November 20, 2013).

political order where the role of the state is severely curtailed or entirely eliminated, and neither do my colleagues. Because the case for Christian libertarianism is not consequentialist, I have not emphasized the likely outcomes of political adherence to the Non-Aggression Axiom. However, as we look at world events for the last several decades, we see in country after country that when the state recedes, society advances, economies grow, and ordinary people escape from poverty.[7] On its face, this fact alone belies their contention that non-aggression helps only the few and the powerful. The answer to Phillips' *"Cui bono?"* is this: in the short term, everyone who is currently the victim of aggression; in the long term, everyone in the society.[8] I think it should be clear that in an environment of political non-aggression, the overall social and economic results will conform to the collective character of the people in that society. Perhaps my colleagues will deny this assertion and state that no matter how virtuous the "little guys" are in society, powerful and wicked interests will rise up and oppress them. In that case, I will remind them that right now, today, the state is the primary tool those interests use to oppress people, so it seems unlikely that removing it from the equation could make things worse than they are already.

On the other hand, we have plenty of evidence of what happens when the state is given more power and influence. In nearly every case, special interests and rent-seekers flock to it and in short order turn that increased power to their purposes.[9] This is why I asked in my foundational essay

---

[7] See, for instance, Julio H. Cole, "The Contribution of Economic Freedom to World Economic Growth, 1980–99," *Cato Journal* 23.2 (2003): 189–98, http://object.cato.org/sites/cato.org/files/serials/files/cato-journal/2003/11/cj23n2-3.pdf (accessed November 20, 2013). Even the much-derided Somalia—what libertarian has never been encouraged to move there?—has fared much better than its peer group of countries in sub-Saharan Africa since its state collapsed in 1994. See Robert P. Murphy, "Anarchy in Somalia," *Mises Daily*, June 30, 2011, http://mises.org/daily/5418/, accessed November 20, 2013; and Benjamin Powell, "Somalia: Failed State, Economic Success?" *The Freeman Online*, April 1, 2009, http://www.fee.org/the_freeman/detail/somalia-failed-state-economic-success#axzz2kpObNhBR (accessed November 20, 2013).

[8] Objections against non-aggression in the economic sphere most often follow from the mistaken belief that the only beneficiaries of a system of private property and free exchange are property owners. In reality, even those with little or no property benefit immensely from living in a society that has accumulated material wealth and increased productivity through these institutions. For example, an American working at the minimum legal wage earns more than enough money in one hour to pay for a day's subsistence diet. The same cannot be said of many developing countries where little accumulation of capital has taken place.

[9] Even the food stamp program in the United States has become a thinly disguised vehicle of corporate welfare. See "Profits from Poverty: How Food Stamps Benefit Corporations," Government Accountability Institute, September 2012. http://www.g-a-i.org/wp-content/uploads/2012/10/GAI-Report-ProfitsfromPoverty-FINAL.pdf (accessed November 20, 2013).

why, assuming the ends of my colleagues are desirable, they think it most effective (or even possible) to achieve them through the state. George Mason University economist Peter Boettke has written words to the effect that the only thing as dangerous as an economist with no moral sense is a moralist with no economic sense.[10] I do not accuse my colleagues of being the latter, but I am disappointed in their failure to address the issue of the negative incentives—what economists call "moral hazard"—their proposed policies create everywhere they are actually put into practice. Nonetheless, I would like to thank all the contributors to this volume for the opportunity to learn from them and for their attention to my own perspective.

---

[10] "Nothing, perhaps, is so dangerous intellectually in the policy sciences as an economist who knows only economics, except, I would add, a moral philosopher who knows no economics at all." Peter Boettke, "The Significance of Mises's *Socialism*," *Laissez Faire Today*, September 20, 2012. http://lfb.org/today/the-significance-of-misess-socialism/#sthash.z5ZNW6Lh.dpuf (accessed November 20, 2013).

Political Liberalism:
A Concluding Response

Daniel A. Dombrowski

In a way, the very success of the present volume indicates the degree to which all of us, even those who do not claim to be political liberals, have been morally improved as a result of the slow development over the past few centuries of politically liberal institutions. We need not despair regarding the fact that the authors in the present volume affirm comprehensive doctrines that are at least partially different from each other. But we can also agree that there is much work that needs to be done to build the realistic utopia for which political liberals hope.

A just society would clearly be one where the interests of women would not be denigrated, as Stivers correctly argues along with Susan Moller Okin and Martha Nussbaum. I remain confident that the views of Okin and Nussbaum are largely compatible with Rawlsian political liberalism. Indeed, both Okin and Nussbaum acknowledge a great debt to Rawls. Obviously there are conceptual problems that remain in this regard, as in the lack of justice in many families and in the uncompensated labor that occurs within many families that is gendered (reproductive labor) or that is often gendered (care of the young or the old or the infirm). Okin's solution, as Stivers notes, is not to repudiate, but to enhance and extend Rawls's original position in that we are to imagine in various ways behind the veil of ignorance that we might be the victims of sexism and uncompensated labor in families that tend to be gendered. As a result of such deliberation behind a veil of ignorance we would be provided an incentive to eliminate such unfair practices. That is, the sort of criticism leveled at Rawls by Iris Marion Young can be forestalled. As I read Rawls, reasonable/rational beings in the original position would obviously not choose oppressive ideologies or sexist practices because, behind the veil, one could easily be seen as the recipient of such injustice. As I see things, we are in the middle of a shift in our view of women that has largely been fueled by politically liberal ideals. The long-term prospects look quite bright even if sexism persists in the present. To repeat a point I have made before, however, although the hypothetical agents of construction in the original position are abstract, the Rawlsian view is *not* that human beings in reality are abstract. The original position is a tool in the overall effort to approximate a just society.

I would also like to emphasize that political liberalism is not to be confused with libertarianism or with what is sometimes called neoliberalism. I think that Jewell agrees with me regarding this claim in that both of us are a bit skeptical of the "Rawlsekians" who try to bring together in a grand way the politically liberal thought of Rawls and the *laissez faire*, libertarian thought of Friedrich Hayek. Granted, there are *some* ways in which Rawls and Hayek are compatible. For example, the first principle of justice described above in my initial essay, the equality principle, does *not* mean that a militant atheist has a fundamental civil liberty to enter a church and shout down a minister during a Sunday service (Jewell's example). Here political liberals and libertarians agree. But Jewell is correct to note that there is a fundamental disagreement between political liberals and libertarians regarding the second part of the second principle of justice, the difference principle. Regardless of Rawls's own religious beliefs (he started out as an Episcopalian and ended up as a religious believer without institutional affiliation), his stance provides philosophical support for the view found in different Christian denominations in terms of a preferential option for the poor, a stance that is not a real option among libertarians and their desire above all else to protect the rights and privileges of the well-to-do. This is perhaps uncharitable on my part, but this is how I view the libertarian position even when it is defended by those who are not well-to-do. As before, although in reality some people defend the libertarian view, no reasonable/rational person would do so in a fair decision making procedure behind a veil of ignorance. Further, Rawls is not as far away from natural law theory as Jewell thinks. Rawls largely *assumes* that human beings have rights and then tries to derive a fair decision making procedure to determine how these rights can be developed and ordered. But the source of these rights may very well be best explained on a natural law basis.[1]

As with libertarianism, there is much that links political liberalism and the liberationist approach. But there are also several claims in De La Torre's response to my essay that would have to be explained in more detail in order for meaningful rapprochement to occur. For example, I doubt if the liberationist approach is necessarily "diametrically opposed" to political liberalism, as De La Torre alleges. If it were so opposed, then I would fear the implications of the liberationist approach. Is the state to be identified with a single comprehensive doctrine (*the* truth)? If so, are those who affirm

---

[1]   See my *Rawlsian Explorations in Religion and Applied Philosophy* (University Park: Penn State University Press, 2011).

different comprehensive doctrines from the official one to be harassed, as was the case in the Soviet Union and as is the case in China? I doubt if De La Torre has this in mind. Further, De La Torre moves back and forth between critiques of libertarianism and political liberalism as if there were no differences between the two. But there *are* significant differences between the two, as Jewell and I notice. Or again, how is political liberalism complicit in empire building? Rawls's book *Law of Peoples* clearly indicates an opposition to wars to expand territory or to build empire. However, De La Torre's challenges to political liberalism are welcome in the sense that they force a defender of political liberalism to point out the radical implications of the view. As I have mentioned previously, a consistent application of Rawlsian principles would lead to the most egalitarian society on the face of the earth today, even when the Scandinavian social democracies are considered, and especially when Marxist governments are considered wherein there is no real egalitarian distribution of political power and rights. It is odd that De La Torre accuses Rawls of being both overly subjectivistic, on the one hand, and of engaging in abstract theorizing that tries to achieve some sort of objectivity regarding our concept of justice, on the other. Finally, there is no textual support whatsoever that the Rawlsian veil of ignorance could be used to justify white slavery of blacks, as De La Torre suggests. Nonetheless, I am glad to hear that the biblical Greek *dike* is routinely translated as *justicia* in Spanish. This really is good news!

Phillips and I are on the same page regarding the need to show the compatibility of agapic love and justice. This is Rawls's view as well. Further, Phillips and I are not as far apart as she thinks regarding the need for a theory of the good. The problem is that *in politics* we cannot, if we wish to be fair to all reasonable citizens, stipulate in any great detail which theory of the good should prevail. It must be admitted that the Rawlsian view that I defend must be "freestanding," but this crucial word could mean one of two quite different things. One meaning is that justice would be free of *any* view of the good. Phillips is correct to wonder if this is even possible. But another meaning is that the politically liberal understanding of justice would be freestanding in the sense that it could be embedded in any one of a number of views of the good so long as they are reasonable (i.e., so long as they are compatible with what would be decided in a fair decision–making procedure). This versatility itself is a good thing. Citizens in a liberal democracy can affirm religious, nonreligious, utilitarian, Kantian, etc., concepts of the good.

Constructive engagement with Phillips can be made regarding her very interesting comments regarding violence. I take it as a given that the wars of religion in the early modern period were horrendous and that the rise of liberal political philosophy was the primary cause of their resolution as people came to realize that human beings could live together in peace without reaching agreement on ultimate questions. This case has been made many times before. But Phillips has several queries. First, she wonders whether one can come up with an airtight definition of "religion." Even she notices, however, that by using the Rawlsian term "comprehensive doctrine" rather than "religion," we can avoid the problems associated with trying to find the necessary and sufficient conditions for "religion." I am more than willing to admit that Marxism, for example, may very well be a comprehensive doctrine, as is utilitarian capitalism.

Second, she thinks that I am in favor of a secular state meant to replace the dangerous religious one. This is not my view. It is true that I think that a just society is, in one sense, post-religious in that it would not be fair to have a religious comprehensive doctrine be the official one to which every knee should bend. But it is crucial to note that I also think that it is, in another sense, post-secular, in that a state that was officially laicist or officially atheistic would be (and has historically been) a disaster. Here Jürgen Habermas, Rawls, and I are in agreement. What we need is a freestanding conception of justice that does not treat unfairly *any* reasonable citizen, whether he or she defends a religious comprehensive doctrine or a nonreligious one. As before, this freestanding view is not divorced from a concept of the good altogether, but can be inserted into any one of several rival concepts of the good so long as they are reasonable. For example, we can talk about roughly the same phenomenon of human dignity in terms of human beings being made in the image of God or in terms of their possessing basic human rights.

Phillips thinks that liberalism has had a hand in the major wars of the twentieth century. Here I do not exactly understand her view in that in World War II, for example, neither Nazi Germany nor Imperial Japan was a liberal democracy. Far from it! However, Phillips rightly notes that whereas liberal democracies have never gone to war with each other, they have at times fought unjust wars against non-liberal peoples. Rawls himself, although he fought in World War II and thought that the Allies fought for a just cause in that war, was a staunch opponent to the American war in Vietnam. This latter war was, *contra* Phillips, not so much an extension of political liberalism as a violation of its principles as articulated by Rawls in *Law of Peoples*.

Although Phillips is on the mark in her opposition to unjust wars waged by liberal democracies, as in the American war in Vietnam, this legitimate opposition should nonetheless be contextualized. As described in Steven Pinker's book *The Better Angels of Our Nature*,[2] the overall effect of liberal

---

[2] Steven Pinker, *The Better Angels of Our Nature: Why Violence Has Declined* (New York: Viking, 2011).

democracy on world history has been very positive, hence I do not think that the felicitous things that I say about political liberalism and the diminution of violence are hyperbolic, as Phillips alleges. Even when atrocities like those that occurred in Vietnam are factored in, the percentage of people killed in war when compared to the total population of the world has in fact dropped. That is, the *Pax Americana*, as inadequate as it is, is nonetheless a peace that is quite remarkable. Despite talk about The American Empire, we are, believe it or not, living through one of the most peaceful periods in human history from 1945 until the present. Brace yourself: it may very well be *the* most peaceful period in human history when the total number of people in the world is compared to the percentage of people who die violent deaths, again as detailed by Pinker.

The role that Christian thinkers (like Martin Luther King) or those that come from the Christian tradition (like John Rawls) have played in the development of peaceful ways of dealing with differences should not be underestimated. But there is obviously no room for complacency, given the fact that distribution of wealth is still scandalously unjust and the extent of human violence is still brutally high. In response to Phillips's query regarding my own view, it is that the pacifistic implications of political liberalism are still underappreciated, even by politically liberal thinkers themselves, including Rawls, who was a just war theorist.[3] Political liberalism, like Christianity, is still on the way.

---

[3] See my *Rawlsian Explorations in Religion and Applied Philosophy*, chapter 2. Also see my *Christian Pacifism* (Philadelphia: Temple University Press, 1991).

Liberation Theology:
A Concluding Response

Miguel A. De La Torre

Scholarly debates are always exhilarating. The clash of concepts usually moves us to a deeper and more nuanced understanding of important ideas. The richness of a book like this is the bringing together of very different thinkers to discuss among themselves what is the meaning of justice. With the mindset of an academic, I carefully read the responses to my essay as advanced by my colleagues. As I read these responses I was reminded of G. C. Spivak's important question, "Can the Subaltern Speak?"[1] More importantly, if the subaltern does speak, will anybody listen? All too often, subalterns are dismissed as being angry, unscriptural, lacking academic acumen, or when all else fails, Commies.

It is humorous that several of the critiques revolved around my usage of the word Eurocentric. While some had difficulty understanding what was meant by my usage of the word; there appeared no confusion when words like Latin American, Hispanic, Black, etc., were used. While we all know what is meant when the noun "Latin American," "Hispanic," or "Black," is used as an adjective before words like ethics or theology; we become confused when Eurocentric is employed in similar fashion. And yet, to name what is seldom named unmasks how the construction of ethics is an arbitrary venture that makes the views of Euroamericans normative at the expense of the marginalized. Far too often the marginalized then develop a false consciousness that supports these ethical paradigms that are detrimental to their very being. Eurocentric ethics employs institutionalized violence to maintain it superiority and legitimizes power and privilege.

Ethical assimilation to Eurocentric models, whether they be total or partial, destroys the worldview of the marginalized by supplanting it with a new Eurocentric way of being. Still, some scholars of color recognize that even that which should be rejected remains part of who they are as a people. The challenge is how to delineate and reject those parts of Eurocentric ethics

---

[1] Gayatri Chakravorty Spivak, "Can the Subaltern Speak?" *Marxism and the Interpretation of Culture*, eds. Cary Nelson and Lawrence Grossberg (London: Macmillan, 1988), 271–313.

with which there can be no compromise or reconciliation (i.e., complicity with the US Empire) and consider those segments of Eurocentric analysis with which we can converse. To that end, liberative ethics becomes an attempt to move away from Eurocentric religious capital toward a grassroots spiritual capital.

Another word which I used in my essay which caused dissonance was the word Empire. Not understanding why Eurocentric ethics is first and foremost a product of empire and colonialism becomes the main reason why liberative ethics, to many Euroamericans, makes little sense. While some within the dominant culture may question the appropriateness of the usage of the word Empire, the wretched of the earth have no problem whatsoever in recognizing that the cultural influences of the Greek Empire, the imperial might of the Roman Empire, the religious supremacy of the Holy Roman Empire, and the global reach of the British Empire all pale in comparison to the cultural dominance, the military might, the capitalist zeal, and the global influence of the US Empire. The term "empire" can no longer be narrowly defined as the physical possession of foreign lands that must pay tribute. Rather, empire is a globalized economy that provides economic benefits to multinational corporations whose influences are secured through the military might of one superpower.

An ethic that normalizes and legitimizes Euroamerican empire, an ethic that remains silent and impotent during a history of conquest, enslavement, and neoliberalism represents the ethical manifestations (conservative and/or progressive) that refuse to challenge the status quo. This is what I define to be Eurocentric ethics. So that there can be no misunderstanding: Eurocentric ethics are any ethical models or paradigms that legitimatize social structures based on a worldview that fails to question how power relationships privileges the social location of people of a certain race, ethnicity, gender, class and/or sexual identity.

When, however, Euroamericans stand in solidarity with the colonized and struggle with them to overturn the injustices that flow from ethical paradigms that privilege their race and class, then I will argue they are no longer engaged in the Eurocentric project of maintaining and sustaining empire. This is not, as Stivers proposes, "dualistically creating an 'enemy' discourse of Eurocentric justice;" rather it is simply an unambiguous rejection of any and all Eurocentric discourses of justice which fails to critically analyze their own complicity with empire building. And yes, just as some Euroamericans have found their salvation in standing against empire ethics, so too have some people of color found a false salvation in parroting Eurocentric ethical principles, even when they have been detrimental and damning to the disenfranchised communities from which they come.

Finally, some of the respondents to my essay challenged me to explain what a society shaped by liberative impulses would look like. This is difficult to describe because a liberative justice-based society is a utopian concept, best illustrated by Isaiah's messianic dream where "the wolf shall stay with the lamb, and the leopard shall lie with the kid" (11.6). Even though liberative ethics stands in open rebellion against the "opium" of otherworldliness, the "utopias" of Isaiah and of the marginalized are still affirmed with an open-eyed awareness of the present power structures, all the while moving toward a future reality.

A justice-based society is not a utopian dream based on the fantasy world of imagination; it is usually a feet-on-the ground utopianism anchored in the realism of the disenfranchised. Gustavo Gutiérrez insists that pessimism comes from reality because reality is tragic, while optimism comes from action because action can change reality.[2] Commenting on an ethic of solidarity, Gutiérrez claims:

> Today, more than ever, is the time to remember that God has given to all humanity what is necessary for its sustenance. The goods of this earth do not belong exclusively to certain persons or to certain social groups, whatever their knowledge or place in society may be. The goods belong to all... We can call this a utopian perspective, but in a realistic sense of the word, which rejects an inhuman situation and pursues relationships of justice and co-operation between persons.[3]

Hence, the desire for a utopian justice-based society is not a flight from present reality to an illusionary world; it is a struggle to perfect our reality and prevent the status quo from absolutizing itself. The utopianism called for by liberationists is not some naive idealism where a future perfect social order is established. Utopianism, as understood here, is a rejection of the present social order grounded in structures designed to perpetuate heterosexism, racism, sexism, and classism. It protests the way things presently are, and imagines, based on the reality of the oppressed, how society can be restructured to create a more just social order. The function of utopian thought is to guide praxis.[4]

As stimulating as intellectual ethical discourse concerning what justice

---

[2] Gustavo Gutiérrez, *The Power of the Poor in History*, trans. Robert R. Barr (Maryknoll, NY: Orbis Books, 1984), 80–1.
[3] Gustavo Gutiérrez, "Liberation Theology and the Future of the Poor," in *Liberating the Future: God, Mammon and Theology*, ed. Joerg Rieger (Minneapolis: Fortress Press, 1998), 121.
[4] Miguel A. De La Torre, *Doing Christian Ethics from the Margins* (2nd Edition) (Maryknoll, NY: Orbis Books, 2014), 54–6.

can and cannot be, more important for liberative thinkers is the actual transformation of society toward a more just-based condition. This is never to dismiss nor demean the work of ethical contemplation. Rather, it is to locate it in its proper place, as a reflection of praxis—not the foundation or source from which praxis flows.

Scholars not in solidarity with those yearning and crying for justice cannot comprehend this logic, so to illustrate the point, allow me to provide an example of the indecent liberative ethics with which I ended my first essay, an ethics *para joder*. Reverend Fife is best known for his felony conviction during the 1980s as one of the architects of the Sanctuary Movement.[5] These days he is one of the leading activists of the organization No More Deaths, responsible for walking the migrant trails providing food, water, and medical attention to the undocumented traversing those trails of terror in December, 2012, *La Lucha Sigue* Conference was organized by Borderlinks, Samaritans, and the 1980 Sanctuary Movement. Representatives from over a dozen immigrant rights groups participated. I had the honor of joining them as a keynote speaker explaining liberative ethics, specifically an ethics *para joder*.

According to Fife, what was useful about an ethics *para joder* is that it provided activists with new ways of thinking, moving the conversation away from repeating past praxis simply because these were the liberative praxis always employed. Ethics *para joder* allows us to imagine new possibilities. Fife provided a concrete example. Representatives from different immigrant right groups gathered to discuss how to implement liberative ethics. Till now, when they tried to think of what to do, they were trapped with having to figure out what dramatic change would look like and then, what actions needed to be taken to get to that end goal. When they accepted the hopelessness of the situation, they were emboldened to simply screw with the system, subverting the prevailing oppressive structures. "Screwing with structures of oppression is our calling," according to Fife, "as we prepare and wait for the movement for justice to take off. Hopelessness frees us to imagine creative ways to struggle for this justice."

The group decided to screw with Operation Streamline, implementing as their methodology, the liberative practice of *jodiendo*. Operation Streamline

---

[5]   During the 1980s, US policies in Central America created military conflicts in places like El Salvador and Guatemala. On March 24, 1982, Reverend Fife, pastor of Southside Presbyterian Church in Tucson, Arizona, along with five churches in San Francisco, declared their worship space a sanctuary for those fleeing the violence in El Salvador and Guatemala. Eventually, some 400 religious congregations and twelve universities joined the sanctuary movement, establishing safe havens where over 70,000 refugees could find refuge.

is designed to quickly move undocumented immigrants through the legal system. Prior to 2005, those who entered the country without proper documentation were not prosecuted but were simply repatriated. However, since then, an elaborate legal procedure has been created ensuring that before the undocumented migrant is deported, a criminal record is established. To house one of them costs taxpayers $2,000 a month, more than the approximately $850 we spend to educate a child in our public schools. Not surprisingly, prison corporations who benefit by incarcerating undocumented immigrants spends millions lobbying politicians to pass stricter anti-immigrant legislation. Operation Streamline, besides being oppressive to the undocumented, fuels a billion–dollar prison industry.

It is hopeless to think that a few activist organizations will defeat the prison-industrial complex and establish a just society. But the focus of these activists was no longer on how to shut down Operation Streamline forever, but rather, how to screw with the system. To that end, they have been successfully *jodiendo*. Recently, in early October, 2013 their actions of linking their arms around prison transport buses carrying the undocumented to trial resulted in temporarily shutting down Interstate 10 and bringing attention to the travesty of this justice system. They also locked themselves around the federal court entrance. They succeeded in temporarily shutting down Operation Streamline as the seventy undocumented were deported without trials or creating criminal records for them. More important, the victims of Operation Streamline witnessed that they do not stand alone; a faith community accompanies them.

This example is offered to underscore what is crucial in the doing of justice from a liberative perspective. All the intellectual contemplation about justice is meaningless if it is not directly connected to the real-life trials and tribulations of the disenfranchised. If praxis is not transforming society then what is being contemplated fails to be ethics.

Christian Feminism:
A Concluding Response

Laura Stivers

Jason Jewell, responding from a libertarian perspective, argues that the concepts of structural injustice and oppression are foreign to scripture and to the traditions of Christianity. Daniel Dombrowski, from a Rawlsian perspective, is concerned that approaches to justice ought to be neutral in relation to religion and the private realm of the family (except in cases of abuse). Elizabeth Phillips, from a virtue standpoint, is concerned that Christian understandings of justice not simply reframe secular or non-Christian sources. Miguel De La Torre and I are largely in agreement in our respective essays, so for the purposes of this conclusion I intend to reply to these substantive critiques of Christian feminism. I will focus the bulk of my concluding essay, however, responding to the libertarian premise that addressing cultural, institutional, and structural oppression is not relevant to a theory of justice.

Christian feminists agree with Dombrowski that a concept of justice ought to be fair to all, religious believers and non-believers. Justice-making and solidarity with those who are oppressed and exploited requires co-operation between people of different traditions and worldviews. Furthermore, there must be some standards of justice external to all religious or secular traditions that serve to critique forms of injustice. Christian feminists certainly want to critique patriarchy in the Christian tradition. They can use norms within the tradition to do so, but these norms are not particular to Christianity.

Christian feminists agree with Phillips that hope for a just world resides in God(dess). They are less concerned, however, about whether they have "baptized" non-Christian perspectives in Christian language and concepts. They are more focused on the responsibility we have as disciples of Christ for treating each person as sharing in the image of the Divine and for challenging and changing cultural, institutional, and structural forms of injustice. In the Christian feminist approach that I have outlined, prophetic resistance to structural forms of injustice and oppression is central to scripture, even if the prophetic response, as Phillips notes, has often been "denied or neglected" within the Christian tradition.

Christian feminists, along with liberationists, argue that justice for women and other groups that are oppressed will entail more than formal equality (e.g., claims to equal opportunity) in the public realm. They also argue that injustice is not primarily an issue of individual discrimination. In this respect, Christian feminists depart sharply from the libertarianism that Jewell defends. Jewell seems to imply that being treated with indignity and disrespect is simply a matter of being insulted by people with bad manners. The implication of Jewell's response to Christian feminism seems to be that all forms of injustice can be reduced simply to the (im)moral actions of individuals. I disagree. Indeed, the critical difference between libertarianism and the Christian feminism I advocate may well be that libertarians deny that cultural and structural oppression—oppression that is systemic and not reducible to the actions of individual agents—are realities that just societies must address. While libertarians treat oppression as the mere byproduct of individual choice, Christian feminists argue for a more dynamic, complex understanding of the sources of oppression that hinder human flourishing.

Granted, Jewell's reduction of personal circumstance to individual choice or personal virtue is quite common in modern parlance. While substantial evidence shows many societies come up short in terms of equality and opportunities for democratic participation, public opinion often holds that personal traits rather than structural factors explain success or failure. If people have power and wealth we assume they must be people of superior intellect, diligence, and character who used their talents wisely. In turn, we assume that people who are impoverished and marginalized must not have the innate capacities to take advantage of opportunities offered. No attention is paid to the structural inequities that gave certain groups a head start and kept certain groups from cultivating capacities for success. Instead, people on the margins are accused of lacking the skills, intellect, or middle-class mindset that they never had the opportunity to acquire. We view people as autonomous individuals independent of their social location.

The better-off believe they have gained their social position through hard work and diligence alone because they are usually unaware of their unearned privileges. The libertarian vision of wealth generated through personal initiative is, no doubt, a deeply soothing one to those who are already well off. But too often, we who are privileged are unable to step out of our own social location and see that others do not have the same privileges. Not everyone grows up in safe neighborhoods, is treated with equal respect in commercial stores, or fits in with the dominant cultural image of a successful person. Social theorist Peggy McIntosh speaks of these privileges as "an invisible package of unearned assets that I can count on cashing in each day, but about which I was 'meant' to remain oblivious."[1] If the better-off are ignorant of their "backpack of assets," then they are more apt to believe there is a level playing field for all. They will often point to the handful of people who made it without unearned privileges, like Oprah Winfrey, to prove that equal opportunity exists.[2]

Women and other marginalized groups routinely deal with forms of cultural oppression that serve to disadvantage them. For women, the primary form of cultural oppression is the devaluation of anything that is considered "feminine." Biblical interpretations, even now, routinely see women as helpmate to men (Gen. 2.18-23), not as autonomous (Gen. 2.21-3), and, in the extreme, as responsible for sin in the world (e.g., Eve temped Adam, Gen. 3.6). This legacy, whether in the form of patronizing patriarchy or outright misogyny, continues to be oppressive for women today. Apart from the liberation perspective, the theories of justice represented in this book do not address cultural oppression. They do not emphasize the ways that people are judged and treated in relation to the socially constructed meanings about them based on their gender, race, class, sexual orientation, or physical and mental ability. Nor do they note that people internalize cultural messages of dominance and submission. It is problematic to base justice on individual merit when the standards for meritocracy preference male, White European culture, middle- to upper-class, heterosexual, and able-bodied people. Even professing a color- or gender-blind system is not sufficient because it masks the fact that we often do not recognize when we have constructed gendered or raced understandings and judgments.

For women, oppression is not simply an issue of being devalued by society, but also an issue of internalized meanings and self-conceptions that shape their individual choices. Feminist philosopher Susan Okin explains, for example, how through socialization women at a young age internalize understandings about what it means to be female that set them up for vulnerability within marriage, and after marriage (considering the high divorce rate these days). The culture places more emphasis on marriage for girls than boys. The result is that women put a high value on having a good marriage and family life, which in turn heavily influences their occupational aspirations. They are more likely to "choose" work that accommodates their

---

[1] See Peggy McIntosh, "White Privilege: Unpacking the Invisible Knapsack," in *The Meaning of Difference: American Constructions of Race, Sex and Gender, Social Class, Sexual Orientation, and Disability,* eds. Karen Roseblum and Toni-Michelle C. Travis, 5th edition (New York: McGraw-Hill, 2008), 368.

[2] See "10 Rags to Riches Billionaires," *Smart Money Daily* website, July 10, 2008, http://www.smartmoneydaily.com/celeb-finance/10-rags-to-riches-billionaires.aspx (accessed October 30, 2013).

role as a parent and as a consequence end up in a more vulnerable economic position than men.[3] The libertarian, Rawlsian, and, to a lesser extent, virtue theories of justice assume a "neutral" agent who makes choices without attention to the ways we are socialized based on our social location.

From a Christian theological perspective, we are *all* created in the image of God. The meaning of this claim can be interpreted in different ways, but for Christian feminists, it means we are all created with equal human dignity and with a need for connection and relationship. Christian feminists argue that the core of Jesus's ministry was centered on making this theological concept a reality. He challenged the purity codes in his culture that humans had constructed to elevate some over others. Women, lepers, tax collectors, and anyone with a disability were considered unclean or impure, yet Jesus purposely chose to be in relationship with them. He was challenging the oppressive cultural messages of his time, just as Christian feminists argue we ought to do today if we take seriously Christian discipleship.

In addition to cultural oppression, women and other marginalized groups experience forms of institutional oppression as well as structural oppression that negatively affect their capability to flourish. Institutional oppression ranges from more overtly oppressive policies such as women not being allowed to serve in certain professions to less obvious institutional realities like female full-time workers making only 77 cents for every dollar earned by men in the United States.[4] Similar forms of institutional oppression can be cited for all marginalized groups. Christian feminists argue that it is not productive to focus on whether cultural or institutional forms of oppression are the product of bad intentions. Rather we should channel our energy into changing our societal worldviews and our institutions so that they are conducive for everyone to be capable of flourishing. The Liberation, Rawlsian, and Virtue theories of justice all have some affinity for just outcomes, not simply a just process between individuals; however, achieving just outcomes will require more than either Rawls's difference principle or Aristotle's doctrine of the mean can produce.

Structural oppression, as I outline in my chapter, is the hardest form of oppression to identify or to envision changing because it is the result of everyday decisions and actions made by people, many of whom do not intend to oppress anyone. Structural oppression is a series of patterns and positions that become visible only when one takes a broad look at the actions of individuals. As Iris Marion Young points out, blaming individuals

---

[3]   Susan Okin, "Vulnerability by Marriage," in *The Feminist Philosophy Reader*, eds. Alison Bailey and Chris Cuomo (Boston: McGraw Hill Publishers, 2008), 600–22.

[4]   "Pay Equity and Discrimination," Institute for Women's Policy Research, http://www.iwpr.org/initiatives/pay-equity-and-discrimination (accessed October 30, 2013).

for injustice, as perspectives that frame prejudice and discrimination on an individual level tend to do, is inadequate since we would not consider most people, while participating in oppressive structures, to be blameworthy. Furthermore, we identify the results of structural oppression by outcomes. For example, I don't think anyone would say I was acting oppressively when I chose to live in a well-off suburb over a poor inner city so that my children would have good schools and a safe place to play. Yet structurally neighborhoods are segregated by class and race in our society, offering benefits and privileges to some and not others. The non-moral (not necessarily immoral) choices that people make can contribute to social patterns that are harmful to people. The concept of structural injustice might be hard to get a handle on, but it is not a concept that "stretches to encompass any social outcome that an author dislikes" as Jewell claims. Outcomes of massive inequality and oppression negatively affect many people and are not something people simply "dislike." While our actions can contribute to structural injustice, we can also work to change the way things are structured in our society. For example, we can organize with others to make sure *all* children have good schools and safe neighborhood to play in. Structural inequality is not inevitable but a result of policies, and can therefore be challenged and changed.

Focusing primarily on "legal equality for women" as libertarian feminists do will not address these unjust outcomes. Simply telling a poor single mom like Sandy (example from my chapter) that she has no legal barriers and can choose to live in my neighborhood does not address all the actual barriers, such as expensive housing and inadequate public transportation that prevent her from doing so. And offering Sandy charity from voluntary organizations like food banks, while perhaps necessary to meet her basic needs, does not constitute being "treated with dignity and respect." Funding all schools well, paying everyone a living wage, creating clean neighborhoods with ample green space, and promoting quality public transportation to all areas are examples of policies and practices that would offer Sandy and her children dignity and respect and would support her ability to be capable of flourishing. Humans will not always flourish despite a supportive environment and people can always be blamed for misconduct, but to assume that the poverty individuals find themselves in is due to unvirtuous behavior is simply to blame the victims without addressing societal injustice and oppression. Addressing cultural, institutional, and structural oppression is about promoting substantial equality and justice, not simply formal opportunity and equality. Faith in a liberating God/dess is our source of hope that such justice is possible and the formation of deep relationships in our solidarity with one another makes prophetic justice-making a process of joy.

Virtue Ethics: A Concluding Response

Elizabeth Phillips

Sincere thanks to my co-authors for their responses. I will first reply to items in their responses which I wish to challenge, and then to criticisms with which I agree, seeking both to explain and critique my essay in light of these criticisms.

Daniel Dombrowski suggests that I do not recognize the distinction between political and comprehensive autonomy. I do, and am very pleased to see that Dombrowski and I agree in our rejection of comprehensive autonomy, which suggests that human beings are essentially autonomous in their being. However, we will still be at odds in our articulations of political autonomy. Political autonomy has its place, but in my approach it must be inseparably related to human interdependency and to the common good. Dombrowski also states there is no "assurance that liberal societies will always progress," because, "liberal societies could regress as well as progress, despite what Phillips says." I did not claim that liberal societies always progress, rather that liberalism in general sees human history as a story of progress. This is not my own contention; as cited, this comes from Song's summary of the traits of liberalism. Finally, Dombrowski laments that I disparage the "liberal attempt to articulate and defend the concept of universal human rights." I am entirely at a loss here, as in no part of my essay are human rights mentioned.

Jewell suggests my contention that "libertarianism is more about the freedom of the individual than the common good of the society" is based on a misunderstanding of libertarian freedom, which (he argues) includes "non-aggressive" restraints on individual freedom in the interest of the common good. Such "non-aggressive" restraints may arise from "contracts, covenants, and social pressures from voluntary associations." First, if individual freedom is only constrained by voluntary associations, why should we expect libertarian individuals to voluntarily constrain their own interests in favor of others? Second, this erroneously assumes that everyone is already equally free in their ability to exercise voluntary choices, as I have already discussed. Finally, how does libertarianism account for associations which limit individual freedom and are non-voluntary? My infant daughter's individual freedom may someday be limited by the demands of caring for aging parents. Are we aggressors for binding her in this involuntary association which is the human family?

Jewell's example of homeowners' associations (HOAs) is an especially good example of why libertarian dependence upon voluntary associations is inadequate. The voluntary restrictive covenants which are required by HOAs have often prohibited homeowners from selling properties to people who are Black, Jewish, or Latina/o. These covenants were legal in America until 1948, and the clauses remain in many property deeds, though they can no longer legally be enforced. I would call the prohibition of such covenants, enforcement of their illegality, and promotion of equality in housing opportunities acts of justice. Would Jewell agree, or would he call them acts of government aggression against voluntary association?

Jewell says that if I insist "that only the state can perform this task of advancing the common good, and that it must employ aggression to do so, then certainly the libertarian will find her position unacceptable." As already indicated, there are acts which I would call just which Jewell would call aggressive. Our views will remain unacceptable to one another there. However, I most certainly do not believe that *only* the state can advance the common good. The virtue approach creates a healthy suspicion in two directions: suspicion of political frameworks which neglect the common good as if it is not part of the *telos* of government, and suspicion of the claims of the modern nation-state to be *the* provider and protector of the common good.[1]

Both Dombrowski and Jewell seemed to misunderstand my section on communitarianism. I cannot know whether this is due to my lack of clarity, or to precisely the same persistent misuse of the label which I sought to address. Dombrowski indicated that my view was a combination of virtue ethics and communitarianism, and Jewell discussed at length the advocacy type of communitarianism (personified by Amitai Etzioni) from which I attempted to distance my approach. He recognized that I was not "putting forward a comprehensive communitarian theory of justice," but perhaps did not recognize that this was because I am not a communitarian. Let me reiterate that there is a difference between communitarian ontology which says that human nature and human flourishing are matters of community (not isolated, autonomous individuality), and communitarian advocacy (perhaps we should call this "Communitarianism") within the politics of the modern, liberal state. Virtue ethicists tend to resonate with most aspects of

---

[1] I am largely in agreement here with William Cavanaugh. See especially *Migrations of the Holy: God, State, and the Political Meaning of the Church* (Grand Rapids, MI: Eerdmans, 2011).

the former but most Christian virtue ethicists distance themselves from the latter.

Both Jewell and Stivers mention the doctrine of the mean. Jewell embraces virtue "as a mean between extremes," while Stivers rejects the doctrine as incapable of encompassing the radicality of prophetic activism. While Jewell and Stivers view the doctrine differently, they seem to share a common misunderstanding. I attempted to emphasize that the mean is not a mid-point on a spectrum, rather the proper ordering of a specific aspect of our character and behavior contrasted with two ways in which that aspect can be wrongly-ordered. Perhaps I was not clear enough on this point. The doctrine of the mean is neither a supposedly sensible suggestion to seek moderation in all things, nor a suggestion that virtue is only found in the moderate mid-point between any two radical options. Remember that justice is the cardinal virtue which guides and orders all other virtues, and that the Christian tradition has not let Aristotle's virtues or doctrines stand alone, but has incorporated the theological virtues of faith, hope, and love. Where love and justice are properly defined through scripture and theology, their normative shaping of our understanding and practice of the other virtues will not advocate a comfortable resting place which abhors the radicalism of the prophetic.

Stivers also criticizes my approach for not taking "the experience of those on the 'underside' of history as the proper starting point for reflections about justice." The centrality of attentiveness to those "on the underside" will fall within my comments below on the criticisms with which I agree. However, I cannot claim this as my "starting point." First, human reason does not work this way; we cannot identify one specific starting point where reasoning begins, or claim that one source like experience can be sealed off from other sources such as our situation within the Christian tradition, or our interpretation of scripture.[2] Second, would it not be entirely dishonest to say that the experience of those on the underside is my "starting point" when it is not my experience? I do not know the life stories of Laura Stivers or Miguel De La Torre, and I do not know if in other times of their lives they would identify themselves as having been on this underside. There is surely a sense in which as a Latino Miguel has experienced at least something of the underside, and that as women Laura and I have also seen something of this experience. However, we are all now in extremely secure jobs in institutions of relative power and privilege. Simply saying "I take the experience of the least of these as *my starting point*," cannot make it so. What we can and should—say with

---

[2] I am simply echoing here the point I made more fully in a footnote in my response to Miguel De La Torre (p. 106).

both philosophical accuracy and moral honesty is that we seek to make listening to these experiences and standing in solidarity with them central to our thought and practice.

Stivers also comments that "Feminists would clearly not support Yoder's vision of the 'kingdom of Christ.'" Whether she means that feminists cannot support Yoder's vision in particular, or the concept/language of "kingdom" in general, she is painting all feminists with too broad a brush. Different feminists respond differently to Yoder's work.[3] Likewise, some feminists reject the continued use of all patriarchally-charged language in scripture, while others believe that some of this language should continue to be used while being redefined through non-patriarchal interpretations. I believe that the first-shall-be-last, upside-down character of Christ's kingdom so necessarily mitigates against exclusion or marginalization, that I am not willing to stop speaking of "the kingdom" because of the oppressive freight of the word "king." The whole point is that Christ is king in an entirely different way from all previous and future kings.

Throughout my reading of Miguel De La Torre's response I wondered what he could possibly mean by "virtue." He claimed that "good Christians with virtuous characters" cause marginalization, oppression, and death; virtue is "personal piety;" virtue ethics employs a "myth of objectivity;" and it creates "a false sense of righteousness." No understanding of virtue employed by any Christian practitioner of virtue ethics coheres with these statements. Virtue ethics has no interest in either personal piety or objectivity. Where there is self-righteousness, and most certainly where people of privilege are maintaining structures which cause suffering, oppression, and death, there is very obviously an utter lack of virtue! He also equates virtue ethics with "character" to the exclusion of "praxis," an entirely mistaken notion which I have already discussed at length. De La Torre notes that "virtues are hollow whenever the struggle for justice is absent," and I could not agree more. Perhaps he too is forgetting that justice is the cardinal virtue which is meant to order all the virtues? I sincerely begin to wonder whether De La Torre has simply read very little from the virtue tradition (other than

---

[3]   In the time we have been working on this book, shocking information about Yoder's life has become available to the general public. It is clear now that Yoder had an appalling pattern of sexually abusive treatment of women. For some feminists this will make his work irretrievable; for others it will mean that all his work must be systematically critiqued in the light of what we now know about his life. I became aware when the following article was published, not long after I had completed my essay for this book. Mark Oppenheimer, "A Theologian's Influence, and Stained Past, Live On," *The New York Times* (October 12, 2013): A14, http://www.nytimes.com/2013/10/12/us/john-howard-yoders-dark-past-and-influence-lives-on-for-mennonites.html?_r=0 (accessed January 21, 2014).

early Stanley Hauerwas),[4] or if he wilfully disregards what we argue is central to our own approach to ethics. In either case, the reader should be aware that when De La Torre uses the word "virtue," he speaks of something that I, as a virtue ethicist, do not recognize.

In the end, however, the most important criticism raised by my co-authors is one with which I ultimately agree. Stivers noted that in my essay I did not "adequately deconstruct how people are currently marginalized by dominant understandings of virtue," and that I failed "to couple [my] defense of virtue with a full commitment to doing sophisticated analysis of how social structures and systems of power contribute to oppression." De La Torre made a similar point, although he mistakenly applied his criticism to the entirety of virtue ethics (and to all "Euroamericans") instead of to my very limited introduction to the approach: "Virtue ethics lacks a thorough analysis of how the power relationships within society construct and define what Euroamericans consider virtuous." I agree wholeheartedly that sophisticated critical analyses are a vital component of any ethical system. I also agree that the importance of this component was nearly invisible in my essay (though I did gesture in this direction in multiple places). I am happy to "repent" of this, though I will say that it was a "sin of omission" rather than a "sin of commission." Given more space, or given the task of introducing virtue ethics more comprehensively, I would not have made this mistake. In this limited space, I chose to focus on how justice as virtue differs from other approaches. I was too brief in my comments on how my approach resonates with liberative theologies. I hope that my co-authors and readers have already seen something of how virtue ethics and critical analysis work together (and how this is in no way inimical to a virtue approach) in my brief response essays.

There is a difficult balancing act which I believe is important for ethicists. On the one hand, we must allow our work constantly to be interrogated by the voices of marginalized others. I do not agree with the many theologians and ethicists who are "post-critical," by which they mean that liberation, feminist, and other so-called "contextual" theologies have had their day, and now it is time to move on (or to allow their work to continue as a curious sideshow). On the other hand, the entire work of the Christian theologian and ethicist is not deconstruction; it cannot be critical analysis alone.

---

[4] Miguel De La Torre included several quotations from Hauerwas in his response. I chose not to use my limited space here to defend Stanley; he has proven himself perfectly capable of defending his own views. More importantly, no presentation of the centuries-old tradition of virtue stands or falls in dis/agreement with one of its advocates—even Stanley Hauerwas. I will only note that these quotations must be understood in context and our able readers should follow the citations and make their own judgments about Hauerwas's arguments.

Christian theology is always, necessarily, about liberation, but it is not *only* about liberation. Thus I am in agreement with some other theologians and ethicists who are "post-critical," if they mean that their work must be constructive and that it must be *about God*. I seek to employ critical tools, but I see them as one set of tools in my tool box. I am grateful to Laura Stivers and Miguel De La Torre, whose criticisms have reminded me to be more explicit and intentional in indicating that I am the latter type of "post-critical" theologian, and not the former. When I speak of "the Christian tradition" I mean to include all the critical theologies of recent decades, not only the mainstream, majority views and practices which can ignore or silence the voices we hear in these theologies. My critical co-authors have reminded me that if I am not more explicit about this aspect of my approach, I leave myself open to the assumption that I am anti-critical or counter-critical, or unsophisticatedly and immorally unaware of the critical. While this almost certainly falls short of what they would consider an ideal response to their approaches, I am nonetheless thankful for the sharpening effect of their critiques.

Index